THE PHOENIX RISES

Medley of prose and poetry

BY TANYA TURTON

Order this book online at www.trafford.com
or email orders@trafford.com

Formatting and digitalizing – by Frauke Nonnenmacher, Creative Cats
Cover artwork and most photographs of paintings – by the author
Author photograph – by Paul Turton

Most Trafford titles are also available at major online book retailers.

Note for Librarians: A cataloguing record for this book is available from Library
and Archives Canada at www.collectionscanada.ca/amicus/index-e.html

Printed in Victoria, BC, Canada.

ISBN: 978-1-4251-9147-4

*Our mission is to efficiently provide the world's finest, most comprehensive
book publishing service, enabling every author to experience success.
To find out how to publish your book, your way, and have it available
worldwide, visit us online at www.trafford.com*

Trafford rev. 10/27/09

 www.trafford.com

North America & international
toll-free: 1 888 232 4444 (USA & Canada)
phone: 250 383 6864 ♦ fax:812 355 4082

FOR MY FOUR CHILDREN

RURIK, NICHOLAS

MARY AND PAUL

CONTENTS

PREFACE

When reading a book do you ever wonder what inspired the author to write? Of course, we all know that it comes from something that the writer had experienced, had seen. Like the phoenix, it's a rekindling or "rebirth" of memories that act like a trigger for the imagination to take over.

I'm now almost eighty years old. I've lived in three very different countries: Lebanon, the United States and England. My holidays have taken me around Europe and further afield. I met relatives for the first time in Moscow. I greeted our present century in New Zealand. Before that, I clambered up some of the steep steps of the Great Wall of China. The mist had just lifted when I looked down into the Grand Canyon in Arizona.

The people I have lived with and met are all individuals with their own characteristic mannerisms and thoughts. And they, too, come from different countries.

An amalgam of all this is somehow built into me- as is the case with everyone. However, some people, like me, have the urge to write and that is why I've been writing ever since I could hold a pencil.

My letters are almost always long (very difficult for me to write short e-letters, but I'm trying!). The stories in the collection have been written over many years. Some of my poems reflect raw emotions and others, simply descriptive, reflect an artist's outlook as painting, too, is an important part of my being.

Someday I might write my autobiography, but meantime I offer you, the reader, snippets of my experiences and memories so that they may add a "second layer" to my stories.

Thank you to friends in Lois Palmers' Medau class who kindly "edited" my stories and to members of the Aspiring Writer's group for their positive comments and help.

My thanks, also, to my family, friends and others who have unwittingly made me who I am, so if you don't enjoy at least parts of this book- I'm not the only one to blame!!!!.

- Tanya Turton

BRIEF BIOGRAPHY

Origin- Russian; Education- American; Nationality-British
Parents: Ivan Alexander Rubinsky &
Alina Francevna Braun–White Russian émigrés
Children   Andrei (born in Port Said, Egypt)
Elia (born in Damascus, Syria)
Tatiana /Tanya (born in Beirut, Lebanon)
All attended the American Community School in Beirut
On graduation Tanya went to Wellesley College, Mass. 1949-1951
Attended Harvard Summer School 1950
Worked in the United Nations Secretariat 1951-1955

Married Cecil Nigel Turton in London, UK, 1955
Children: Rurik, Nicholas, Mary, Paul
First solo art exhibition, Darien Connecticut, ~1970
Assisted husband as Freelance Translators 1955-1975
School Art teacher, part-time, 1972-1976
After twenty years my husband, Nigel, died (1975)

Medical copywriter with Smithkline & French 1976-1981
Public Relations Officer of the Natl. Pharm Assoc. 1981-1989
Member of the Institute of Public Relations
Hamilton Andrews- partner for fourteen years (d 1998)
 Development Officer-Natl.Assoc.for Colitis & Crohns 1989-1991
Art tutor for U3A group 1992-2003

Art exhibition in Borlase Gallery, Blewbury, Oxfordshire 1994
Art exhibitions Boxfield Gallery, Stevenage, Herts, 1995, 2003
David Best- partner for seven years (d 2008)
Freelance writer of articles for local magazine 2000-2007
Organised web-site Artisttanyaturton.co.uk 2007
Edited, wrote, revised material for this book 2008

STORIES

SHORT AND LONG, HAPPY AND SAD

SERIOUS AND FRIVOLOUS

A MATTER OF HANDS

A crowd of enthusiastic visitors stood around the main exhibit in the gallery. It was a delicate statue of a Grecian maiden. The fine lines, chiselled by some great master long ago, were of music suddenly stilled into the coolness of marble.

"She's wonderful! How delicate!"

"You can almost imagine her breathing!" gushed another.

"Or jumping off her plinth and running away!" An elderly gentleman chuckled. He was polished and groomed from the shiny bald spot on his head to the two black mirrors of his shoes. The smoothness of the statue pleased him immensely.

A little boy standing patiently by his mother was watching everybody's shoes passing by him and counting how many of them stepped on the crack between the tiles. One lady's red heels missed almost all, except her toe stepped on one right close to the boy.

"How lovely! Why it's perfect!" her exclamation was completely spontaneous.

Disgusted, the boy shook his head and looked up at the lady. He was getting tired of all these people.

"No, it ain't perfect. She ain't got a hand!" and he pointed at the statue.

The little marble maiden had one hand patting down the creases in her gown, but the other – an arm lifted up towards her hair as if to tuck in a strand escaping from her combs- had a rough wrist, jagged, where somehow, somewhere long ago her hand had broken off.

Strangely enough, at her feet on the pedestal lay another hand, bigger, cruder than her own, but made of the same white marble- as if an offering to her. Showing more the ravages of time, the hand was missing several fingers, and it was obviously cut by a poorer sculptor.

"Oh, what a pity!"

"If her hand, her real hand could be found, wouldn't she be the most perfect, I mean, the best in the world! Better than the Venus di Milo!" And other visitors, overhearing, nodded, agreeing.

The neatly printed card under the statue explained its history "Grecian Maiden, found by Dr Schtoller, Byblos, July 28, 1930"

"But why that huge hand?"

Suddenly there was a livening among the crowd, a slight buzz and people turned to find out why the excitement.

"Its Abdul Khoury, that tall man. He's the organiser of the exhibit."

"You mean the famous archaeologist?"

"Do you know it's that fellow who lived for years with Dr Schtoller out in the desert finding all sorts..."

"Mummy, what's an archaeologist?" the boy pulled at his mother's sleeve "Mummy what's an archeo...."

"....Out in the desert, as a young lad too. They say the doc was awful to get along with. Never talked except when excited..."

"....Mr Khoury was his only pupil. Never took anyone else along..."

"Sh....." and the crowd's buzz rose then quietened as they parted to let through the tall, intense-looking man. Everyone silenced, waiting to overhear what the famous man would say.

He was smiling, talking with his companions, then, almost as if to himself, he described the eminent doctor. "A fantastic man, he was! He always stressed that logic is everything. Scientific. No place for emotions." Mr Khoury gestured to the low cabinets displaying maps, plans and calculations.

"If you examine the doctor's work, you'll see it's all so logic! Exactly where the statue should be found...."

"But, Abdul," a lady smiled charmingly at him. "Why have you got this, this almost monstrosity here?" She pointed at the crude, mutilated hand.

Abdul Khoury stared intently at the hand. Then slowly shaking his head, he looked up. "I don't know." There was only a slight accent in his near perfect Oxford English. "Doctor always insisted that this hand be placed with the statue. I could not understand and one could never question him. You know, he had his own ideas." and Mr Khoury chuckled, remembering.

"It's a very ordinary piece of sculpture," he continued. "Hand that was probably part with two others of a base for a vase or a plate. Quite, quite ordinary. But doctor wished it – So..." Turning his palms up in a foreign gesture, he shrugged his shoulders. "I wish I knew!"

His companions started questioning him on his next trip and they moved through the crowd to look at other exhibits.

An elderly lady wearing a subdued suit had come hurriedly into the hall and had just overheard the last part of the discussion about that grotesque hand lying at the feet of the statue. She edged into the crowd to look at it, then stopped startled. The printed sign for the statue read- July 25, 1930. She stared at the hand. Then brusquely she turned and hurried after the archaeologist.

"Mr Khoury! You're Abdul, aren't you? We've met before!" He raised his eyebrows slightly, in surprise.

"Well, yes, I'm Abdul Khoury."

The lady laughed, waiting for his recognition. "We've met before" she repeated, "Long, long ago, in Byblos, exactly on July 25, 1930! I'm Eleanor Brook and my husband Eric was with me"

"Madam?" The archaeologist was startled.

"Yes, and I can tell you why that hand is there with the statue! You see, I found it. I mean the hand. That does sound strange, doesn't it?" And she gave an embarrassed little laugh as Mr Khoury, completely puzzled, looked at one of his friends for his reaction.

"Your strange Doctor Schtoller, he was a great sentimentalist after all! Yes, Eric and I found the hand. We decided to go to Lebanon one summer. Funny place to choose, isn't it? Yes, we decided to go in July 1930."

July 1930

The country had been just a small spot on the map in the atlas. A little yellow strip on the flat end of the Mediterranean and its name was too long to write across the country so "Lebanon" started quite a few letters out on the blue of the sea and ended cramped against the black line that was the border of Syria.

Now it was no longer a map that Eleanor was looking at but a land that was coming closer and closer to their ship. Grey mountains sloped down into the lush green valleys. The slowly curving beaches of startling white sands were broken here and there by bleak cliffs rising abruptly from the waves.

Lebanon. She had never thought it really existed. There was a small town called Lebanon not far from Newport, New Hampshire, where they had spent a summer once. Perhaps someone had remembered the story of Solomon building his temple from the cedars of Lebanon!

Yet, there it was. Slowly the ship passed the black and white lighthouse and turned into the harbour of Beirut. Her husband Eric leaned down on the rail beside her.

"Excited? Last time we went shopping, rubbed elbows with Macy customers. What'll we find here?" He smiled, pointing. They were close enough to see a string of camels walking, dipping, carrying some heavy load on the harbour street. Then fast, leaving a cloud of dust, a huge red truck whirled past the camels and was lost behind the white-washed houses.

Eleanor burst out laughing ., "And just when I was thinking here's the real Orient!"

Their first stop was the Thomas Cook office.

"You must include Byblos in your itinerary! It's the oldest, continuously lived-in town in the whole world! From cave men to the present day...." and on top of the pile of brochures the Cook representative had selected for them was one on Byblos. "It's only a short drive from Beirut."

And that is how they came to be in Byblos. The taxi deposited them at the entrance to the huge castle. The old gateman at the bottom of the stairs held out a hand. "Just fifty piasters, please, for entrance," he muttered, scratching his grey straggly beard. "The guide, he is inside, there."

Massive, weather-beaten, the castle loomed above them. Lines of huge blocks of stones fitted on top of each other, almost grown together, the castle seemed a silent monument to some great powerful race long extinct. And Eleanor's skirt was too narrow for the steps.

Sitting at the top of the stairs, a sheet of paper laid on one of the steps beside him, was a young, dark-haired lad. Almost motionless, except for the bright, steady movement of his eyes, he was completely engrossed in counting the number of stones in the great vaulted ceiling of the entrance. He did not seem to notice the two tourists, but when they asked him for the guide, he quickly sprung to his feet, a lively smile on his face. All absorption had vanished.

"Abdul, my name. I know everything here. I will show you."

Eleanor hesitated. "Eric, don't you think they might have a more experienced, I mean older, guide here? You see, Abdul, we'd like to hear the history, everything, and, well, could you tell us if there is an older guide?"

Abdul's smile flickered and his eyes became serious. "No, madam, I do not have paper in archaeology," he stammered over the long word, "But, missus," He smiled broadly again. "Believe Abdul, he knows. See..." He quickly picked up the paper he had laid on the steps. Drawn hesitantly, but what looked like the exact proportions was a small plan of the entrance. Even the exact number of stones was recorded at the end of each row.

"What do you do with this, Abdul?" Eric put out his hand to take the plan, but the lad quickly folded it and stuffed it into his pocket.

"No, mister, this just fun." and he asked them to follow him.

The American gentleman and lady had come from far, far away to look at the ruins and Abdul knew what and how to show them. First he had to take them to the tower from where they would be able to see all of Byblos and its harbour.

He led them to the tower with its stairs, solid, worn, bearing the smoothness of many centuries of footsteps. Cut into the wall, the thin slits of windows cast thin slashes of sunlight onto the opposite side.

"These," Abdul explained, "for archers, men with arrows, to shoot at the enemy. The Crusaders, they built this castle." Glancing out of one of the slits, Eleanor saw that now spiders and other insects had made their homes in the safe cracks of the rock.

The sun was hot and dazzlingly bright as the three emerged onto the roof. A flock of pigeons swirled away, down to the village clustering near the castle's foot. Before them stretched the castle yard and further out, towards the sea, they could see rising between piles of rock and sand a few columns, pointing up at the sky.

"That is Greek temple. Doctor archaeologist says to Greek god Dionysus."

"Abdul, did the archaeologist teach you?" Eric was intrigued. How did this lad know so much?

Abdul shook his head. "No, doctor talks to himself, to his guests, I listen. I learn some." He smiled again. "Dionysus is the god for drinking. Very happy god!"

"Did the temple just break up? Wind, storms?" Eleanor wondered.

"No, after Eskander and his Greeks left,"

Eleanor interrupted "Eskander?"

"Yes, " Abdul chortled. "Eskander is Alexander the Great for you. When he go away, then the Roman came. Then the Bedouin of the desert came and pulled down some of the columns. Also earth shake, and storms so temple become ruin."

"That's just about when the Crusades must have come here to liberate Jerusalem." Eric held up his guidebook. "About 12th century AD. End of history lesson, Abdul. What can we see in the castle?"

The sun was too hot to stay long in its glare.

"Abdul will show all!" and he led them through the various rooms and corridors. In the great hall he pointed out where the lord of the castle had sat on a raised platform.

Then they followed him down into the vault. There the great sarcophagus of a crusader knight, probably the builder of the castle, loomed dark and huge in the dim-lit cavern.

But Eleanor didn't want to linger there to listen to Abdul's explanation of the carvings on the marble tomb. Nor did she want to know how old were the half-buried jars with the remains of much earlier inhabitants of Byblos!

"I'm sorry, but I can't help thinking this is just the place for snakes and scorpions! Please Abdul, take us out…" Abdul shook his head sadly. He must have thought it was always the same with tourists. They seemed to want to see everything, but they were too impatient to listen.

"Abdul, may we go to the temple, please? There might be a cool breeze from the sea.

The five slender white columns stood on a raised stone platform. Lying around broken among the stones were the remains of other pillars and of great blocks of marble with little bits of sculpture still clearly seen in them.

Abdul pointed out the different designs. He even drew them a rough plan in the earth how all the columns were erected in a circle and where the figure of the god must have been placed, facing the sea.

They could hear the lapping of the waves and the mumble of talk from a group of workmen not too far away. They were carefully excavating trenches in the soil.

Eric looked at Abdul. "Who? What are they doing?"

Abdul spoke quietly. " They dig for the doctor. Chicago Institute doctor. They look for antiquities, old things from the past." He nodded towards a figure sitting on a nearby rock.

A small man in a shabby suit, dirty with earth clots sticking to the trouser legs, was examining a shard of pottery. He did not look up from his magnifying glass when the two Americans and Abdul approached. His hat, no longer white, was thrown carelessly behind him.

Oblivious of the hot sun, the flies and the grumbling of the workmen he was completely absorbed in his study, the little piece of pottery the only interest he had in the world.

Whispering to the Brooks Abdul's voice took on a note of admiration or even perhaps adoration. "He knows everything, everything at all!" and he almost bowed to the silent, unhearing little man.

Suddenly a workman started shouting excitedly and waving his arms, "Shoouf! Shoouf! Talahon!" Come see, come here!. All the other workmen clambered out of their trenches and came running to him. They stood around, talking, looking down into the excavation, happy for any excuse to stop working.

The man in the brown suit rose quickly, carefully putting down the pottery piece, and, waving the other men back to their digging, cautiously climbed down to the excited workman. The hole he was in was not very deep, only a few feet.

The Brooks and Abdul, fascinated, watched as the doctor very gently dug with his fingers around what looked like a dirty piece of stone. The dry, soft earth crumbled under his hands as he cautiously cleared it away. And then, breathlessly, through what seemed like hours they saw him uncover bit by bit a small marble statue.

With the dirt still clinging to it they could see that the statue was delicate, beautifully proportioned. A statue of a maiden in a Greek gown, perfect except that one little hand was missing, broken off at the wrist.

Gently, lovingly the little man lifted out the statue and placed it on a pile of soft earth. Overwhelmed, he stared at the exquisite piece of art, his face transfigured, completely alive, flushed with excitement.

He started wiping off the dirt and dust with his handkerchief, very cautiously, and the white gleam of the marble appeared.

Still excited, he started talking to the Brooks and Abdul, or, perhaps to himself, slowly, almost incoherently. "A treasure! Priceless treasure. About a hundred and fifty B.C. Some two thousand years old. And perfect! Perfect made in Athens, Athens at her best. And almost whole."

Very gently, as if the marble maiden was really hurt and could feel pain, his fingers felt the jagged edges of her wrist where the hand had broken off.

He turned back to the workman standing next to him. "Mohammed, get Usif to help you. You must search for the hand. It may be there too." He looked down at the statue, shaking his head.

He went on talking to himself, "No, probably the hand will never be found. The statue had probably been in another place, pushed off its plinth, hand broken off, then dumped here."

Somehow, suddenly the outside world intruded itself into his consciousness. He got up, dusting himself. "I must telegraph the Institute. Right now, imperative! What a find! Greatest in our generation! Oh, pardon me." He turned to the Brooks, but didn't really see them. "I'm Hendrik Schtoller of the Chicago Institute." He put out a hand to shake hands, but then, forgetting his purpose, turned back to the statue. Eric smiled amused.

"I must telegraph the Institute, find out how much reward can be given to the workman, how much reward for the hand. What a treasure!" He bent down and picked up the little statue. The Brooks and Abdul looked after him as he carried away his beautiful find.

"So," Eric was the first to break the silence. "That is the famous Dr Schtoller, Eleanor, and probably we have just seen the greatest discovery in years! Perhaps a second Venus of Milo!"

Eleanor broke in, "Eric, Eric just imagine if the hand could be found! She's so perfect, only the hand missing. How exciting! Just finding her there in the earth! All that beauty just waiting for someone to dig her up. It could have been you or me!"

"Oh, no!" Eric laughed. "You don't just find things like that. It probably took the doctor years and years of research to discover that that statue could be found here, that this was a good spot for digging around. Really exciting, wasn't it, though!"

Abdul was not following the conversation, but he understood what had happened and he felt elated, excited that he had been there too and that in his land, in his park, that famous man had found such an exquisite statue. Abdul knew it was priceless for he had never seen the doctor so excited before.

And suddenly he felt that it should have been himself, yes, it should have been him, Abdul, who had dug out the statue. Then he heard the American tourist speaking "it probably took the doctor years and years of research…" Yes, he knew that himself.

He had often watched the little man working in one of the castle rooms, studying books and maps. It took so much time, so much patience.

Abdul had helped clear one of the better rooms of all the rubble and had helped fit a door to it. There, with boxes for tables and shelves, the doctor had his collection and laboratory equipment. He'd be soaking little bits of pottery in various solutions to bring out the painted designs. And he would talk to the quiet lad watching him work.

That was how Abdul learnt about Byblos, its history and its archaeology.

He would have loved to have followed Dr Schtoller now to see him clean the statue. But that was impossible with tourists here. Mrs Brook was asking him something, pointing to a little glistening spot on the wet beach sands close by.

"Abdul, could that be a coin, washed up?" He jumped down onto the beach and ran to pick up a wet shell.

He came back and, laughing, gave the shell to Eleanor. "No gold coins, am sorry! Me, I have a collection of coins, but not very good. What the doctor doesn't want, I can keep, he says." And sounding like a professional guide, Abdul told them a story of a fabulous ship, loaded with gold that had sunk close to the harbour. From that time onwards coins have been washed up.

"You see my collection?" He sprinted up before them into the castle keep and when they arrived Abdul was holding a cardboard box. Some thirty coins, rusty green with strange shapes, some square with square holes in the middle, others round, chipped, bent, but a few in good condition with their Greek, Latin or Phoenician inscriptions still legible.

"This money," Abdul was explaining, "coin from age of Justinian, and this one, quite new, Frankish, from the castle, only eight hundred years old." As Abdul talked he seemed to forget he was talking to anyone.

Eric watched the lad, more than the coins. The boy knew what he was talking about, knew it well. There was something of Dr Schtoller's excitement in this young boy. He had the same kind of love for the old and the infinite patience to search for it.

"Abdul," he interrupted the explanations, "Why don't you sell these coins and go where you could study archaeology? You know, be like Doctor Schtoller."

For a brief moment the boy flared up excited. "I could ? It would be wonderful!" But then he turned back to his collection. "No, I do not have the money. These, they are not rare. Doctor has many of each. He has many workmen. They dig all day, they find much. I find only after they go away."

Through the narrow window came the sound of talking and footsteps. It was time to go. The workmen were leaving.

"They go now. I look before night, perhaps doctor has thrown something away. Too much of it, then I can take." And carefully the young collector put away his coins.

The sun was starting to set when the Brooks reached the small hotel in the centre of Byblos village where they were staying for the night. After supper, sitting out on the balcony they listened to the town settling down to sleep. Donkeys braying, a wail of a baby and then the haunting strains of an aoud, the Arab guitar, coming from some lit window near by. Beyond the houses, they could see the glisten of the sea and hear as background to the other night music, the quiet lapping of the waves.

"What a day! Could you have ever imagined being there when Schtoller found that statue!" Eleanor shook her head in wonderment.

Eric interrupted her thoughts, "You know, Eleanor, that boy Abdul, I wish there was some way of helping him. He seems so eager, and bright. If nothing is done, he'll just grow up to be one of the workmen. All his eagerness, and, yes, his knowledge, for nothing!"

"Perhaps we could talk to the doctor about him. Don't you think, Eric, perhaps he would take him on as an assistant?"

Eric was quite sure. "No, that's out of the question. Quite impossible! Have read about him. He's always unaccompanied; refused, even the best students of the Institute. And who are we to ask him?"

Most of the village was asleep as the moon rose up over the mountains. It was too beautiful to go inside the house. They decided to go down to the sea, out of the village and down to the beach, away from all the houses and the castle.

The slight breeze had died away and the water glistened, completely still in the bright moonlit night. They wandered barefoot on the wet beach, Eric stooping down now and again to pick up a pebble and whirling it into the sea, making it skip over the calm surface.

Eleanor bent down to pick up a stone, to see if she could throw as far. Part of it lay buried in the sand and she gave it a little tug. Suddenly she gave a cry of surprise. She was holding a small marble hand, broken, mutilated, only a couple of fingers still left, but definitely, quite definitely the hand of a marble statue!

"Yes, Dr. Schtoller, it was there in the sand. Eleanor picked it up." They were standing at the open door of the archaeologist's room in the castle. Excited over their find, Eleanor and Eric had hurried to the castle hoping, and indeed finding, the little man still working in his laboratory. He was standing in front of them in the doorway, holding in his hand the marble piece that Eleanor had found. He seemed strangely calm over such a find. Eleanor was still very excited.

"Goodness, Mr Schtoller, I mean doctor, with the hand found, the statue is completely perfect! I wonder ..."She hesitated. She wanted to look again at the statue and hold the hand up to the broken wrist to see the lovely maiden whole.

Dr Schtoller stood stolidly in the way, as if on purpose, and then Eric interrupted her when she wanted to ask his permission to go in.

"I believe you mentioned earlier that there would be a reward for the finder of the hand?" Eleanor, startled, looked up at her husband, ready to protest, but he motioned her to be quiet. Dr Schtoller nodded, a slightly amused look flickered through his eyes and he looked at the hand he was holding.

"Yes, yes quite right, Mr... ah...? I didn't catch the name."

"Brook," Eric seemed so businesslike, the way he was when trying to get through with something that wasn't very pleasant. "Could you tell me the exact sum of the reward?"

Eleanor was starting to get indignant. Eric was spoiling an exciting moment by becoming money-minded. She had found it, after all. She almost said so out-loud, but Eric laid a restraining hand on her arm.

"Its quite a big sum, I suppose, I really don't know." Dr Schtoller again half-smiled, but not pleasantly. "But you seemed so interested in having found the hand, it is quite usual in the circumstances to present the museum with it. Is your trip here to look at the ruins only so that you can now tell your friends you have seen Byblos?"

There was a coldness in his voice. He seemed to be getting tired of them or of some joke that he was playing on them for he never even thanked them for their find.

Eric quickly set him right. "I'm sorry, Dr Schtoller, that you should have got such an idea. Quite on the contrary. You see, we would like to have the money used for a scholarship- if Eleanor would agree- we would like to make a bargain with you."

Dr Schtoller was silent, waiting. Eleanor suddenly smiled remembering what Eric had told her about the famous man. She understood now what was happening.

"You have here in the castle a young lad, Abdul. He works as a guide, seems a clear-headed fellow, very interested in the things you are. Has quite a collection of coins." The doctor nodded.

Eric continued. "We'd like the money to go for his training, with you as his sponsor." Eric was starting to lose his courage before the unmoving man. After all, what right did he have to bargain with the famous archaeologist about some lad or other.

The famous man had been listening patiently. Now he smiled. "I believe you left unsaid a part of the bargain. Abdul should become my assistant, perhaps, before getting his formal education?" Somehow he had read Eric's thoughts. "Is that so?"

Both of the Americans smiled. The doctor half turned away from them and looked at the statue standing on a rough wooden crate. "I think on a day such as this, one can break a lifelong habit. Of course," he turned back to look at Eric. "You do realize that he will become my successor at the Institute and in the world of archaeology? I doubt if it will be too hard to convince Abdul!"

He walked over to the statue and carefully put the marble hand down behind her on the crate. Eleanor was disappointed that he did not put it up to the broken wrist.

"Please, Dr Schtoller," she hesitated to enter the room. He turned back to them showing impatience. "Could you, maybe, just hold the hand up to her wrist so that we could see her whole. Just for a moment?"

Dr Schtoller turned to the statue abruptly. "No!" It was curt and final. "But the hand will always be with the statue." Then forgetting completely that they were still standing in the doorway, he started to clean away with a minute brush the little particles still clinging to the marble. The Brooks watched him silently for a while then turned to leave. The famous man did not even hear their "goodnights!"

Next morning, after a late breakfast, Eleanor and Eric went down to the castle for a last look around before leaving. They asked the gateman for Abdul, the guide. The old man shook his head, smiling toothlessly.

"No, no more guide. Abdul now working with digging man. No more guide!"

THE HOLY WAR

Ahmed lay unmoving, camouflaged by the shadow of the grey boulder.

In front of him stretched no-mans-land, rocky grey, with the dry bluish bushes of sage and emaciated thistles thrust upright against the brilliant blue of the sky. He turned his head slightly and looked down. Below him, the black road snaked its way between the hills to the small yellow custom's house on the Israeli side.

Behind him the black road, shimmered in the heat. It lead back first through the bare rocky hills above the sea, then dipped down next to the white beaches. Then through the orange and banana groves, the white, dusty villages, past the bamboo stands of the dried-up rivers, the Crusader castles in Sidon and so to Beirut. Beirut, his home....

How he would have liked to be sitting in the café now, his favourite one, in the eight-floor building overlooking Pigeon Rocks and the sea! It was cool, air-conditioned, at night a club, decorated in the latest "pirate" fashion. It seemed like years since he had been there, but it had been only a month ago.

Now, in his thoughts, Ahmed was there. He smelt the strong aniseed as he poured water into the arak and watched it turn milky white. The waiter brought a tray crowded with the little plates of mezze, green and black olives, meat wrapped in vine leaves, pine nuts strewn liberally through the kibbeh, and the raw meat of the kibbeh had been pounded in a stone mortar so it was just right.

He leaned back and looked out through the closed window at the heat glimmering on the uneven pavements. A group of young lads were leaning languidly against the wall opposite, their banners proclaiming "Holy War" and "Death to Israel" piled pell-mell together at their feet.

He watched them. If war continued for much longer it would mean fewer tourists would return to Lebanon. That meant no more sales in his father's souvenir shop where the iridescent brocades from Damascus had been piled together, leaving space for the embroidered tablecloths from which his father had removed the Hong Kong labels. Ahmed would have to find another job.

He walked slowly out to the car park. His battered turquoise Buick was so hot that he could hardly touch the door handle. It was like a furnace inside, but it cooled as he drove through the traffic. He dodged a green tram, crowded with passengers hanging outside, he honked loudly at a crossing pedestrian and cut through a one-way street.

The destruction of the last few years was slowly being cleared away. He bumped around a crater in the road, dug by a shell. The rubble was still piled high at the sides.

El Hamra had been a beautiful, modern street. The tall glass and concrete buildings, vying with each other in the splendour of their shops, displayed the latest cameras from Berlin, the latest purple-pink minis from London.

The dark, cool coffee bars with glittering expresso machines were always crowded then – before the war. Now most of them were skeletons of buildings with the sky showing through their naked metal ribs.

Strange to think that only forty years ago there were family houses along here like the one he was living in, but that was very long ago, before he was born. As a teenager he had tried to convince his father to sell their home, although it was in another part of the town.

One of the booming engineering companies would have paid a small fortune for their garden alone. Then an oil sheik from Kuwait would have paid a fantastic sum to the company for his glass skyscraper. Before the war....

He drove on to the old Moslem quarter of the city. It was cool and quiet in the house. The thick, white walls and high painted ceilings kept out the heat and noise. He heard only the fountain splashing in the garden beyond the arches of the terrace and the murmur of the women preparing supper in the kitchen. They had been lucky. In the shelling of the town by one side or the other their house had been spared somehow. Only some windows had blown out when a bomb exploded nearby.

It was that evening he had received his call-up papers.

His mother had immediately sent for her brother. His uncle said he knew someone whose father was in the government. Perhaps he could fix things up, for a price. But the young man was bored. It might be fun to go.

The loudspeaker on the minaret proclaimed the Holy War!

The shadow of the grey boulder shrank as the sun, hot and glaring, rose higher above it. Nothing moved except the heat waves dancing on every rock in front of the soldier. Then he heard a sound, clear, distinct, the tinkle of a silver bell.

He moved his gun and looked around. Slowly, a scraggly goat edged its way along the rocky ground, pulling at the dry thorns, then moving on, its bell tinkling with every move of its thin, grey beard.

The soldier raised himself onto an elbow. He picked up a small stone and threw it at the goat. He missed. The goat glanced at the puff of dust from the stone and moved further into no-mans-land. The soldier hurriedly picked up another stone. If only he could hit the goat on the side, perhaps the goat would turn back.

The soldier laid down his gun and sat up. Just as he threw the stone, a shot rang out. A clear, shattering burst of noise. The goat, terrified fled behind the rocks.

The soldier turned slowly and fell back, his eyes wide open, surprised, staring up at the glaring sun for by now the shadow had gone. And again nothing stirred except for the heat waves on the grey rocks.

FOR BETTER... FOR WORSE

"Giving us the boot already?" Eileen laughed and, pushing her long, blond hair back, snapped on her helmet. Its shiny black contrasted vividly with the soft flush of her radiant face, making her look like a magazine cover photograph of a with-it bride.

Her black leather jacket glistened like her new husband's and matched his down to the last curlicue on the grinning red skull painted on the back.

A glistening motorbike stood ready, with another by it. The guests and parents crowded laughing, joking as Roy, the best man, tied an old brown shoe to the back of Mike's bike.

"I don't feel like going yet!" Eileen smiled at Mike, but he was impatient, ready to go. He stroked the handlebars of his motorbike lovingly. He had had enough of the polite reception and his hand touched the starter. The revving engine drowned out all the goodbyes. Eileen's mother wiped her eyes and tried to shout above the noise...

Then, with a rising roar, the motorbike sprang forward. The other bike, escorting, roared in answer and, also carrying a couple dressed in black, swung into the road behind them.

Just before the corner the young wife looked back and caught a last glimpse of the squat figures of her parents silhouetted against the sun. Her father's arm was around her mother's rounded shoulders. They looked solid and strong together, as if they were two old gnarled oaks with roots deep down keeping steady against all winds.

Eileen smiled. Yes, of course they couldn't understand how she could get married so young, how she could then live with Mike in his cold-water flat, sharing a bathroom with neighbours.

"But, dear," her mother had argued. "Mike isn't old enough either. He's only a year older than you. Just twenty! He doesn't know what it means, all the responsibility."

"Of course, I could just move in with him, like everyone is doing..." Her mother looked shocked. She prodded her husband, but he had just grunted and patted Eileen on the top of her head. And so now they were man and wife.

The motorbike gathered speed and Eileen pressed her cheek against Mike's back. She could feel his body relaxing and knew that the tense, forced smile on his square face was smoothing away.

At the end of the thirty-mile limit the escorting motorbike stopped. Roy waved and revved the engine in farewell. Behind him, Amanda, his wife of two years, rubbed her ring against her sleeve and held up her hand.

"Keep it shining!" she shouted tossing her head back to throw the burnished bronze strands of hair away from her glowing face. Eileen laughed and waved back. Her new ring glinted as it caught the sun.

Mike nodded as slowly their machine glided away. "Wonderful, huh, darling?" His hand reached up and squeezed hers gripping his shoulder.

"Yes, my husband!" Her blue eyes sparkled. Except for that new, exciting phrase, everything seemed the same. They could have been going to Southsea for the weekend instead of a week's holiday in Cornwall.

But one week is a very short time.

"Oh, Mike, why can't we just forget everything, our jobs and all and stay longer?" Eileen wailed as she pushed her rolled up jeans into a bag. Mike muttered something in reply, not really hearing as he polished the mirror on the motorbike and then swung onto the seat.

The road home seemed very short. The bike wove in and out of the traffic and she rode as if she was part of it, feeling like Mike did, the thrill of the smooth roar of the engine and the rising, shouting elation as the wind whistled passed.

The winding back road near their town trapped them behind an old grey Ford chugging painfully up the hill. Mike slowed down, waiting for it to turn off.

The big "For Sale" sign towered above a mound of builder's rubble. Behind it Eileen glimpsed the bright new terrace houses strung out in rows in the sea of dried mud.

She tapped Mike on the shoulder and pointed to the sign.

"What for?" he asked, but he swung the bike to the left and bumped to a stop on the unmade road leading to the estate.

Eileen slipped a hand into Mike's. She nodded towards one of the houses. "That's ours! Its got an orange door. Right?"

Mike guffawed. "Number Twelve. Okay, let's go see." He pushed open the door which seemed to have caught some of the sun in the glow of its orange paint. They stepped onto the raw wood floor.

Mike pulled her to him and kissed her in the tiny kitchen where the water pipes were jutting out of the unpainted breezeblock walls.

"Now don't get any ideas, Eileen. It's all very fine, but we don't need a house now."

"Sure, I know," Eileen nodded, but her face remained shining and excited. "The curtains in the living room should be striped orange and brown." She laid her hand against his jacket. "And pink with little blue flowers in the small bedroom, just in case."

He raised her chin with one gloved hand and looked down at her. "Someday, Eileen, sure, someday but not now, huh? We don't need it now," he repeated. "Haven't got the money, anyway." He looked worried for a moment, his eyebrows drawn together and his young face creased into an unaccustomed frown.

"But I've saved two thousand, well, almost two, and we've both got good jobs. What about the wedding presents from our parents?" She spoke wistfully.

"Oh, come off it!" He pushed her towards the front door. "Don't start getting all soft!" He laughed uneasily, but his brown eyes did not even smile. "That's chicken feed for a deposit and anyway, Pop's gift is for a garage for the bike. Can't have you riding a shabby one, you know."

Eileen stopped outside the doorway and her finger followed the large, bold figure twelve fixed to the wall.

Mike took her hand and pulled her along. "Come on, time to mount. Work tomorrow." He wheeled the bike around and patted the solid leather seat with his glove. The engine started with one twist of the key. He chuckled, pleased.

At first Eileen wasn't with it. She wasn't riding with the bike. She was just sitting on it. She took two corners badly, but then on the long smooth stretch of road leading to the centre of town, she relaxed. They were both smiling and breathless when

28

he drew up before the old Victorian house where they were going to live together.

The calendar on the wall had lost quite a few sheets since that date circled with a heavy red pencil- their wedding day. Eileen stared at the calendar and counted to herself. Seven months. It could be October then. She shivered although the coal fire had flushed her face with its heat.

"No, no, no!" She shook her head emphatically as if to get rid of the thought that haunted her. Mike had looked worried in that new house. He had said not now.... he had meant it. He did not want to be chained down.

It was her day off from work. Mike had gone very quietly, thinking she was still asleep. She had kept her eyes tightly closed as she lay in bed, trying to relax, but it didn't work. As soon as the door shut behind him, she had run to the toilet and was sick, miserably sick. And this was the third morning. She was due at the surgery at nine.

Eileen sat on the bench leafing through the tattered women's magazines, waiting her turn. Hardly thinking she counted five full-page and at least nine half-page ads of gurgling babies in long frilly frocks, polished-pink babies in nappies and fat, podgy babies with dimples looking up from the arms of their neat, model mothers. And the photos left her cold and numb.

It was the tenth advertisement for baby powder that made her throw down the fourth magazine. A model father stood bending over his baby, cooing at it, poking playfully at its naked belly. She tried to imagine Mike like that, bending over their baby, but the baby vanished and it was his motorbike that he was bending over.

"Well, well dearie!" A familiar raspy voice shouted to her and she looked up to see her neighbour lowering herself into the chair opposite. "You do look poorly! It wouldn't be that you're in the family way?" and the raspy voice cackled.

Eileen felt her face flush and she glared down at the brown, laced-up shoes of her neighbour. She wished that they'd shuffle away.

"Come, come, it's to be expected." And the voice became intimate, the shout sank almost to a whisper. "You know with my last, I was so poorly every morning that my husband had to stay at home and look after me. Mind you, that was our fifth!"

A fat hand smoothed down the creases of the worn purple coat. "Yes, he was on piece work, too, but he stayed home to look after me." The woman sat up a little straighter and looked triumphantly around the room.

The doctor's door opened and gratefully, Eileen slipped into the surgery.

"Yes, I know you were on the pill, but as I had warned you, the contraceptive doesn't work one hundred percent. In about seven and a half months," the doctor repeated.

The grey, dull day dragged into a grey, wet evening. A motorbike came noisily down their street. Suddenly it reminded her of their honeymoon, of the two motorbikes revving, then bursting away. Amanda, tossing back her mane of bronze hair, smiling behind Roy, both free, carefree. And Mike had pointed at them "Married and nothing different, wonderful!"

The engine outside their house died down. Eileen rose wearily from the chintz-covered settee and pushed her hair away from her face. She glanced into the mirror hanging above the brown gate-leg table. She had forgotten to put on some lipstick. She ran to the bathroom.

A purple and yellow striped towel hung draped over the mirror cabinet. She grabbed it and threw it wildly onto the grey lino floor. The neighbour with her brown laced-up shoes! She just wouldn't learn to hang up her towel! Nothing seemed to have its proper place, not like it used to be at home.

Mike found her sitting on the rickety stool, sobbing, her face hidden in her arms.

"Eileen, darling, have you hurt yourself?" Anxious, he knelt down in front of her.

She shook her head, her face still hidden. Slowly her sobbing quietened. She put her arms around him, clinging to him, her tear-stained face pressed tightly against his chest. He half-carried her into their room.

"What's wrong? Please tell me. Aren't you feeling all right? Shall I call a doctor?" Very gently he started wiping her face with his handkerchief, his dark eyes looking intently at her, worried.

"No, I'm all right." Eileen's wavering smile didn't reach her eyes. She drooped on the settee, like a wrung-out wet rag. "It's just that I'm... I'm... that towel... I'm so tired. That towel, she always hangs it on the mirror... I just couldn't take it...I'm..."

"Oh no!" Mike hooted and stood up. "So that's what started it!" He grinned relieved. "And I thought you were coming down with a bug or something, that you wouldn't be able to come to the race!"

He threw off his coat and eagerly pulled out a bulky envelope from his pocket. "See? All the rules and the route, the lot. I've signed you on as the passenger and there's a meeting tonight." He stopped and looked down at her, the envelope held in mid-air.

"You do want to come to the race, don't you?" It was a plea, not a question, like a little boy afraid he won't get the sweets he's been promised.

Eileen's head drooped down. She did not seem to hear him.

"I haven't made tea. Sorry." Her voice was flat. You'll have to get some fish and chips. Sorry." She repeated dully. "Just fish and chips for one." She stared at the faded pink flowers on the worn carpet at her feet.

The door closed quietly behind him. Out in the corridor she heard the voice of the neighbour greeting him and then the raspy voice sank to a whisper. She could not hear the words, but she could hear the tone, solicitous. Then the front door banged shut and the motorbike roared away.

As far as Eileen knew it could have been minutes or hours or days when he came back. She sat listening for him, dreading his coming and dreading that he might not return. Then without the usual warning of the revving engine, he was there. He stood on the carpet in front of her, not looking at her, and tossed a little package into her lap.

"Present for you," his smile was hesitant, shy, not his usual grin.

She looked up at him dumbly, the words seemed meaningless. She made no attempt to unwrap it. He knelt down and took it, quickly flicking off the brown paper.

It was a toy- a small, black motorbike moulded out of plastic, cheap, poorly finished with the edges rough. She looked up at him from the toy, her eyes questioning.

"Well," he half-chuckled as his big thumb rubbed the seat of the bike. "I know it's cheap. Couldn't find a better one, but thought you wouldn't want to live without one. The other is sold." His voice cracked and he swallowed hard, staring at the toy.

Eileen whispered, "Your bike? Sold?"

"Well, yes, you know, one's got to pay a deposit," His voice became strong again. "Besides the mortgage…" Slowly the words started making sense to her. Slowly the puzzled look in her face started fading away.

"Mortgage?" Something like a smile started to brighten her eyes.

"Remember Number Twelve?" He raised her up very gently, but even then she could feel the masterful swagger in his movements. He was beaming now as his chin pressed down against the top of her head. He did not try to kiss her, he just held her tightly against his chest.

"Oh, you are thick!" he laughed and then tipped her chin up. "Now, no crying!" as he saw her blue eyes filling. He glanced down at the bike lying on the settee. "I thought our kid would like the bike to play with, huh?" And he held her closer again so that she couldn't see his face.

"And if he's a girl, he could push his dolls on it…" It was then that she burst out crying and laughing at the same time and her arms went around him. She pressed her cheek against the cold black leather of his jacket. He felt strong and steady to her like a tall tree with roots deep down.

LIFE STORY

Eloise moved closer to the edge. The canal was deep here - cool, inviting. The dark green water was still; the weeds floating on it lay motionless. Only the skim of oil kept changing patterns, skeins of reds, greens, blues and silver.

She pushed back her hair and straightened the collar of her worn dress. She grimaced.... always dresses. Her father wouldn't let her wear jeans.

"Damn it! No daughter of mine will be in those abominations." He had slapped her hard and sent her weeping upstairs.

That had been six years ago, when she was fourteen. His pub customers wanted women in dresses. Funny that she should have thought of jeans right now. So unimportant.

Eloise smiled, looking at the water, and the smile dispelled the haunted look on her face.

It looked so easy, just a couple more steps.

Suddenly the peace was shattered by a child's desperate, high-pitched scream. Eloise swung around towards the cry.

Further down along the towpath a bulky man in blue overalls was dragging, half-carrying a scraggly little girl towards the copse of trees close to the arches of the bridge. Her thin, stick-like arms were flaying out, her feet trying desperately to kick at him, to free herself. His massive hand clamped down on her mouth; the scream was cut-off short.

Eloise sprang towards them. She was thin, hardly more than a shadow of a woman, but she was quick and wiry. In a mad fury she threw herself at the man, hitting him, biting, scratching. With the harshness of his overalls against her face, she smelt the sweetish alcohol and sweat odour permeating him.

When others came they could hardly drag her off. Someone told her later that she was like a wild cat. Then she had fainted. The man had stepped back hard on her foot and crushed it in his struggle to get her off.

The little girl's father came to see her in the hospital. He looked down at the drawn, ashen face framed by her dishevelled hair. She seemed so slight to have tackled his daughter's assailant.

"Thank you, thank you for saving Alice. She's my only daughter." His voice trembled. "My wife died five years ago. Alice, she's everything to me. How...how can I repay you?"

"No, don't want money." Eloise whispered so quietly that he had to bend down to hear her. "No money."

"Would you like something else?" He was begging her. He needed to thank this stranger, whose hair was as black as his daughter's, with more than just an oral 'thank you'.

"No, no, don't need anything."

"You saved her from..." His voice choked. He couldn't bring himself to say aloud what nightmare horrors he had imagined could have happened.

"Please, no, nothing." She turned away from him towards the wall so that he couldn't see her crying. His voice showed such tenderness when he talked of his daughter.

He knew from the nurses that Eloise had had no visitors. She gave no address.

"I do have a vacancy at the warehouse," he hesitated, looking at her thin back covered in the white hospital gown. "There's a cleaner's job. If...if you want it, it's yours." He waited for a reply.

Eloise lay motionless, staring at the crack in the wall that looked like a spider. Unsure how to continue, he added "That is, if you haven't got a job?" She shook her head slightly.

He came back again next day, with a colourful bouquet of chrysanthemums. He held out his gnarled hand to shake hers, but she shrank from him.

"Thanks." Her eyes wouldn't meet his. Eloise looked only at the flowers.

As he was leaving the nurse called him to her desk at the end of the ward. Her smile was almost apologetic.

"I'm sorry, but I should tell you. We've had to change Eloise's doctor to Dr. Hardcastle, our female doctor. She doesn't accept men right now.... Traumatized."

Alice's father frowned anxiously. "Oh, I didn't think. It must have been hard on her too. I was so concerned about Alice. Should I stop coming?"

"No," The nurse was quite adamant. "It's good that she has someone coming to see her."

So Alice's father continued to come every day. He had to repay his great debt to her.

On her last day there the night storm had washed away the greyness and the morning was crisp, sparkling. Eloise almost smiled, looking out of the window.

Her foot wasn't hurting that much, just an ache. Perhaps she should think about the job, after all. She would tell him- yes, please. He'd left his card and some taxi money with the nurse. She'd work hard....

The heat of the summer afternoon danced on the black tarmac in front of the warehouse. The two workmen paused, resting, having stacked the heavy boxes of tools neatly on the conveyor belt.

"You'd think I was trying to rape her, the way she ran off!" The small man's falsetto voice pitched higher with his indignation. "George, all I did was try help her move that flamin' box."

He wiped his brow with the sleeve of his denim shirt, leaving a wet streak of dust on his forehead.

George chuckled. "You've just got to ignore her, John.

"Ignore her?" The small man was angry. "Who on earth would want to lay her, anyway? Old, skin an' bones an'...."

" Hey, nobody talks of Eloise like that!"

"Christ almighty! Her name Eloise? Eloise for that mousey thing?"

The conveyor started clicking, moving its load steadily into the dark, cool interior.

"She couldn't lift the box. What's she doing here anyway?"

"She's useful. Cleans the place." George shook his head. "Won't see her doing it though. Tools put away, coffee machine full- that's Eloise's doing, what she gets paid for."

"Surely not a week's wage for that?"

"Ya, there's more than that. Hadn't heard her story then?" George relaxed and leant against a pile of boxes. "She's been around coming up for over thirty years, ever since I've worked here. Saved the boss's daughter from some old creep. Come to think of it, the daughter was something like Eloise must have been - weedy, thin." He suddenly stopped talking and motioned with his head.

A gaunt, grey woman slipped silently along the wall from around the corner of the warehouse. One foot was dragging slightly. Not looking at them, she disappeared into a small side door.

The men stared after her.

"Ya, that's her place," George grunted.

It was still and quiet in her cubbyhole. She was used to the slight smell of machine oil. It was part of her "home". Eloise took off her coat. She always wore it outside whether it was hot or cold. She stroked it, as if the grey woollen cloth was the fur of a beloved pet. Then carefully she hung it up on a plastic hanger dangling from a nail.

An armchair was pushed against the huge wooden crate that was one side of her corner. The wall of the stairwell leading to the boss's office formed the other so that she was completely shut off from the other workers. Their talking, swearing and laughter, the groan and clack of machinery penetrated only as a subdued murmur.

Eloise sank slowly into the armchair, letting out her breath in a quiet sigh. She smiled contentedly. How peaceful!

Somewhere, far away, a siren wailed. Soon the other workers would be leaving and then it was her turn to do her work.

"Goodnight, Eloise," a gruff masculine voice shouted to her through the wall- as it did every working day.

"Goodnight, sir," She unconsciously straightened herself in the chair.

"Don't forget to lock your door."

"No, I won't." She automatically checked her pocket for the key as she had done for so many years.

Eloise rose slowly. Stumbling awkwardly against the side of the armchair, she glanced down at the floor where her right foot was caught under the chair. She pulled it out painfully, shaking her head. No, she would never get used to it. And suddenly she found herself trembling.

"That man! That man! May he burn in hell!" Her voice was full of hatred. The whole scene from that morning by the canal flashed in front of her eyes, as it had through the years, haunting her. Eloise felt again the overpowering red fury as she threw herself at the man.

She remembered the feel of his body- solid, stocky. He had a moustache... She shook her head. No, he didn't. He couldn't have had one- because the newspaper photo showed him clean-shaven. And yet she remembered it - it was black and curly.

She was hitting him, making him let go of that thin, crying child. Then the overwhelming pain in her foot and everything went black.

So many years ago. She snorted disparagingly, annoyed at herself that she kept remembering.

Before going into the warehouse Eloise picked up her mug, embossed with the late king's portrait. She placed it next to the teapot and the biscuit tin so that they were neatly aligned on the upturned box that served as table.

She looked around, half-smiling. It had taken her some time, but she had managed to build up her cosy private corner.

Her bedsitter was like that too- cosy and private. Only twenty minutes away by bus.

She knew someone had been in her house even before she opened the door. The pot with the straggling geranium had been pushed over onto the cracked doorstep. The window above it was ajar.

Could he still be inside? She drew a deep breath and pulled her old grey coat closer to herself. The door, as always, creaked. She slipped in and stood with her back against the corridor wall, leaving the door partly open for escape.

Deep empty silence. It wasn't the usual welcoming safe and tender silence of her room. It was darkly menacing. Could he still he here?

Her back against the wall she edged to the living room door, quietly, stealthily, hardly breathing. It was the smell- the mixed acrid odour of a sweating man, alcohol and stale tobacco that hit her.

Instantly she was there in the crowded, low ceilinged pub. Her father, his eyes almost glazed, laughing with his mouth wide open, his black moustache wearing an outline of white foam from his beer, pulling another pint, his shaking hand spilling the dark brown froth.

"Here, Eloise!" he shouted to her over the noise. She ducked between the drinking men and grabbed the tankard from him before he'd spilt more. "Give it to Mike, over there." She plonked down the glass in front of the heavy man sitting at the second table.

"Yes, as I was saying, Joe, they're all growing up." Her father was in his verbose mood. The violent one would follow later. "My lads gone already to the plant. All five of them and Eloise, here, Eloise, come here!" She had learnt to keep out of his way when he was drunk, but this time she was hedged in by the bulk of the three sweating men lounging against the bar.

"See," he suddenly grabbed at her blouse. His wet, thick fingers slid under her collar and with a jerk he tore her blouse open. "See, see! She's starting to grow tits!"

Clutching at her torn blouse, her eyes blind with tears, she clawed her way desperately through the men and out of the pub. The raucous laughter followed her.

No, there was no one in the small tidy room. But a man had been there. The washed-out blue cover of the settee where she slept had been pulled partly off, showing her patched flannelette sheet. He had looked underneath it. The mattress still held his imprint where he had sat down.

She backed away and standing in the middle of the room, slowly turned around, looking at all the familiar things.

The small wooden shelf standing under the window was usually crammed full of paperbacks, but now several had been pulled out and lay scattered, open, their grey pages gaping at her. And the rest on the shelf leaned sideways. The six china owls on the mantle shelf were all there but pushed untidily to one side. Someone had looked under the embroidered runner.

Even the worn faded rug had been lifted and dropped down askew. The wooden floorboards did not have a hiding place. But the ground-out cigarette butt had spilt ash onto the faded pink roses.

No damage. Nothing stolen. She tiptoed out of the room, as if afraid to wake someone up. Slowly she closed the door behind her and leant against it for a moment, her eyes full of despair. It wasn't her room anymore.

Pausing in the hallway she looked unseeing at the mirror. Its mahogany-dyed wood was cracked but dust-free, polished, and the mirror was spotless. Her face, pale, drawn, the wrinkled flesh almost as grey as her wispy hair, stared back at her. Involuntarily she brushed her hand across the glass. He must have seen himself in it.

She shuddered and then made herself walk to the bathroom. If he was looking for money, he wouldn't have gone in there.

Her hand smothered her cry. The toilet seat had been raised. He'd used it. She stretched over to push the lever down. Then pulled her hand away as if burnt. He must have flushed the toilet himself. She glanced at her hand almost expecting it to show dirt sticking to it.

"Must wash it! Wash it!" She murmured hysterically and turned to the basin. The cold-water tap was open. Water was dribbling down.

"Have to wash...have to wash..." and she saw herself again a youngster, so very many years ago, desperately washing herself, scrubbing her shivering thin body almost raw, in the half-filled bathtub. She had felt dirty, unclean.

It was not only her father with his crude thrusting way. It was her oldest brother too who had cornered her in the empty pub when she was cleaning up.

"Dirty, unclean!" She could never get rid of their stink- the sweat, the vile breath.

Trembling she staggered to the kitchenette and it was there that she started sobbing. He had opened the fridge door brusquely and an egg had crashed down onto the lino, its pale yellow yolk spreading in rivulets over the congealed white.

And it was there that her neighbour found her. Crouched on the floor, her shaking fingers were trying to put together the shell of the egg.

FOR THE LOVE OF OMELETTE

"And what have you there, Timmy?"

He watched apprehensively as the low-heeled shoes approached his desk. His eyes stole up to Miss Greenacre's ample brown belt.

"My...my...pet," he stammered, his face flushing red. He was cradling a large coffee jar in his arms, its contents hidden by a jungle of leaves.

Miss Greenacre waited, her round face smiling kindly.

Slowly, almost reluctantly, he unscrewed the top and put his hand into the jar.

"It's all right," he bent over the jar, "It's me," he whispered so quietly that no one could hear him. His classmates crowded around.

"Ugh! A worm!"

"No, he's...he's not!" Timmy stammered. On his hand, arching its back, was a velvety yellow and black caterpillar. Its black head with shiny button eyes, much too big for its size, swayed from side to side as if looking at the youngsters.

Miss Greenacre put her hand gently on Timmy's shoulder. "Why, Timmy, its beautiful! What do you call it?"

Timmy glanced up at her. "He...he...he isn't a worm, is...is...is he?" he enquired anxiously.

She shook her head. "A caterpillar."

"He's a caterpillar!" Timmy repeated loudly, proudly, his stammer gone.

"What do you feed him?"

"Nettles, every day."

It looked plumper, softer than when he had found it on a nettle leaf a few days ago. And his mother had told him to throw it away!

His mother didn't need company, couldn't understand that he did. She'd said "No!" when he had asked for a puppy. It was also "No!" for a kitten. But now he did have a pet.

"What's his name?"

"Omelette."

Bernard sniggered. Alice asked what omelette meant.

"Broken eggs, fried..." Paul piped up and the others laughed.

"Eggs!" "Eggs!" "Fried eggs!"

But the giggling stopped abruptly when Miss Greenacre held up a hand.

"Omelette? Very original, Timmy. Why did you call it that?"

"I found him in the nettles in our garden. He was curled up all yellow and the bits of black like bacon. Mum makes omelettes for my tea..." his voice faded away. He didn't add that that was very rare. It was usually baked beans on toast.

"So, it's the most original? Huh?" Bernard growled as he caught up with Timmy going home. "Gimme! Let's see it."

Timmy clutched the jar tightly to himself."No ,no...you've seen him." Bernard grabbed the jar and pulled.

Stronger, at least a head taller, he easily broke Timmy's grip and stood back, paring off with one arm Timmy's frantic attempts to get his pet back.

"Hey, what's the fuss?" Both boys stopped tussling. "What's in the jar?" John was in the top class.

"It's a caterpillar." Timmy's thin voice wavered.

"Let's see!" It was a command.

Bernard unscrewed the lid and held up the caterpillar dangling between two fingers. He laid it on John's outstretched hand. The caterpillar rolled up and lay unmoving, only the soft black hairs twitched slightly above the velvety yellow body.

"Well, whose is it?"

"Mine!" Both boys spoke simultaneously.

What was it the teacher had said on Monday? Something about a baby and a wise king. The story flashed through John's mind. He didn't remember it all, just a part.

"O.k. I'll cut it in two then." John grinned as he pulled out his red pocketknife. "Half each."

"No, no, let him have it!" Timmy burst out, "Don't hurt him!" He turned and ran for home so that they couldn't see him crying. But their mocking laughter followed him.

As he reached the gate of his home he jerked at the string around his neck and pulled out the door key. His mother wouldn't be back from work for a while.

He ran up the stairs two at a time, burst into his small room and fell on the bed sobbing. Under the bed no Omelette, only his old trainers and dust. Timmy rolled himself up into a ball, hugging his knees, trying to stop the convulsive sobs. He was alone again.

"Hey, Timmy!" His mother was back. He could hear the staccato of her heels on the tiled floor of the kitchen.

He straightened up quickly, ran into the bathroom, dashed water on his face, just in case she looked at him. She didn't.

"What are you doing inside?" and she gave him a shove towards the garden door. "Call you when tea's ready."

"Mum, Bernard stole my caterpillar." Timmy's voice trembled and he bit his lip not to burst out crying.

"Serves you right." she snapped. "Should 'ave put it down the loo long ago." She bustled about in the kitchen, took out a frying pan, some bacon and eggs. Before she broke the eggs Timmy had fled into the overgrown garden.

Next morning on the way to school Bernard rang the doorbell. Timmy, still chewing a piece of toast, opened the door. His mother had already gone to work. Bernard held out Omelette's jar.

"Here, take it back." Timmy's eyes flashed with happiness, then became anxious as Bernard added, "It's sick or something."

Timmy cuddled the jar in his arms, caressing it. "Did you feed him? Fresh nettles?"

Bernard shook his head. "I'm no prat! Nettles! Yuk! I don't want to be stung."

"But...but..."

"There's plenty in there." Bernard turned on his heels and walked off, whistling.

Timmy backed into the house and pushed the door shut with his shoulder. He sat down on the bottom stair. With shaking hands he unscrewed the top as he murmured, "Hello, Omelette, hello...."

He looked into the jar. He couldn't see the caterpillar at first. He took out some of the wilted nettles. Then he saw the yellow and black shape, but it wasn't quite right. It lay motionless and wound around it were grey threads holding it to a twig. He stifled a sob, biting his lip.

The clock in the kitchen buzzed. Nine o'clock. School! He screwed the top on and slid the jar carefully onto the hall shelf. "'Bye, Omelette!."

The school hours dragged. Miss Greenacre had to repeat her questions to Timmy because he didn't hear her and then, stuttering, he gave the wrong answers.

Finally the last bell. He rushed home. He picked up the jar.

"Omelette, I'm home. Are you okay, Omelette?" He opened the jar carefully and looked in. The caterpillar had disappeared. Instead a small crinkled bag hung strapped to the twig. There was a glint of yellow at its top but the rest of it was a dull greyish brown.

"Oh, Omelette!" Timmy tried not to cry, but his face puckered up with the effort.

After that, first thing every morning Timmy pulled the jar from under his bed.

"'Morning Omelette." he whispered hopefully, but when he unscrewed the jar he could only see the grey bag.

In the afternoon, back from school, he took the jar out into the garden and pulled out the wilted leaves, and put in a few fresh nettle tops, just in case. He picked them carefully so as not to get stung but, if the wind was blowing his hand brushed against the leaves.

"It's okay, Omelette, it doesn't hurt, not really." though the weals that sprang up on his skin itched and burned.

It was eight o'clock on a sunny Thursday morning when, as usual, Timmy pulled the jar from under his bed and unscrewed the top. He peered in.

"Hello Omelette." It was hard, but he always tried to sound cheerful.

Timmy stared…the grey bag had trembled slightly and as he watched astonished, a slit widened and out of it crawled a butterfly, its wings folded and crinkled.

"Omelette?" His mouth opened wide with surprise. Carefully he slid a finger into the jar. The butterfly's tiny claws grasped his finger and he pulled it out gently.

"Omelette?" he repeated uncomprehending.

Its wings were like a tiny, multicoloured silk handkerchief, wrinkled as if just washed.

"I think, maybe, are you wet?" Timmy whispered. Holding his hand very still, he moved to the window where the sun was gleaming through the glass.

As he watched, the limp reddish-orange wings started to dry out, to stretch. Timmy counted the brilliant black and yellow spots on them, six in all. The lower wings lay unmoving against his finger. Then, as they too dried, tiny blue crescents, delicately outlined in black appeared, sparkling like sapphires.

"Oh, Omelette!" Timmy let out his breath slowly. "You're beautiful." He stopped bewildered. "You can't be Omelette!"

The butterfly twitched its antennae. It flapped its iridescent wings, slowly, laboriously at first, then lighter, faster. The tiny clutching feet let go of Timmy's finger and the butterfly fluttered up to the lampshade, a splash of orange against the white. It perched for a moment, then flitted to the curtain.

Timmy grabbed the jar, threw out the nettles, stealthily crept up to the curtain and popped the jar over the butterfly. He closed the top with his hand. The butterfly beat its wings wildly, desperately, trying to fly.

"Don't you want to stay with me?" Timmy pleaded. "I'll be good to you. Please!"

In reply the butterfly flapped against his hand and he could feel the wings tickling his palm.

"I'll get you flowers, nettle flowers, as many as you want!" The butterfly, exhausted, fell to the bottom of the jar. Almost immediately it rose again, its wings flapping against the glass.

Timmy's eyes filled with tears. "You want to go, don't you?" Stretching over to the window he pushed it open and turned the jar with its mouth facing the sunlight.

For an instant the butterfly was still. Then it rose gracefully, circling near the ceiling. It glided down close to Timmy. He held out his hand, its wings brushed his fingers as it flew towards the window and out....

He watched it drift down, brilliant against the greens of the garden. It hovered over a wild daisy and settled on a white nettle flower. A moment later, with a final flash of orange it floated over the fence and was gone.

"'Bye butterfly, 'bye Omelette." Timmy murmured and swallowed hard. Then slowly, through his tears, he started smiling. The butterfly looked so lovely gliding down to the garden. And it was free!

GRANDDAUGHTERS

When the eleven-thirty bell rang the teacher took out the big storybook with the picture of a beautiful flower on its cover. The whole class quietened down. Bill didn't even try to catch the fly sitting on his desk and Mary forgot to answer the very secret note that Patsy had passed to her.

Miss Curtis read a long story about a little girl, how she grew up and married a nice boy from next door. The story continued with the tale of their life together and their exciting trip to Africa. Mary could almost see the lion's hunt- the dark, dark night, the jungle trees, and she could almost hear the cracking of a twig as the lion crept nearer...nearer. Finally the story brought the little girl and boy to old age.

Mary's blue eyes were tearful when the teacher stopped reading. It was so sad that the little girl had grown so old that she couldn't go to Africa again. She could only sit before the fireplace and dream.

On the way home both Patsy and Mary were quiet, each one busy with her own thoughts. Patsy forgot to ask Mary to come over and draw dresses for her new paper-doll. Mary wouldn't have wanted to stay anyway as she had a question to ask Granny.

Granny was the old lady who sold apples at the corner of the street. However, she wasn't at all like the poor woman in one of Mary's books who had to sell fruit to keep alive. No, this Granny wasn't dressed in rags and she wasn't even poor. She enjoyed getting up early in the morning and picking apples in her little orchard. Then she sold them for a penny to the passing school children.

Mary tried to creep up quietly to Granny's bench so as not to scare away the squirrels playing tag near her, but they heard Mary just the same . They scampered up the tree so fast that she didn't see Granny's favourite- the one that had a white spot on his nose. Granny smiled and her face all crinkled up like a sand-pie cake drying in the sun.

Mary stopped shyly. She really didn't know exactly what she wanted to ask Granny, but it was something very, very important. She looked down at the redness in the apple basket, then she looked up at the sun and that made purple blotches everywhere.

"Oh, Granny, please, were you ever as old as me?"

Granny looked slightly startled. "As young as you, Mary?"

"Yes, Granny."

Granny chortled, "Of course, I was! What funny questions you ask, Mary. And my pigtails were longer than yours!"

Mary looked puzzled. She kicked at a leaf lying on the pavement and it fluttered up like the small bird that Tommy had caught.

"But Granny, did you want to grow old and not go to Africa anymore?"

Granny shrugged her shoulders and started rearranging the apples. "No, Mary, I never wanted to go to Africa. I wanted to go to Italy, but that was long ago, before I got old and tired."

"Granny, Granny!" Mary insisted that the old lady listen with all her attention. "Granny, why did you grow old if you didn't want to? Did your mother tell you….."

But, no Mary knew that couldn't have been true. How could Granny have a mother when she was so old and didn't need one? She could get up alone in the night and she probably wouldn't even see the black spooks in the corners.

A grey squirrel started scolding in one of the trees overhead. He chattered and sputtered and both Granny and Mary laughed.

"You see, Mary, you've disturbed him. He was sleeping peacefully."

"Then, Granny, you were as old as me?"

"Of course, of course, Mary. Now run along home. Your mother is probably waiting for you."

Mary walked away and started watching her shoes catching up with each other… How could Granny have been as old as Mary; how could Granny have played hop-scotch? That was impossible. Granny had always been there, that is, when the sun was shining. Mary could remember her, that way, way back always sitting there at the corner, a part of the old bench.

Here at last was Number Sixteen and Mary started hopping up the path, three times on one foot and three times on the other, trying to miss all the cracks in the pavement.Her pigtails bobbed up and down with each hop. She soon forgot about Granny and that sad, sad story where a little girl grows old and can't go to Africa anymore.

The teacher had finally closed the book, but time continued to pass. The leaves on the calendar were torn off many, many times...and new calendars were placed on the hook by the dining room door. The colour of the wallpaper behind it faded and was changed to a new pattern and that, too, faded. Another pattern took its place.....

It was morning and a little girl ran eagerly down the path of Number Sixteen. Seven trees down the street was Janey's house . Janey, swinging on the garden gate, was already waiting for Mary. They always raced to school and the one who touched the door last was a slow-poke..

At recess all the children were out playing in the yard. Johnny and Peter were climbing up the old tree that wanted to fall, when the teacher came out and called Peter. Soon after, the children saw Peter walking past, going towards his home.   He didn't even wave goodbye. During the last class Miss Moore told them that Peter had to go home as his uncle was very sick. She didn't read any stories that day.

Mary knew Uncle Ted very well. He had a squeaky voice and whenever she came to see him he would give her cough drops and would tell her stories about the time when he went hunting.

Next morning Peter's father called Mother and Mary could hear the sadness in her footsteps when she left the phone. At lunch she told Father that Peter's uncle had died and that the funeral would be next Saturday.

"Mommy, what's a funeral?"

"Well, Mary, when somebody dies there is a church service and then they bury the person in the cemetery. You know, that place behind the church where all those white stones are."

"But, Mommy, if Peter's uncle has died and he's going to have a funeral, when will I see him again? I want him to give me some more cold candy."

"Sorry, Mary, but Peter's uncle has gone now , for always. You can't see him again. You see, dear, he's dead".

"But why? Did he want to be dead?"

"No, nobody wants to die, but one gets old or sick and then one has to die."

"Why, Mommy, why?"

"Well, dear, if everyone lived on and on there wouldn't be room for all. So we have to die and somebody nice will take our place."

Mary couldn't understand it. Nobody would want Uncle Ted's room. It was always dark and tobaccky. His rocking chair, too, had a limp. He could have stayed there and nobody would have taken his place, anyway. Maybe Grandmother would understand.

Mary was very serious when she came into Grandmother's room. There was always a heater in her room even when it was summer outside. She could never get warm enough even though she was all wrapped up in her quilt, the one that had ten different colours in it.

"Granny, why did Uncle Ted die? Mommy says that he died so that someone else could have his room. But his room is awful. Nobody would want it!"

Grandmother was startled by the question. She looked at Mary for a long time. Mary saw that Granny was beginning to forget the question.

"Granny, please, Granny, why?"

"Why did he die, Mary? Well, he was old and sick and it was time for him to die. And then....but, what did Mother say?"

"Mommy said that somebody nice wanted his place. But will somebody be nicer than Uncle Ted?"

"Yes, Mary, of course, of course. Someone young and full of life like you and Peter."

"Oh, but Granny, Peter isn't nice. He always shoots peas at me. They hurt. Uncle Ted is much, much nicer. He gives me candy, so why did he have to go away?"

"Mary, please, my dear, don't bother me with such silly questions. Why don't you run along and play with your dolls?"

And Mary left Grandmother alone to dream in front of the heater. She seemed to remember something, vague, indefinite, a story, an old woman selling fruit. And then her quilt slipped and she forgot what she was thinking about.

IBIZA AND TURTLE OIL

Joy glanced down at the notebook lying in front of her. "Plan for a perfect holiday."

Mabel had written it in the office and underlined it twice with a red pencil. After saving for two whole years for Ibiza, it just had to be perfect! Nothing was going to be left to chance. Mabel and the others had worked out the Plan during coffee breaks.

The warm sand trickled through Joy's fingers. She closed her eyes and stretched, feeling luxuriously comfortable. The breath of the sun was untying all the nervous knots of a nine-to-five girl's existence.

"May I join you? Name is Robert Arnold." A quiet male voice spoke above and she looked up at a tall, smiling young man. He didn't wait for an invitation, but sank down onto the sand beside her. She closed her notebook and mentally crossed out Point One.

"Hi! I'm Joy." She smiled at him. "Isn't it wonderful here?" They both glanced over across the bay where the white buildings of San Antonio Abad shimmered in the heat waves. The still blue water of the bay reflected the grey palm trees edging the quay.

Point Two had vanished from her mind. She just couldn't be "aloof but alluring" right now. Mabel couldn't really blame her for looking pleased at his company- not when that company was a well-built six footer with a shock of brown hair, laughing eyes and a grin that was friendly and warm.

"Are you also from the hotel?" She nodded towards the long, pink building stretching behind them, its terraces shadowed by tall pine trees.

"Yes, arrived this morning for two weeks. Judging by your colour, you've only arrived too. Right?" He smiled, looking at the ivory colour of her back, not yet tinted by the hot sun.

"You just wait! I'll be like a native Ibizan soon!" She pouted smiling and turned to lie on her back. "Half an hour more on my back and then into the shade. I have this all well planned, you know." She wrinkled her nose to push her dark sunglasses into a more comfortable position.

"You're probably right, but what about a swim right now?" He brushed the sand off his legs.

"Oh, dear, do I have to?" Joy sat up and wriggled, shaking off the sand. It was all very well having a sleek bathing suit that made her look so stylish, but sand filtered down the low-cut back.

"Yes, quite definitely." He stood up and held his arms down to pull her up- and then he froze, staring towards the hotel. Joy glanced over her shoulder.

The girl coming down the beach was magnificent. The brilliant emerald of her tiny bikini contrasted vividly with the shiny bronze of her lithe body. Her golden hair was plaited into a glorious crown on top of her head. She walked proudly, deliberately, towards the small wooden quay jutting out into the bay, as if knowing that every man on the beach was staring at her.

She paused at the edge of the platform and slowly, languidly, pulled on a bathing cap. For a second she posed...then rose on her toes and flashed straight into the water, cutting it cleanly, without a splash.

Robert looked down at Joy. "Wow! And I thought Wagner had invented the Walkeries!"

The Walkeries?"

"Sort of German goddesses in an opera."

Joy sighed and started drawing patterns in the sand. "Her name is Gretel and her room is number 34, just next to mine." She frowned and stared down at the squiggles she had drawn.

"She's really quite nice. Would you like me to introduce you?" she added, trying not to sound miserable. She took off her dark glasses and looked up at him, her large blue eyes serious.

Robert burst out laughing. "Not my type, little girl!" and he kicked some sand onto her doodles. "Come on swimming."

Joy frowned again. Yes, after all, she would have to use Point Two of the plan. "Be aloof but alluring", Mabel had lectured her. "Can't be your dear, sweet self, you know. Any man good enough for a romance will treat you like the kid next door!"

Robert had called her "little girl" already. Just like Mabel had warned. "You're pretty, very pretty with your curly hair and so on, but you've got to learn how to smile slowly. You know, come hither-like or cat-like...Stop beaming as if the whole world is wonderful."

Then Joy forgot about Point Two for a while. He dared her to swim out to the small yellow sailboat moored to a buoy in the middle of the bay.

Panting hard she swam up to the boat and Robert pulled her up, holding her wet and dripping against himself for just a moment to steady her, and her heart missed a beat. His smile was so warm when he looked down at her.

They lay on the front of the boat, drying in the sun, talking as if they'd been friends for years.

Robert took her hand and turned it palm up. With one finger he started tracing the lines of her hand. "Just as I thought." He nodded seriously, but the glint in his eyes was mischievous. "I know all about you. See?" He pointed to a line. "You like animals, right? Have you got a cat?"

She nodded.

"No, no don't tell me." He frowned, concentrating. "Here, see this zigzag? Means you have a cat!". He grinned. "And you're taking care of your mother in her old age...and not leaving home so as not to hurt her."

She giggled. "Not quite!"

Then a while later she suddenly remembered Point Three. "Flatter the male ego. Ask him about himself. Leave yourself mysterious." But too late. She'd told him all about herself- even that yellow roses were her favourite flowers.

She laughed out-loud, thinking of The Plan. "Quite impossible!" she guffawed, and then rolled off the boat hitting the water with a splash. When she came up sputtering, Robert wanted to know what was impossible.

"You!" she teased. "Quite impossible! And I've known you for years, too", she added and he nodded understanding.

They raced back to the beach and then lolled in the shallows still talking. And the hot sun beat down upon them.

It was when she started dressing for dinner that she realized that something was wrong. Very wrong. She turned her bare back towards the mirror and stared over her shoulder.

A hot, burning V shaped exactly like her bathing suit was painted in bright red on her back. She touched it gingerly- hot, painful. Even the light weight of her cotton blouse was too much.

She changed again, slowly pulling on her electric blue strapless sheath, moving her shoulders as little as possible. Smiling wryly at herself in the mirror she thought –not bad, really- now that her shoulders were covered with the light net stole. The dress did make her look svelte and elegant, the blue bringing out the silvery blondness of her hair.

Joy paused in the doorway of the dining room, looking around for her table. Robert had promised that tomorrow he would arrange to share a table- that would take care of Point Four. Mabel had insisted on it, saying it was very important. However, tonight she was dining with a group of elderly French tourists.

He was staring at her when she caught sight of him. She smiled and he grinned back and blew her a kiss. She caught her breath and looked away fast because she hoped he meant it.

Someone brushed past her chair and she winced as the stole pulled tight against her shoulders. Even the back of the chair was painful and she sat straight, hardly moving, like a royal princess sitting for her portrait.

The waiter placed her dessert peaches in front of her just as Robert came up.

"You look absolutely royal, Joy!" He sounded almost breathless. "What about going dancing? There's a very nice place, I've been told, called Los Tres Guitarres, the Three Guitars, open air, pase double as well as everything else..." He looked down at her eagerly, his eyes shining.

He put one hand out to pull up a corner of her stole that was slipping and laid it gently on her shoulder. She jumped, shrinking away from his touch. He drew his hand back immediately.

"Sorry!" He smiled automatically, but that did not hide the hurt, questioning look in his eyes.

"Robert, I'm awfully sorry. I just can't go dancing. I'd really love to, but, you see, I've had too much sun....I..." Gretel came up to the table just then.

"Joy, you will come with us on excursion tomorrow, ya?" The German accent was heavy.

Joy shook her head. "No, I don't think so." She had forgotten the excursion around the island, but she could imagine the agony of a bumpy ride in a bus.

Gretel turned towards Robert. "You will go then." She did not ask, she stated. Robert glanced down at Joy, but his eyes revealed nothing. He seemed to wait for her. Then he turned towards Gretel, smiling.

"Sure, I'd love to." He walked out onto the terrace with Gretel.

Joy pushed one of the fragrant peaches around on her plate. She didn't feel hungry anymore, just miserable.

As she marched back to her bedroom she remembered Point Two. Yes, she was being aloof to Robert, unwillingly. So here she was alone while he must have gone off to dance with Gretel.

Her back radiated heat, burned painfully. She burst out crying as she gently smoothed some sunburn lotion onto her shoulders.

"A perfect holiday!" she sniffed and then guffawed with laughter. Her nose was now as red and shiny from weeping as her back was from the sun. The lotion didn't help.

Next day breakfast tasted flat. She kept thinking of Robert and Gretel scaling the walls of the capital Ibiza together, poking around in the dark, medieval shops clustering at the foot of the fortress.

The morning was already breathless when Joy stepped out onto the white, dusty road leading to the town. San Antonio was half asleep although it wasn't yet time for the siesta. She brushed aside the strands of beads hanging in the doorway of the Casa Figueres and stepped into the dark coolness of the little shop.

Piles of straw hats zigzagged up to the ceiling in the corners. The shelves behind the counter were laden with gypsy dolls dressed in flounced scarlet gowns and wooden carvings of emaciated Don Quixotes. Dusty bottles of French cologne alternated with piles of toothpaste boxes, looking familiar, but the names written boldly in Spanish.

"Buenos dias, seniorita!" The dark-haired woman dressed in black suddenly appeared behind the counter.

"Buenos dias! Por favour..." Joy faltered. She pointed to her shoulders. "El sol, the sun...have you anything for a bad sunburn?" She smiled helplessly at the woman.

The shopkeeper nodded and made sympathetic clucking noises. "Si! Si!" She disappeared behind the counter and reappeared holding a little plastic bottle.

"Very, very good this!" She smiled broadly, showing golden teeth. "Turtle oil, in English. Turtle oil."

And it was good. It worked miracles. It soothed and cooled and almost healed in a day.

But that day was very long. She didn't see Robert till next morning. He was sitting under one of the bright umbrellas on the sand, dressed in his swim trunks and a gaily striped shirt, his face set, completely absorbed in a book.

She started walking towards him, dragging her canvas beach bag by the strap when she noticed Gretel in front of her.

The brilliant emerald bikini had been changed for one of shiny tropical flowers and the crown of golden hair was now twirled in two flat coils above her ears. Men turned, men stared, but Robert was too engrossed.

Gretel paused next to him. She smiled down and said something. He looked up, grinned and rose. Joy could not hear what she said, but he shook his head. Playfully Gretel put her hand on his back and pushed him towards the sea. He twisted away from her.

"I said no! Thank you!" He sounded angry and Joy stared surprised. "Just go away. Go find Sigfried or Sigmund or whoever" Gretel pouted and walked off, her hips swinging.

Robert sat down again and opened his book. Joy interrupted him. "You were rude!" She stared at him. "Absolutely rude!"

She was angry because she never imagined him as being rude.... and she had been imagining him in all his moods and ways every waking hour since she had met him- all of two days ago. His behaviour just did not fit.

"Hi!" He looked up at her and she saw the flicker of pleasure in his eyes and then his eyes became expressionless, just like they were when she had refused to go dancing with him. "I'm not sociable today, so you might as well go on." He grunted and turned back to his book.

"Why were you rude?" she demanded taking a step closer to him and swinging her beach bag menacingly. He shrank from her and turned to face her.

"Look, look just leave me alone." He put up his hands as if to protect himself. "Now just run away like a good girl, will you?"

Joy frowned and turning on her heels walked away. She glanced over her shoulder when she had gone a few paces. He was sitting very erect, like a sultan under his stripped umbrella- with a book instead of prayer beads.

And then she started giggling. She walked back to him still giggling. He shrank away seeing her shadow approach and looked up warily.

"I've come peacefully." Her blue eyes smiled tenderly at him. He looked startled. She sank down on her knees beside him in the shadow of the umbrella and pulled open her bag. She rummaged in it and took out the little plastic bottle of turtle oil.

"This," she waved the bottle in front of him, "This little bottle works miracles! I don't mean to be indecent, but take off your shirt!" she ordered.

He looked puzzled, but he slipped off his shirt gingerly, trying to move his shoulders as little as possible.

"Just as I thought! Painful, isn't it?" She tried to look sympathetic, but started giggling again. "I guessed why you were sitting so royally. Just like me!"

Carefully she poured a little of the oil onto the palm of her hand and gently started smoothing it onto his burnt back. "So that's why you were rude!"

Slowly the oil soothed and cooled and his natural grin returned. He caught her other hand and squeezed it.

"I knew it! You really are a good kid underneath!" And Joy knew suddenly that that was the highest compliment he could pay her.

She smiled or rather beamed as if the whole world was really wonderful. She would tear up the Plan that night.

Except she forgot because it was so late when they wandered back to the hotel, hand in hand, watching the pink dawn slowly blossoming into another perfect day.

LOVE IN A TAXI

"When exactly does your train leave?" The taxi driver had a quiet voice. "Is it the ten twenty-five to Scarsdale?"

Startled, Sara frowned at the back of his head. He was occupied with driving now, but his car was the last in the pack, almost dawdling. You could tell it was Sunday, she thought, because there were fewer cars racing with them down the four lanes of the avenue and the driver had smiled at her in the mirror. Usually no time for smiles during the week day in New York .

"Yes," she nodded, puzzled how he knew she was going there, couldn't remember mentioning it when she had jumped into the taxi standing right outside her door.

"Grand Central Station, please hurry," she had told him.

She sat back and glanced into the square reflection of the mirror in front of him. No, she had definitely not mentioned Scarsdale. One usually didn't to drivers or waiters or bell boys. They always expected a bigger tip as if only the rich commuters lived there.

The traffic lights turned green . The group of taxis leaped forward as if the light had suddenly pulled them. Just like a pack of jackals, snarling, dodging around each other. Sara sat up straight as if to push the car faster, but he stalled the engine and slowly started it again, ignoring the impatient hoots of the cars behind.

Annoyed, she glared at him, but he seemed completely oblivious of her, started whistling tunelessly, his hands relaxed on the wheel. She leaned forward. "Please, please hurry!" Then she slumped back. Somewhere, above the roar of traffic, she heard a clock chiming.

"Oh, I'm so sorry!" The driver tried to look contrite but she noticed that the corners of his mouth quivered and he looked away quickly from the rear mirror. "Its really dangerous driving that fast." He sounded apologetic as he nodded at the other cars passing them on either side.

Suddenly he burst out, "I know what, I'll drive you up! That's it. Make amends."

"Drive me up!" She almost shouted. "All the way to Scarsdale?"

"Wait, wait, don't get me wrong". The car was now barely crawling in the middle of the avenue. "I made you late, right? Any decent professional taxi driver would have got you there on time, but I didn't. Right?" He glanced at her over his shoulder. "Next train to Scarsdale on a Sunday may be an hour or even two hours from now. Right?"

"Eleven forty-five," she intoned wearily.

"Well, that's more than an hour in that ant heap," he stated as the taxi passed the station entrance and turned the corner to cross the town.

She sat up suddenly, "Wait, let me out! I can't afford a taxi ride all that way! Stop! Stop!" She clutched at her handbag and grabbed at the door handle, waiting for the car to stop.

"Hold on, don't jump out right under a car! I'm paying for this ride, okay?" He glanced up at her. "I made you late, so I pay. Now, just sit back and enjoy it!"

The taxi dodged around a slow car and gathered speed. "Soon on your left you'll see the majestic Hudson and as we leave the dusty, dirty city behind us, the highway will curve along its shore." He grinned at her in the mirror. "The dogwood is all in flower and if you look up as we drive along, you'll see towering above us the flowering cherries of the Monastery."

She chuckled and sat back. "I didn't realize you have time to look at flowering cherries when driving around New York!"

"Heck, taxi drivers are human too, you know. Its spring and these greying locks do but beguile a young and fervent heart beneath," he declaimed dramatically. Sara giggled. She'd been right to put on her new suit- the blue matched her eyes exactly and it brought out the poetic in a taxi driver!.

Sara frowned. "Quote, unquote. From where?"

"From me. John Michaud." He laughed half-embarrassed. "Somehow every spring I can't help gushing half-poetic nonsense. Does that happen to you?"

"No, its autumn that gets me. The golds, reds, oranges, sad and happy."

"You mean all this doesn't affect you?" His wide gesture included the blue river, the distant, abrupt shore dressed in brilliant green with splashes of pink and white flowering trees.

"Yes, but not as much. The river seems to flow slower in the autumn. It lingers."

"But autumn is a thinking time. When you re-think values, life."

"Tell me, why are you a taxi driver?" Sara suddenly interrupted him. "Somehow it doesn't suit you." She glanced at his dark hair brushed with grey.

He guffawed. "Why not? You meet all kinds of people and people talk to taxi drivers, you know, like they talk to a psychologist or a family doctor. Simply, a driver isn't a person," He shrugged his shoulders, "A sounding board, I guess, and it's interesting. So why not me?" His eyes smiled back at her.

"It's just a feeling I have, that somehow you should be something else."

"Like what? A writer perhaps?" His tone was serious now.

She thought for a minute. "Yes, almost." She paused, "Well, thank goodness you aren't" she added vehemently, so vehemently that she stopped, surprised at herself.

She stared out at the river flowing grey-blue and calm and at the tiny dot of a boat moving slowly across it, but she didn't really see them. No more writers for her, thank you!

It had been hard to persuade her father that she had meant it. He had even asked her to join him for lunch on Friday to convince her to come to Scarsdale next day to his publisher's party for a new writer. After all, even as a baby there had been books and book writers. Her milk went cold while her mother scribbled another sentence of her latest story on the back of the baby cereal box!

Sara smiled wryly to herself. It had taken only four weeks of wearing Patrick's ring. Her world had revolved around him and his books. But when she realized that Patrick, too, thought that he made the world go round, her whole world shattered.

"You need to marry a tape recorder or, or....a robot, not a human being...You need someone or something to listen to you from morning to night....You don't care a hoot about who it is, as long as they, it, she can hear you and admire you...you great author!" She remembered her last shouted words and the angry, final bang of the door.

"No more writers, no thank you," she had repeated to her father at lunch. "I'll come on Sunday." Her father smiled and shrugged his shoulders.

"All right dear, not this time. Perhaps you'll come to the next party?" They had then gone down to the ground floor in the lift. The bellboy said "Good morning, sir" and winked at him, but she had been too engrossed to really notice him, except that his brass buttons shone like new.

"Well, that certainly started a long train of thoughts!" The driver swung the car to the right. "And you really looked furious there for a moment." He smiled, "Why so much against writers?"

"They're a self-opinionated, self-centred, egotistic lot, that's why! And I hate the whole bunch of them!" Then she burst out laughing. "Except, of course, my father and brother and mother!"

"Well, you should know! Self-centred, huh? Maybe its not just writers, you know. For example, the people I've taken in this taxi and I started only yesterday."

"Only yesterday? So that's why I was late for the train!" she teased.

He ignored her. "Yesterday an old, distinguished-looking dame, pearls and purple hair 'an all climbed in. 'Yes, ma'am, where to? says I respectfully. And her answer- 'I wish to ride around Central Park, but please go slowly, really slowly like a horse and cab'" The taxi started jerking slightly, rhythmically, like a horse-drawn cab. Sara burst out laughing.

"For two hours we jogged about and every time I wanted to stop she would wave me on imperatively and continued to pour out all her troubles to my back. All I could say was 'yes, ma'am' and she was no writer!"

"Yes, but most writers..." He interrupted Sara.

"Most writers self-centred? No! On the contrary. They have to listen, observe." He spoke passionately. "Listen, I can't argue with you like this, with your reflection. What about a beer and a pizza tomorrow evening in the Village after your work?"

She shook her head. She did not go out with men she hardly knew.

He persisted. "After tomorrow? Look, there is my photograph staring at you. Grey eyes, straight nose, no special markings, five feet eleven, single, and not really a flirting type. All right? Proper enough introduction?" He glanced back at her over his shoulder. "Please say yes!" She laughed.

"All right! I'm Sara Montane and you are John Michaud, number 73844."

"Sara Montane. Montane?" He reflected seriously, but the twinkle in his eye was mischievous. "Well, I guess you're heading for Number 43 on Peter's Street."

Sara stared at the back of his head, surprised. "How did you know?" He just shrugged his shoulders and looked ahead. Very soon the taxi stopped outside the open gate. He jumped out and opened the back door.

"I'll pick you up tomorrow evening at six o'clock outside your flat. Okay?" She was going to protest, make some excuse because after all, somehow it seemed wrong. But he held up his hand, silencing her. "And please, do wear this blue suit. Really lovely on you!" He said it as if he meant it. He slide onto the driver's seat, the motor revved up and he was gone.

Sara suddenly realized, she hadn't even thanked him for bringing her all this way. And she had enjoyed the ride!

Monday- John was at her door at six o'clock. He drove her back at eleven, feeling vibrantly alive with all the talking and arguing.

Tuesday- he took her to a comedy put on by an amateur group. They tore the play to shreds, but applauded the gusto of the actors.

Wednesday- she was occupied- a hen party with colleagues from the office.

Thursday- she refused to go out with him, saying that he had to earn his living- and she had to stay late to finish some work.

Friday- he arrived punctually at six, victoriously waving two tickets to the opera …and two hot dogs to eat in the park before they went there. There seemed more magic in La Traviata that night. When he brought her home, he kissed her gently, very gently, in the shadow of the doorway.

Saturday- they joined her friends at a bring-your-own-bottle party. They danced in the semi-dark and he held her close and kissed her… And she wondered how she could have ever thought of living a full life with Patrick. She stopped suddenly.

"Right now and here I swear I'll never have anything to do with writers, ever again!" She raised her hand up in a mock boy's scout salute.

John was puzzled. "Why not?" He held her at arms length to look down at her.

"You see, I was engaged to one and what a fool I was!"

"Yes, I know."

Indignant, she drew herself away. "What do you mean? You know I was a fool?"

"Oh no!" He burst out laughing. "I knew you were engaged and it almost broke my heart!" He took her hand and drew her close again. "I see I was right in being worried about losing you- even though I hadn't met you then!"

She looked up surprised.

"Oh yes, I had seen you before. Several times at parties, but you never saw anyone else besides your fiancé."

"At parties? You?" She asked amazed. He nodded, then bent down and kissed her, holding her so tightly that she forgot all her questions.

At the end of the month her father sent her a formal invitation to his next party and across it he had written:
" they're awfully dull without you. Please try and come this time. Mum wants to know how to make the bacon-banana canapes. Phone her."

Sara phoned and promised to come early, if she could invite John over for the party. She giggled, thinking of her mother. "Why, yes, Mother, John works as a taxi driver. Where did me meet? Why two months ago, in his taxi of course!" She had never found out what he had been doing before that. Something in a hotel, he had told her vaguely and changed the subject.

He was too busy to take her down to the station that Saturday and somehow everything felt grey to her, even her favourite blue suit looked faded. But just as she was going to leave the flat the doorbell rang. A florist boy stood at attention holding out a small silver box.

The three tiny white velvet orchids lay on a cushion of moss and his message was brief. "Missing you" it read and three very black Xs followed.

Her spirits soared. The trip home to Scarsdale seemed very short. The party preparations were so easy… Her mother smiled.

"What's your magic recipe for shiny eyes?" Sara laughed and took the little card with his message from her pocket.

"See? Just two words!" She twirled around, "And three white orchids." She touched one of the flowers pinned on her dress gently with the tip of her finger.

The ice clinked in the tall frosted martini jug and Sara laughed hearing her father's senior editor repeat his story about the Dutch man and his donkey for the third time. She turned towards a tall, thin man standing alone, ill at ease, leaning against the marble fireplace.

"Why, your glass is empty! Let me fill it for you." She smiled. "You know, if you'd prefer something else, I know just where to get it." She winked at him laughing and pointed to the side door leading to the pantry.

He relinquished his empty glass with obvious relief. "Do you think I could have something like an ordinary orange juice?" he asked hesitantly.

"Why, of course," Sara nodded, and she knew that the three young men from the printers standing together across the room were all staring at her and hoping the party would end with dancing…

She turned around and was going towards the pantry door when she saw John enter the room. She stopped absolutely still. Her father was taking John by the elbow, leading him to her mother. Her mother, the very gracious hostess, was shaking his hand, and a few of the words reached Sara.

"Congratulations, Mr Michaud! A second success so soon after the first. Most unusual". The bar man held out a drink to him, but he shook his head and murmured something in reply. Her father had looked startled at first them smiled. They both turned to look around the crowded room and she knew they were looking for her.

She thrust the empty glass back into the moist hands of the bewildered tall man and turned towards the pantry door, keeping herself from running. The few steps to reach it were an eternity and she kept a smile frozen on her lips till the door shut behind her. Then she ran sobbing up to her room. She grabbed her handbag and ran down the back stairs.

No one saw her go out the back door and there was a train that left immediately for New York. No one could have caught up with her, even if they had realized she had fled.

"John Michaud, John Michaud," she kept repeating as the train wheels clicked. "Why? Why did it have to be him?" She remembered the two novels propped up in her father's study. If only she had listened to her father when he had talked about his latest find!

One cover had a bell boy standing to attention in front of the lift and the title was written flamboyantly in a fluorescent blue "Bell Hop Blues!". Yes, of course, the man in the lift had winked at her father! She couldn't remember the title of the second book. It was not out for sale yet, but it was something like "Hey Taxi!"

Clever, her father had said, very clever.

The telephone was ringing when she unlocked the bright green door to her flat. She let it ring. When finally it stopped ringing she took the receiver off the hook and laid it on the table.

Sunday dragged on and on and on and her thoughts were like wild squirrels going around and around in an empty cage.

As she turned the alarm off on Monday morning after a sleepless night she hoped the routine of the week would help... and then she burst out crying again.

The doorbell rang suddenly, loudly, insistently. She glanced through the spy hole and saw the dark blue uniform of the postman. When she opened the door slightly he silently thrust a brown paper package at her. She locked the door again.

She untied the string and unwrapped the parcel. On top were two books lying on a tissue paper package. She didn't have to read the titles to know whose they were. The second one, and she was right about the title, had a piece of paper stuck in it. Opening it to that page she saw that the print was bold and clear- "To my favourite passenger- the lady in blue."

Pushing the books aside, she pulled off the tissue paper. Inside it the taxi driver's cap still looked like new, while the lift boy's jacket lying under it had lost one of its dozen brass buttons. Surprised, she stared down at them, not knowing what to think.

The doorbell rang again. She opened it. It was the postman again. He pushed the door open wider and taking off his cap threw it on top of the other things. Sara gasped as she recognised him. She wanted to slam the door shut, but he was already in.

"Okay, lady in blue, choose!" He looked down at her unsmiling.
"I tried ringing you all of yesterday." His voice was pleading as she backed away from him. "You never gave me a chance to tell you, not after you blew up about writers. What could I do?" He held out his hands imploring. Sara shook her head, biting her lip to keep herself from crying.

"Look, you can choose! The taxi owner would take me on full time. I could get a permit. Or, if you prefer, I'll be a bell boy for ever, or what about a respectable postman?" He pointed to the postman's hat.

He caught her by the shoulders and held her at arms length looking down at her. "But tell me first, does it really matter to you which? Does it?" His eyes were stern, searching. The question hung in the air and she knew it was very important.

She glanced at the pile of things then looked up at him. "You mean..." she whispered hesitantly, trying to sort out her feelings. "You mean, you're you, regardless..." She felt him standing so close to her. Then slowly, a smile started lighting up her eyes through the tears. "No, nothing matters, nothing now that you're here!" She was sure.   When he finally let her go, he grinned. "Good choice. You see, if I had the bell boy's jacket on, all those buttons would hurt you!" Then he drew her close again.

WASHINGTON SQUARE BLUES

The judge frowned, looking like all the university officials rolled into one. "You acknowledge breaking into Reade's store, damaging property therein and using some of it without permission?" The judge's voice was heavy, slow, and his thick finger tapped the police record. Each tap seemed ominous. A student with a police record, tap, tap. No scholarship next year, tap, tap, lost his weekend job, tap, tap, tap!...

"This is your first offence, I understand?" The judge looked up at Peter.

Peter gulped, "Yes, sir, that is, your honour." Peter glanced over at John and Bob, but both of them were staring down at their hands. John was fidgeting, while Bob hardly moved, only he kept biting his lower lip.

It was hot inside the small grey courtroom and there was such a crowd of onlookers. You would think it was an exciting case or celebrities. Much too busy for a morning session in Greenwich Village dealing with petty thieves.

"So, why did you break into the store?" Peter ran a finger inside his collar and stared at the floor. It didn't really make sense his being here. The judge stroked the roundness of his unbuttoned waistcoat and waited. A fly buzzed and buzzed at a closed window.

"Your honour," Peter stopped. His throat felt dry. He didn't know where to begin....

At the beginning? He had sat the whole of the summer term at college two rows behind Amy and to the side so that he could see her profile, almost classical except for the small tilt of her nose.

She bit the end of her pencil and frowned when writing notes, but usually she had a smile that was soft, almost hesitant, like a warm ember that had to be encouraged to glow. Only her yes gave her away with the strong laugh-crinkles at the corners.

It had all started only a week ago. Peter saw her neighbour bend over towards her and say something to her, smiling, but suddenly to Peter it was a leer. Why should that large hunk of a football player talk to his Amy? Peter looked away fast. He had hardly ever talked to her before and here he was getting jealous!

The lecture was over. He could see her collecting her books. He pushed his own together and almost ran down to her.

"I...I say, Amy, ah..." he was sure that his face was scarlet. She looked up at him, smiling. "Amy, I'd love to spend all my worldly possessions on you. All four dollars and a quarter! Yes, please?" She nodded. "A few of us are going after the last exam on Wednesday to Alberto's. Its not..." but she interrupted him. And her eyes were the bluest he had ever seen.

"Oh, I'd love to, Peter," and then suddenly, picking up her books she fled down the steps of the lecture hall and disappeared.

"Well, I'll be darned!" and his grin broadened. It was Amy who had blushed. He strode down the steps, two at a time, whistling.

And before he reached the dormitory his whistling had become a hum. And somehow a few words, or lyrics melded with the hum and the hum became a song. His Irish grandmother's blood made music come easily to him. He'd also inherited her vibrant red hair and jealous disposition!

And jealousy can make a fool of anyone as happened that Wednesday at Alberto's.

Alberto's was a favourite with the students- second street down from Dougall, and on the north side of Washington Square. The scarlet beer ad flashed on and off in the window above the yellow, faded card saying "No Minimum, No Cover Charge."

The small tables had been pushed into the shadows as if elbowed out of the way for the tiny dance floor. Peter sat next to Amy sharing the table with his two friends, John and Bob, and their dates. Their table was close to the jukebox that kept turning purple-yellow-green and white, white because the red glass was broken.

Peter's duty was to punch the record knobs. He studied the list of records and found Number Eight, a smooth, quiet tune to dance with Amy. But he was too late. Bob bent down towards Amy, nudged her elbow, and motioned with his head towards the dance floor.

To Peter that record seemed to go on forever. At last it ended and Amy was back next to him. But so was Bob.

"Trouble with him," he pointed at Peter, "he only writes trad songs. Hey, Peter when are you going to write a best seller?"

John at the other end of the table guffawed in his usual bearish way. "Yes, and then can you imagine Peter's Music Store? Much better than Reade's! You won't have to work there during weekends!"

Peter grinned, but his smile faded as Bob bent down towards Amy, whispering in her ear.

"Oh that's wicked!". She looked down at her beer glass and started drawing circles on the frosted glass. A curl of soft hair fell over her forehead. Bob reached over and smoothed it away, very gently.

Peter flushed, annoyed. He turned quickly to the jukebox so that he couldn't see her smiling at Bob, except that he could see her reflection anyway in the glass panels above the knobs with the record numbers. He knew that Bob always played around, but Peter just couldn't stand it. Not with Amy.

The juke box turned yellow, then slowly faded into green. The last record ended with a low crooning note. He turned around slowly, trying to smile nonchalantly. "Next piece is lovely! Moonshine and Music!" He announced too loudly, "Played by Allen and the Apples." The coin clinked into the slot and he pressed down the two knobs- A 34. He turned to Amy but again he was too late. Bob was pushing back his chair, taking her hand to go dancing. Peter had to stop them.

"I say, do you know this song is a take-off from Gershwin?" he spoke out to Bob, too strongly, he knew. The tune rose in a crescendo and it had a few notes that were slightly off, slightly rising like a piano solo of a Gershwin.

Bob looked at Peter surprised. "That? Nothing like him at all."

"Oh, but wait, its coming now, there, that passage there." Peter was listening intently. Bob laughed and started moving off with Amy. Peter caught his arm.

"There, those notes again…"

The rest of the evening Peter remembered later very vaguely. More like as if he had stood in a corner of a smoky room looking across at their table. It didn't make much sense. He saw himself standing near the jukebox gesticulating, almost shouting at Bob for if he didn't keep talking Bob would go dancing with Amy. And he always held his dance partner close, cheek to cheek.

The record played over and over again as if the machine had stuck. Then Alberto himself, glaring at Peter, strode over the dance floor to their corner and put a coin in the slot, pushed two different knobs.

"Listen, I can prove it to you." Peter banged the table with his fist so that the empty beer bottles rattled. "Its just those two lines. Just like Gershwin. Come over to the store tomorrow. I'll prove it!"

Bob was laughing, "Didn't know you're such a Gershwin fan! You haven't a clue!"

He offered Amy a cigarette, then, gallantly, as if presenting her with a bouquet of flowers, held up a match to it.

Peter picked up his beer and drank it in one gulp. "All right, come on over right now. I'll show you." Anything to get Amy away from Bob...

John roared out, "You crazy? Reade would never stand for that! Anyway, you don't have a key." John's girl giggled and the other started looking around at the neighbouring tables, bored.

Peter shrugged his shoulders. "So, a little thing like that? We can climb in the back window and I'll play it to you. Come on, everyone." Peter took Amy's elbow to pull her up. She stretched her thick yellow stole around her shoulders, her chin nuzzling in the soft cloud, her eyes dark blue, almost black, looking up worried at Peter.

She spoke in a soft whisper, "Please, Peter, don't go."

Peter snorted and looked down at her astonished, "Not go?" His voice was loud and he stuck out his chin. "Why not?" The rest of the group turned to look at them. Amy hid her face in her stole.

She looked up again. "Oh, nothing. Afraid I'll have to get back to the dorm. Its pretty late."

A clock chimed three somewhere in the distance as they walked out of Alberto's and the beer ad was still blinking, reflecting colours on the deserted sidewalk. The girls' dormitory was only two blocks away and soon the door clicked shut behind them. The click seemed to echo dully inside Peter. He knew he had been such a fool with Amy.

The three young men stood for a moment uncertainly. Then slowly they turned down the side street leading towards the music shop. It did not seem like a good idea now, but no one said it. They walked quietly along the sidewalk, but their footsteps seemed to raise a clatter of other feet in the dark corridors of the houses they passed.

The music shop was dark. As they peered into the window the bright red demon on a Faust cover leered up at them.

"I say," John started hesitantly, "Perhaps we'd better...." but Peter interrupted him.

"Come on to the back. That's where the window is", he whispered. A shadow of a cat slunk out of a corner and jumped effortlessly up onto the wall above them and vanished.

Bob was the smallest and after some protests, Peter pushed him up the wall. Bob caught hold of the sill and then disappeared into the black square of the window.

It seemed like an eternity to Peter and John before Bob finally opened the side door.

The place was dark and smelt of newness and polishing wax. Slowly Peter groped his way around the tables. John and Bob followed him through the door at the back into a second room. Peter switched on the light and all the shadows vanished.

It was a small room with shelves of records running along the walls. Phonographs and radios were standing on a table and on the floor, arranged in an artistic chaos with large signs proclaiming the wonders of the machines.

Bob and John started looking around the room while Peter headed for the stairway leading to the basement. "I'll get the Gershwin." He switched on the stair lights and walked down. The basement was large and the shelves stood in straight lines, stretching into the dark corners.

He did not know his way around here very well. During the weekends he usually worked in the radio department, but it didn't take long to find the Gershwin with its cover of gaudy purple dancing girls.

He ran up the stairs three at a time. It wasn't pleasant being here at night. Up in the room he found John and Bob sprawled on the floor, in front of a little wire recorder, laughing uproariously. The little machine, its solitary green eye gleaming, was playing back their off-key version of a well-known football song: "We are poor little sheep who have gone astray, baa, baa, baa." John's voice boomed out the final baa.

Peter glanced quickly at the door leading to the main room, but they had pushed it closed. He stood there looking down at them, annoyed.

"I say, Peter, you're the one! What about your latest?" Bob half-rose, motioning Peter to sit down. "You know, the one about the Washington Square birds. Come on, Pete!"

Peter shook his head, "You're nuts! This isn't the time." He looked at Bob with distaste. "Anyway, they're not Washington Square birds, they're swallows!"

John guffawed and took the Gershwin record from Peter and put it down on the floor beside him. "Come on, Peter, be a sport. Just one song?" He reversed the recorder. It hummed slightly and the green light flickered. John started humming Peter's song off-tune. Peter shuddered.

"If you have to sing, at least sing it correctly," he growled at John and squatted down beside him. "You're both crazy!" The machine stopped humming and John pushed the microphone up to Peter.

Peter forgot about Gershwin and why they were there. He had always loved to sing. His wasn't a Frankie voice, but it had a warm tone. Not the kind to start a bobby-socks craze, but just right to dance to in a soft-lit nightclub: the kind of club with a small band strumming in the background behind a polished dance floor.

"The Washington Square swallows have gone, spread their fan tails …"It was a lilting song, almost a peasant one. "But perhaps they'll come back, come back some day…and my baby, she has followed them, she has followed them…"

Washington Square. He had just left Amy there, and somehow he was singing Amy's song next. He could imagine her dancing with him, her hair just brushing his cheek and her lips, moist, slightly parted, as she looked up at him sleepily, almost like a soft kitten purring and gliding effortlessly with him.

"Aimee, they say in Paris means love, darlin'," his foot beat the rhythm on the floor, "but to me Amy is a much sweeter name, for my Amy is Aimee to me..." It was a simple tune and the words were corny—the kind of a song you just can't forget and wish you could, but it keeps coming back as little bits of humming. The kind of song that sells and keeps on selling till the craze is over and the record in juke boxes worn thin and scratchy.

Suddenly a loud car horn startled them. They looked up. Through the half-closed door the pale-soft light of dawn was slowly smoothing out the shadows and making them grey instead of black. John jumped up.

There was a loud crunch. They all stared down in dismay. The Gershwin record lay smashed at his feet. Quickly, without saying a word, Bob took several dollar bills from his pocket and bending down, tucked them under the record.

John turned to Bob "Thanks! Pay you back later." Then quietly the three tiptoed into the main room and slipped out of the side entrance. The door clicked shut loudly behind them. Peter shuddered. A few hours later Mr Reade would be opening that door and he would find the broken record.

But, a few hours later it wasn't Mr Reade who unlocked that door, as Peter found out when he returned to the store to see him and apologize. The sales girl was busy with a customer and answered curtly.

Mr Reade had gone on holiday for two weeks. His son, Samuel Reade had taken over for that time. Yes, he'd dropped in first thing in the morning on his way to his office at the broadcasting station.

The girl smiled. "Yes, he'll be in tomorrow morning. Can't you see I'm busy?" Peter walked out of the store slowly. Tomorrow morning he would try again and not wait till the weekend when he was due to come in to work.

But next morning was too late. Peter glanced at the headlines of the Greenwich Village Daily as he sauntered passed the corner stand.

He stopped startled and grabbed a paper. It was local news hence the headlines on the first page. "Police search for store breakers. Romantic Records joins the hunt." He scanned the article looking for the address. It was Reade's Store.

Bob and John were studying in their room when Peter burst in. Grimly, he held out the paper to them.

"Nice humour that, Romantic Records joins the hunt!" John pulled on his jacket.

They walked down quickly to the police station. They knew where it was very well- just on the way to their lecture hall. The officer behind the desk hardly glanced up at them. He questioned them in a flat, cold voice, writing down all the details.

The court session was the morning after. The judge was waiting for an answer. No way could he be told that it was all due to jealousy!

Peter glanced at the witness bench, but there was no one there. Only a recording machine. Peter shut his eyes quickly and then slowly opened them, staring at the bench. Yes, the recording machine from the store was there. Neat, compact, shiny and accusing!

"I see you have noticed the main witness," the judge spoke drily. He motioned to a policeman who bent over and pushed down the "on" switch. The machine started humming, warming up, its little green light glowed, but it seemed an ominous eye glaring at Peter and he thought wryly – green for jealousy, yes, quite appropriate.

"You see," the judge's face almost relaxed into a smile. "I missed the song when Mr Reade broadcast it. I have been told you missed it too."

Peter felt hot, burning, and he clenched his hands tightly. He shuffled his feet and stared down at the dirty, faded tiles of the floor. So that explained the large public! Mr Samuel Reade and his sense of humour!

The machine started playing. There was a rustle among the audience like newspapers being folded, then complete quiet, expectant.

"Aimee they say in Paris means love, darlin'," It sounded strange in the bleakness of the court room with the shoddy grey walls echoing, but it sounded good, warm, a bit of a southern breeze blowing in some sunshine, "but my darlin' Amy is Aimee to me." Peter groaned and sank down onto the bench.

The song was over soon and the drabness of the court settled down again like a powder of dust. The policeman switched off the machine, the little green light dimmed out.

Someone on a side bench signalled to the policeman and the movement caught Peter's eyes. Startled, he saw Mr Reade, senior, give a note for the judge.

The public was shuffling, whispering. The show was over for them. Slowly the judge opened the note, his lips moving with the words as he read it. The judge silenced everyone, raising his hand.

"The case is dismissed as all the damage has been paid for. Next case, please...." Peter staggered to his feet and turned to the judge.

"Thank you, judge, your honour, that is..." The judge waved him away.

Bob and John were walking down the aisle between the benches out of the room, talking to Mr Reade. As Peter turned to follow a large man in a wrinkled suit caught his arm.

"I say, Peter, hope you don't mind me calling you that, I represent Romantic Records, Dance section. Name is James". He held out a thick, hot hand. Peter automatically shook it.

"We're interested in that song of yours, that is if you're willing to sell it."

A slight hand curled under Peter's other arm. There was Amy smiling up at him, and her eyes were the bluest he had ever seen. She was saying something to Mr James, something about the song being hers, but, maybe, it would be for sale a little later.

Peter wasn't listening to what she was saying. He couldn't really hear anything when she smiled at him like that! Couldn't see straight either as he bumped into Bob. She laughed at him and started humming his song. It was just that kind of a tune. You couldn't forget it.

NESSY? EGGSACTLY

I still have the cassette.

So typical of Roger! When I awoke him up that night he insisted on recording all I said. However, it's his introduction word by word.

"In the middle of the night, no, exactly three-o-five on the 20th of May 1982 Peter O'Liar- sorry I mean O'Leary- woke me up to tell me that he'd just seen the Loch Ness Monster!"

This is what happened. My latest assignment was in Glasgow to interview a dame who'd started a crazy association : "Save our Nessy from the scientists", SONS for short. Protecting a non-existent monster from the latest one-man sub that some American crackpot wanted to use. She was an aggressive redhead. Attacked me verbally. As if I was after her Nessy!

I had a couple of days leave due from the newspaper. First night stopped on the shore of Loch Ness. Sleeping bag spread out. Moon bright enough to read by. As I was falling asleep heard grinding of pebbles by the shore.

Then I saw it- a dark silhouette, almost ten feet long, with ridges along the back. It slithered into the water smoothly, hardly a ripple in the moon's reflection. I saw its tail, flattish, shaped, well, sort-of like a beaver's, and it held it up...That's why I saw it- a black elongated shape against the moonlit sky with that strange tail. Then it disappeared.

I grabbed a flashlight. Half hidden in a sandy patch was an egg. I knelt down and brushed the sand away- six eggs...

I couldn't help myself. I felt guilty, like a thief, but I took one. It was green, cool, leathery to the touch, size of an ostrich egg. Covered the others with sand. Drove to Roger's like a madman.

The rest I recorded onto the cassette. It was three fifty-four when Roger phoned the town's zoo director. He immediately called his reptile man.

George arrived, took the egg in his hands and shook his head. "Its dead. No use incubating it." The green colour was fading to dull grey.

Dr McPherson at the hospital had the egg at eight forty-five that morning. We stood breathlessly watching the screen as he moved the ultrasonic probe millimetre by millimetre across the surface.

It was a minute creature, curled up, hard to see clearly. Then we saw the profile: a tiny spine with spikes and at its end a protrusion- its flat tail.

The news of Nessy's egg somehow flashed through the town even before I'd organised the press conference.

The hall was filling up fast, but there was a crowd gathering outside. The crowd was shouting: "Murderers!" "Leave our Nessy alone!" "Criminals!" Elbowing through was the redhead from SONS- the Save our Nessy lady. End of news conference.

Remember it was 1982. Next day, May 21st, couldn't write a Nessy article. Was sent to cover the Falklands War.......

All I have is the cassette tape and three ultrasound photos. Somebody stole the egg.

SING-ME-A-SONG, OH!

It was very early when Annie opened her eyes. The sky was gaudy pink like a lady's boudoir, and the birds were still silent on the acacia tree.

Annie wiggled down further under the warm covers. She stretched, feeling her long thin body tightening from the back of her neck down to her toes, then slowly she relaxed, going soft again. Lazily she held up a hand and looked at it smiling. The glossy coral nail polish glowed and yesterday was the first time she had used any. She stretched again and yawned. The drowsiness from sleep was vanishing slowly, like the wisps of mist in the garden.

She turned on her side and looked around. The whole room seemed somehow transparent and pure. The white silk curtains of the open window whispered faintly. She listened. A melody, a few notes seemed to be vibrating in the stillness of the early morning. She started humming almost unconsciously, and some words came into her mind and the tune and words went well together.

Suddenly she sat up, completely awake and conscious. She was composing a song! Again and again she hummed the tune, and the words fitted so perfectly! Hurriedly jumping out of bed Annie opened a drawer in her desk, pulled out a piece of notepaper, a pencil, and scribbled down the words. Such warm romantic words......

The words were written down, but she did not know how to write down the music. Perched on the side of her desk, her bare feet beating the rhythm on the cold floor, she hummed the tune over and over to herself, afraid not to lose that melody that seemed to have come from a dream. Someday, someone would orchestrate it. Someday that tune would be a hit. She had to remember it.

Annie jumped off the desk and danced a few steps. The walls of her room retreated to make a ballroom and the early light was the golden light from a crystal chandelier. The white silk curtains became her Grecian evening gown. She was

76

dancing with a tall, suave gentleman. Her partner bent down to whisper in her ear "…..what a charming song!" and blushing, she murmured that she had composed it in a dream……and he, astonished, pleased, bowed and kissed her hand…. But now, only to remember it till Mother awoke. Her mother had a good musical memory and she would remember the tune till some friend wrote down the notes.

Quietly not to disturb anyone, Annie opened the door of her room and tiptoed silently through the still-dark corridor to her mother's room.

The door to the big bedroom was wide open and on the bed the large hump that was her mother rose and fell rhythmically, giving a little snort now and then. No, Annie could not wake her up. Disappointed, Annie pattered back to her room.

She bent over her desk and picked up the pencil and paper again. Next to the words she drew a rough chart of the music- something like the silhouette of a range of mountains-where the notes went up, there would be a peak and the valleys were the low notes. Annie held up the chart and giggled, thinking what her music teacher would say. But then, perhaps it would help her to remember.

The sun rose and made shadows of the acacia tree on the wall of the bedroom. The birds started twittering and chirping, playing hopscotch in the branches. Annie was still humming her tune, her beautiful dance tune. She looked at her watch. Six-thirty. Perhaps, Mother was awake by now.

She tiptoed to the other bedroom and maybe it was the creak of a floorboard, but as Annie looked in, her mother opened her eyes. Annie jumped onto the bed, excited, full of enthusiasm. She hugged her mother.

"Mother, Mother, I've made up a song! I'm a composer now! Wait, listen, listen to it. I'm afraid I 'll forget it. No, don't say anything. I'll sing it." And she sang the song, her voice trembling a little, and then repeated it several times and asked her mother to remember it. Her mother smiled, said it was very beautiful and told Annie to go back to sleep.

Next day perhaps she could sing it to her choir teacher and he would write down the music. Mother kissed Annie, smoothed Annie's ruffled hair, and turned onto her side and fell asleep again.

Annie returned to her room and crept into bed, but she could not sleep anymore. She looked up at the ceiling and watched the reflections the curtains made changing into different designs and pictures. The reflections on the ceiling changed, became visions of her self on a stage singing her own melodies ..... the audience applauding wildly.....flashing bill-boards announcing the new star.....teenagers swooning.....handsome young men protecting her as smiling she waves to them and, hugging her ermine wrap closer, steps into her white Rolls Royce. Another great song by the famous young star Annie James, the BBC announces excitedly as the main news item......

An alarm clock rang out brazenly next door. Annie jumped and the visions vanished. Annie got up and dressed, washed and still the tune was with her. Perhaps her mother would forget it and then.......

When her younger brother staggered sleepily out of his room, she whistled the tune to him. He would not have liked the words, too romantic for him, but he did not listen to the whistling either. Too early for that.

As Annie was eating her breakfast in the kitchen, alone, no one else was ready yet, the porch door slammed and Jim, the neighbour's son sauntered in. He wanted to borrow Annie's notes for the class he had missed. He perched on a high kitchen stool and grinned at Annie, his freckled face shining from his morning scrub with a smudge of soap still wet behind one ear. He hinted he would join her willingly for a second breakfast, but Annie ignored his comment.

Half-shyly, and yet triumphantly, Annie announced to him that she was now a composer! He was in the same choir class as she and he would understand her excitement. Yes, she had composed a melody and even the words were hers! She did not wait to ask him if he wanted to hear it. She sang the song to him quietly but clearly, she knew it well by now.

He scratched his head and asked her to sing it again. Why, somehow it reminded him of another tune he had heard. He stared at the floor, biting his thumbnail, trying to remember. It was an old tune....The smile on Annie's face slowly faded and the sparkle dulled in her eyes.

Yes, yes, he had it now, an old tune his parents used to dance to...... Begin the Beguine with three notes changed.

VEN – TRI – LO – QUIST

"My lady, you called!" Patsy stared amazed at the green lamppost. A faint figure, like a TV screen off focus, showed up on its metal surface. It grew and grew. And then a boy appeared in front of the lamppost.

"You called. Here I am. Edmund." He bowed gravely though there was a merry sparkle in his eyes.

"I..I..I didn't call" Patsy stammered as she edged away from the lamppost.

He was about Patsy's age and just as tall. He even looked like Patsy with long curly hair, but his eyes were black while Patsy's were blue. He wore a dark brown tunic of some rough material, with a rope tied around his waist. His feet were in leather sandals with straps that wound up his legs.

Ferdy, Patsy's little dog, wrinkled his nose at him, then his tail wagged. One ear went up and he cocked his head, looking at this strange boy. Ferdy had been just as amazed as Patsy because he had been sniffing at the weeds growing at the foot of the lamppost when Edmund appeared.

"Forgive me for asking, but how did you waken the great oak?" His accent was strange but easy to understand.

Patsy shook her head as if to clear it. " Which oak?"

Edmund touched the post. "This is where the oak stood. Now..." The metal was cold to his touch.

Patsy shrugged her shoulders. "I didn't really call you. All I did was use my other voice."

"Other voice?"

Above their heads a grey squirrel jumped from one horse chestnut tree growing on the pavement to another and showered them with pink petals. Patsy looked up. The squirrel squeaked at them, "Hello down there!" and vanished behind a trunk.

Edmund's eyes opened wide and Patsy laughed, "Yes, that's me talking. I'm a ven-tri-lo-quist" She still couldn't say the long word easily.

"Ventriloquist?" Edmund stared at her. "You make squirrels talk! A witch?"

"Oh, no! no!" Patsy was horrified. "I'm no witch! It was hard work..."

"To make squirrels talk?"

"No, how to talk without moving my lips. You try it. It's very hard! Then throwing my voice." It was difficult to explain. "No, directing my voice away, as if it wasn't me talking."

"I don't understand." Edmund shook his head.

"I got a book from the library."

"Library?"

"Yes, and it said how to do it."

"A book! You are very rich!" He was amazed.

"No," Patsy was puzzled. Why should having a book make her rich? "Edmund, who are you? Where do you come from?" She glanced at the slender lamppost.

"Not far from here. Come, I'll show you." Edmund grasped Patsy's shoulders and turned her around towards the road that led to the park.

Patsy gasped. The tall concrete buildings with the flats had disappeared. So had the glistening white hotel with its balconies draped in red geraniums. The road itself was just a mud track. Even the park had changed.

Patsy pointed at the great oak trees, hung with streamers of grey moss. "That's where we play rounders in the summer! There aren't any trees there! And there's grass, short grass for us to play on!" She stared astonished at the bracken, the thickets of blackberries and wild roses sprawling between the massive trunks.

Excited, she turned towards Edmund, " Look, look! Horses!

Edmund chuckled. "Yes, I know."

Several small hairy ponies, one white and two brown and black, were quietly searching out what grass there was between the bushes, their tails swishing at the flies.

Far in the distance Patsy could see a cluster of huts with thatched roofs sheltering close to a high wall. A lazy whiff of smoke was rising from one of the chimneys.

"What's that?" Patsy heard from afar the low tolling of a bell and then another ringing with a high metallic clang.

"It's going to start!" Edmund's face went white and his voice trembled. "We've got to go. Everyone must be there! Hurry!" Then he whistled.

The white pony raised its ears and trotted over. Ferdy backed away from it, but Patsy grabbed him. Edmund jumped lightly onto the pony's back, straddling it, and helped Patsy up.

Suddenly the pony wheezed, "You're too heavy!" Edmund froze and then he saw that Patsy was grinning.

"You again!"

"Yes, don't forget I'm a ven-tri-lo-quist!" she laughed. She was still holding Ferdy as he was trying to wriggle free.

Patsy wanted to ask "What's going to start? Where was she? Who was Edmund?" but Edmund dug his knees into the pony's sides and Patsy, her arms around Edmund's waist, hung on tightly not to fall off. Ferdy curled up his plump little legs and sniffed at the air. Then he licked Edmund's belt. He was jammed tightly on her lap and wouldn't fall.

The pony raced towards the huts, but before they reached them it swerved towards a great gate in the wall. The huge doors, studded with metal caps were wide open. People were hurrying through the gate, many dressed like Edmund, others in multicoloured robes, women in long colourful skirts, some with tall conical hats swathed in veils, others with bright kerchiefs.

A man dressed in a leather jacket and tight leather leggings was leading a brown bear by a chain fastened through his nose.

"Stop, stop!" Patsy prodded Edmund in the back. "I want to see that bear!" Edmund patted the pony and it stopped. The bear looked moth eaten, its fur matted. Its legs were curving in and he seemed hardly able to walk. His master pulled on the chain and the animal tried to walk faster.

"Oh, poor animal! Why has he got him?"

Edmund shrugged his shoulders, "Why poor? He gets fed and the man makes him dance. Gets money that way."

The owner pulled a whip from his backpack and hit the bear. The bear rose on his hind legs, growling with pain.

Then he growled again, "Don't hit me! Don't." The man jumped back and almost dropped the chain. And Edmund dug his heels into the pony's side and they shot away fast.

When they were inside the gate, he slowed the pony down to a walk. He turned to look at Patsy. "Look, if you do that..."

"Do what?" she asked smiling, looking pleased with herself.

Edmund was angry. "Use your other voice. You'll get punished! So, don't!"

The pony caught up with some other people on horseback, but most were walking or running. Two musicians, their guitar-like instruments slung on their backs, strode along, singing together.

Inside the town Edmund and Patsy followed the crowds. Patsy looked around curiously. She'd never seen so many people dressed in theatre clothes before. At least that's what it looked to her.

"That house there and that one and that," Patsy exclaimed, " They're all like the old tavern at home." The buildings were white with black painted beams criss-crossing the walls and they had very small windows.

The road narrowed, squeezed in by the houses that overhung it. The sharp smell of rotting hit Patsy. There were heaps of refuse and pools of dirty water that Edmund just ignored.

The people were noisy, laughing, talking.

"They're talking in English." Patsy was surprised.

Edmund laughed, "Yes, of course they're talking in English."

Patsy shook her head, "But I can't understand all the words." And then she thought- could it be old English, the kind that was spoken many, many years ago?

As the crowd jostled further, the talking became quieter, subdued, except for the crying of babies and barking of dogs. Somewhere a cock crowed. Then the road opened up onto a large square, crowded with jostling people.

"What's happening, Edmund?" Patsy whispered. He pointed ahead to the church standing majestically above all the other buildings. In front of it was a wooden platform.

"Its an auto de fe."

"Auto what?"

"It's a ceremony. The church, they are getting rid of witches." Patsy could hardly hear him because of the booming of the bells.

"Real witches?" Patsy was curious, "What do they do?"

"They're bad women who do bad things," Edmund replied. "like making people ill and putting evil spells so that cows don't give milk and..."

"Do they ride on broomsticks?" Edmund nodded. "And do they have black cats?" He shrugged his shoulders. "I don't believe in witches! That's just make believe!" Patsy stated firmly.

Edmund's eyes opened wide as he stared at her. "Be quiet!" he whispered, " They'll hear you. Of course there are witches. Just wait and see." He added triumphantly.

The church stood at the far end of the square. Its columns of white stone rose in layer upon layer to the shining copper roof. The niches between the columns held delicate marble statues. The great archway of the door was decorated with lines of figures, strange animals and flowers of all kinds cut into the stone. And looming above all was the high bell tower held up by graceful arches.

There were three golden chairs with red cushions on a platform, like a stage, in front of the church. Behind the chairs, fluttering on a short pole was a magnificent gold embroidered flag showing a lion roaring.

Slowly the grand doors of the church opened and a kind of a sigh rose from the crowd and faded away. The ceremony had started.

"What's going to happen?" Patsy leaned over to ask Edmund as he slid off the pony and stood at its head.

He ignored her question or maybe he hadn't heard it. Excited, he stood on tiptoe, pointing ahead. "They're coming! Look!"

The procession from the church reached the platform. Men in full armour, like the knights in one of Patsy's books, with helmets flashing in the sun, strode around its base and stopped in a straight line facing the public.

Then slowly climbing up to the platform came two figures dressed completely in black - long black robes, pointed black hoods that hung close over their heads and black masks, with slits for the eyes.

Patsy shivered and shrank down on the pony as if trying to make herself invisible, they were so frightening, so menacing those black, silent men.

The crowd, too, fell dead silent, even the babies and the dogs seemed to sense the horror clinging to those two figures.

Suddenly the bells boomed out again. Trumpets sounded; a loud cheer rose from the soldiers standing at attention in front of the platform. The crowd joined in the cheering and clapping. The silent spell was broken.

Then the procession started again. Several monks in white robes and black cowls or hoods climbed up the steps and grouped behind the golden chairs. They were followed by monks in brown robes, whose heads had been shaved bare except for a band of hair that formed a circle..

Several very solemn young boys, dressed in long white gowns trooped up onto the platform carrying decorated gilded crosses and on a velvet cushion a small statue of gold and silver. The sun's rays fell on it making it glitter and sparkle.

Then two priests appeared, resplendent in brightly embroidered cassocks. They seated themselves comfortably, folding their hands together and bowing their heads as if in prayer..

A hush fell on the crowd. In the silence a tall, thin figure dressed all in black walked up the steps and sat down proudly on the middle chair. Around his neck was a massive gold chain from which hung a great golden cross encrusted with precious stones.

Patsy stared at the cross. "Is it really gold?" she whispered, " or is it plastic?"

Edmund looked puzzled. "Plastic? Don't know what that is, but its gold. And the green stones are emeralds, the red rubies."

The man in black had on a red velvet cap that matched the red of the rubies. Under it, his face was pale and smooth, the nose curved like an eagle's and the eyes looking over the crowds were pale blue. Then his eyes seemed to gaze directly at Patsy. She felt herself go cold and frightened- the eyes were so cruel, and penetrating, as if he could read her mind.

He rose and raised his arms. His voice was soothing, calm. "Friends, good Christians" His thin lips stretched in a smile that did not reach his eyes. And then his voice rose, it became menacing. "Witchcraft...witches, sorcerers, the wicked of the earth, those who talk with Satan, the devil...!!!" And his voice roared. "We will exterminate them! We will clear our dear land." Patsy couldn't understand all he said. He spoke for what seemed such a long time. Everyone was silent, listening; it seemed they didn't dare move.

Patsy's legs were uncomfortable, so she slid off the horse and stood next to Edmund, jumping up and down to ease the stiffness.

"Silence! Who dares interrupt the Grand Inquisitor, the messenger from our Holy Father?" The voice of the captain of the guard rose over the crowd. The man in black smiled down at him and with his right hand, bedecked with rings, he made the sign of the cross- blessing the man.

Edmund pushed Patsy down and held her unmoving. "Don't, don't" he whispered urgently. His face was drawn and he looked frightened. "They'll take you. They'll burn you for a witch!"

Patsy stared at him. "Burn me?"

"Yes, its a ceremony, to get rid of witches. Those stakes over there, see them? For burning witches."

"Oh," Patsy felt cold, although it was a lovely summer day and the morning sun was hot. "Is that why, those piles of wood?"

"Yes, but hush!"

As he spoke another procession was making its way towards the platform. The crowd opened up in front of the briskly marching soldiers. Behind them staggered five women and two young girls, chained together, their dirty yellow robes in tatters, hardly able to drag their bare feet. On each robe was sewn a cross.

Their faces haggard, looking starved, were marked with cuts from whips, their arms were scarred from the chains that were wound too tightly.

"Why do they look so awful?" Patsy was shocked. She had never seen such a pitiful sight.

"They've been tortured," Edmund whispered back.

"Tortured? How? Why?"

Edmund let his breath out slowly. "The priests want the women to say they are witches, that they are sorry."

"What if they aren't witches?"

Edmund shook his head, "I suppose they'll say they are. Shush, its dangerous to talk."

One girl, her face swollen from an angry red wound, her hair wildly tousled, looked around desperately. Her dazed eyes met Patsy's and Patsy felt as if the girl was asking her- Why? Why was she a prisoner? Then her eyes moved on to Edmund. Patsy saw her start.

Edmund cried out, "Oh. mercy! Katharine! Katharine, my sister!"

He rushed towards her, but immediately a soldier lowered his lance and stopped him. Others among the crowd held him back as he tried wildly to reach his sister. She looked in complete despair at him and then was pushed on by the soldiers. Patsy heard the terrified moaning and sobbing of the other women as they shuffled painfully by.

Patsy felt tears prickling her eyes. "Why is she a prisoner?" she whispered very quietly to Edmund.

He had his face buried in his hands for he was crying. "The Holy Father," he mumbled, "the church says they're witches. They aren't, they aren't! Katharine is no witch." Patsy stroked his arm soothingly. "And her friend, Joanna, she's no witch either!"

Behind the prisoners a small cart trundled along, pulled by a thin, grey donkey. The cart passed quite close and Patsy could see animals crowded in cages. Their fur was matted with blood. She heard a dog whining and a cat meowing pitifully.

"That dog," Edmund's eyes opened wide as he stared at the cages. "Its Robbie! Robbie?" The dog barked excitedly, recognising Edmund's voice.

People around them started muttering. "Probably the witches' helpers" " There'll be a black cat there too." "And pigs, they say the devil loves pigs!" "If they're witches, burn them!" " Burn them!"

"They're not!" Patsy forgot herself. Her voice rose loudly in protest. "Those girls, they're not witches!"

Suddenly she found two soldiers standing next to her. They stared down at Patsy and then motioned for Edmund and her to go with them. It was a one-word order "Come!"

Edmund grabbed her elbow and pushed her along. She felt his hand trembling and she realized that she, too, was terrified. She didn't dare say anything. The soldiers looked so stern in their deep helmets, their faces drawn into a set frown. And they held their swords unsheathed in their hands.

As they were taken to the platform they passed the rough, wooden stakes driven hard into the ground. The prisoners were being tied to them by the men in black hoods. Some already had the wood stacked around their feet. The cages, too, were here, piled one on top of the other.

On the platform Edmund threw himself on his knees in front of the man in black.

"Please, please, my sister is there. She's no witch. Please, please save her!"

"Arise, my son!" the man's voice was kindly even though his eyes were cold. "No harm will befall her now. She will go straight to heaven if she is no witch. And if she is..." his voice rose so that all could hear him, "If she is she can beg forgiveness. Then she will no longer be accursed!"

"Please, save her from burning, she's no witch." Edmund was now crying, his tears falling unchecked. He put his hand out to clutch at the man's sleeve. Brusquely the man shrugged Edmund's hand off.

"And you!" His voice was almost a screech, "If your sister is accursed, is a witch, you too must be tainted!" He arose standing above Edmund. Edmund backed away terrified.

Patsy stood there frozen with fright. Ferdy wriggled suddenly in her arms and she dropped him. The dog growled and baring his teeth he slowly advanced on the man in black.

Ferdy hated black. It was a sign of danger to him. And he could smell fear. His mistress was afraid. He had to protect her.

"Take it!" The man nodded at a soldier and waved at the small animal growling up at him. Edmund moved towards Patsy.

"Patsy, hurry. Make him talk!" Patsy at first looked at him puzzled, but just as a soldier was approaching she realized what Edmund had said.

"Don't touch me" Ferdy said in a wheezy voice. "Him, he...you, you are a wicked man." and Ferdy, his tail between his legs, his brown and white fur bristling, crouched as if to spring.

"Satan speaking!" The man in black stepped back. "Take him!" He commanded the soldier, but the soldier was staring at the small dog who had spoken.

"Go away" Ferdy spoke to the soldier. "That's a wicked man.Don't listen to him. Go!"

The soldier staggered back, turned at the edge of the platform and jumped off, and ran. The crowd around the platform edged away, whispering, worried, some excited, others frightened.

The man in black shouted down to the captain of the guard. "Kill the dog!" But the captain, too, was backing away, not listening.

Patsy dried up. She couldn't think what else to say.

Edmund whispered, " The statue, can you make it speak?"

Patsy stared at the golden statuette still held up high by one of the young boys in white. It was the figure of the local saint, loved for her kindness. Patsy didn't know what she should say.

Edmund then spoke aloud, his voice full of anger. "Those young girls there, they're not witches. If you don't show mercy- you're no Christian!" He looked bravely at the man in black, but Patsy knew he was really frightened because his voice had trembled.

The man stepped forward threateningly. His hand went down to his dagger. But at his feet Ferdy growled. "Don't you dare!"

It was then that the lovely statuette spoke "The young girls there, they're no witches. Show them mercy!" The boy holding the statuette went white and almost dropped it. He just managed to catch it with trembling hands. He then held it high up above his head.

The crowds fell dead silent and then one then another they dropped down on their knees, till all the people were kneeling, bowing down before this miracle.

Ferdy growled again. His enemy still stood there. "Go, go away" he said in his wheezy voice. The two priests edged out of the chairs and bending low, slunk down the steps and into the church.

The tall thin man in black shouted to the soldiers, "Take these people." but none of them moved.

Slowly the crowd arose, they started talking, excitedly, "Did you hear? Did you hear what our saint said?" "He is wicked! she said." "No, that was the dog."" She said show them mercy."

"Christians, these are witches! They should burn!" The man in black shouted hoarsely, but no one listened.

Then the crowd remembered the poor women chained to the stakes. Too many of their families and friends had been punished this way for witchcraft when they were innocent.

The men in black masks held lit torches ready to light the fires around the stakes. Then they saw that the crowd was turning towards them. They threw their torches into the dry piles of wood and ran for their lives.

The fires caught immediately. Crackling and sputtering the flames rose through the dry wood, the smoke choking the poor women tied to the stakes. A light breeze fanned the flames brighter. One woman screamed as a flame licked at her bare foot.

"Help! Help!" People rushed to the fires. They pulled away the burning twigs and branches, stamping on the flames. Someone threw a bucket of water. The fire sputtered, soon the flames died and only the smoke rose circling up from the smouldering wood.

Patsy stood on the platform, no one left there except for the furious man in black and then he turned slowly and walked down the steps. Ferdy snapped at his heels, but Patsy caught him quickly. She looked around.

It didn't take long to free the women. Crying, laughing, their families embraced them, carefully, not to hurt them further. Then they were hurried away, taking their animals with them.

Edmund had his arm around his sister, supporting her. He also found the cage with Robbie and the poor dog came hobbling after him. His head had been shaved and his ears pierced with hot skewers. But he was so glad to see Katharine and Edmund, his tail didn't stop wagging wildly.

Edmund looked at Patsy. "Its time for you to go back," he said sadly.

Patsy smiled, "Backwards or forwards?" He just shrugged his shoulders, then whistled. The white pony trotted up. He helped Patsy mount it and handed Ferdy to her.

Suddenly the pony wheezed, "I don't want to go!" Edmund's sister shuddered, frightened, and tried backing away, but Edmund held her tightly.

"Don't be afraid! Its just our witch here" he laughed as he looked at Patsy. He took her hand and bowing over it, he kissed it. "Lady Patricia, we'll never forget you!" Then he slapped the horse's rump gently and it raced off.

Patsy shut her eyes as the wind streamed through her hair and then the pony stopped.

Patsy blinked. She found herself standing in the park, but the great oaks and the horse had disappeared. Ferdy was sniffing at the lamppost in the street.

THREE DAYS

The airport guard was puzzled. Private calls never came on the internal phone line. "Calling Doctor Knowle!" His voice sounded brusque over the loudspeaker system. He held up the phone as he scanned the passengers. "Doctor Knowle! Daphne Knowle!" he repeated.

She sat up startled, looked across the crowded waiting room to the passport check-in desk.

The loudspeaker crackled, " All numbers from one to forty-five please proceed to the gate." It was boarding time.

Daphne grabbed her coat and hand luggage and dodged between the passengers making their way to the exit. Relieved, the guard gave her the phone.

"Daphne?"

She smiled. It was her husband, Henry.

"Hello, Daphne. Thank God I found you! At last!"

She frowned, puzzled. He sounded tense. "Why, Henry, this is a lovely surprise! I didn't expect you to phone. You obviously got my e-mail. I only sent it half-an-hour ago."

"E-mail? What e-mail?" He hesitated. "Oh, yes, of course. How was the conference? How'd your report go?"

"The conference was great. You'd have been proud of me! And your idea that I should take a break afterwards... well, just what I needed!" She chuckled, "Went off for three days."

"Are you in the waiting room? Is the phone at the entrance?"

"Yes, in the waiting room. But those three days! It was just lovely. Wilderness!"

"Quite a wilderness! Not even a phone!"

"No, and no TV either. Heavenly! After all the noise of the conference."

"Did that bastard of a prof. steal your thunder? "

"Who? Oh, you mean Professor Ellison? No, but I'll tell you about him when I get home."

"Was his talk after yours? That could have spoiled...."

"No, not now Henry. I'll tell you later. Wait, Henry before I go, are you okay? You don't sound quite... Bad cold, headache, something?"

"I'm okay." He was dismissive, curt. "What about the wilderness camp? Daphne, good crowd?"

"Yes, great fun. Can't talk now. They're loading.".

"Where did they take you? I'd love to know..."

"You'll have to wait, dear. I'll tell you all about it, promise."

"You'll forget!"

" No worry! I won't forget it. It was really marvellous. Hold on...They're calling my number now. Got to go. Love you..."

"Please?"

"What? No, darling, I can't, not now. Its too late...."

"Okay. Will you sit down for our usual? You know, just five minutes."

"Oh, Henry, don't be daft! I can't just sit still now, no, not even for a minute.."

"Your mother said we should continue your family's custom, you know, before anyone travels.."

"Yes, I know, Mother always insisted. But I'm alone here, no family. It was always all the family."

"Mummy!" It was her daughter's voice.

"Oh, Kathy! You're there too! Hello, dear. I'll be seeing you very shortly. Has Daddy been taking good care of all of you? Did the boys behave?"

"Yes, Mummy. And you? Did you have a good time?"

"Yes, dear. It was a lovely trip. I'll tell you all about it. Got to go now..."

"Will you sit down, then, Mumsy, like Daddy asked?"

"Kathy, not you too! I know we did sit a minute before I left but you're not here now. So its not right."

"Daddy and I are here- just on the other side of the phone. And Granny always..."

" Well, yes, your Gran said they always did. But its an old custom.."

"But I like it! It was sort of peaceful."

"You liked it Kathy? Even though Jerry was crawling all over you?"

"Daddy and me, we'll sit quietly."

" You'll sit quietly with your Dad? Oh, my dear...."
" And we'll count a minute!"
"And you'll count too? To sixty? Kathy..."
"Daphne!" Henry interrupted.
 "Oh, its you Henry. What's got into you? Its nuts..."
"Please. For the kid's sake."
 "All right, all right! Oh, dear, everyone has gone now. I can't..."
 "For me? If you love me?"
 "Crazy! Yes, yes of course I love you..."
 "Bye, Daphne!"
"'Bye. See you in four hours time!"
 "Just one minute?" He asked again, " Quietly. Sit down just where you are."
 "Yes, yes I'll sit down quietly- just for one minute. Henry, tell Kathy......." but the line went dead.

And suddenly, she knew what troubled her. It wasn't the request for five quiet minutes, crazy as that was. It was Henry calling her Daphne. He called her Daphne only when something was wrong ..... It was usually "sweetheart", even in front of business associates.

They had met at an "Old Tyme" music hall in their town's refurbished cinema. He sat down next to her with his plate of cheese and crackers just as the band started playing that old song "Will you always call me sweetheart..." He looked across at her and said, very solemnly, "Yes, quite definitely, I will..."And that was eight years and three children ago.

The two uniformed stewardesses stared askance at her. She closed her eyes as she sank down into the plush armchair next to the desk and started counting. Just one minute she had promised. "One, two three...." Her watch didn't show seconds.

 "Mrs Knowle!" the tone was urgent, "the doors are going to close in a few minutes. Please..."

 She opened her eyes and looked out across the rows of empty seats. The plane, standing in brilliant sunshine, was framed by the huge window. Baggage was still being loaded into its belly. Daphne shuddered thinking of the bottle of Cointreau she had bought for Henry as the workmen were throwing suitcases from the truck up to someone in the plane's hold. The umbilical cord, the passenger passageway, attaching it to the airport would be kept open for a little while longer.

Daphne closed her eyes again and counted faster. "Twenty, twenty-one, twenty- two..."

Suddenly a thunderous roar of an explosion shook the building. The huge window collapsed shattering with the blast. The crashing of the glass mingled with the screams of terror, the crackling of fire and breaking fuselage. Riveted to her seat she gazed in horror through the jagged remains of the window as the plane became engulfed in flames. The choking stench of burning rubber and fuel invaded the room.

The two stewardesses staggered back from the open passageway their faces distorted, bleeding from splinters of glass.

Petrified, unable to move, Daphne stared at the small figures of burning men trying to crawl away from the holocaust. She could see the flames licking at their clothes, consuming them.

Sirens blasting, the fire engines arrived on screeching tires. Even before they had come to a stop the firemen had broken loose and pulled out the hoses. White foam streamed out in a Niagara fall, but the hungry flames raged higher over the silhouette of the plane.

For a moment she could see a face in one of the round windows; it could have been that little blond girl who had been sitting next to her sucking a lollipop. Then the flames and foam covered all.

Pandemonium broke out. The waiting room became a mass of people... The stewardesses, hysterically weeping, were led away. Someone came up to her, but she couldn't see, her vision was full of the burning plane and the tiny face with open mouth screaming unheard.

A hand touched her shoulder. "Are you all right?" It was a uniformed attendant.

"Come, are those your things? " He picked up her smart blue coat and matching briefcase. He held her elbow and led her out towards the main hall. "We can't do anything here. It's horrible...."

She didn't answer. Dumbly she let him lead her to a table and give her a cup of hot coffee. She couldn't taste it because of the acrid smell of the fire. A photographer raced past them, followed by others. Several were carrying television cameras.

"Vultures!" The man frowned. "It'll be in all the papers tomorrow, ..TV tonight."

Daphne looked up at him. "In papers? TV? In England as well?"

He nodded. "All over the world."

Daphne staggered to her feet. "I must phone. I must find a phone to call my husband.." Her voice was desperate. "He's coming to meet me, meet me with the children."

When her call finally got through, she sighed with relief. She pictured her sane, quiet hallway. Away from all this tragedy.

It was her neighbour's voice. " Oh, Daphne we've been trying to find you." Her voice broke. "Even the police..."

Daphne interrupted her, " Helen, the plane, the plane that I was flying in.. it's exploded. A bomb or something, it was horrible! Please, please let me speak to Henry. He'll be worried when the TV, radio, the news...I wasn't on it... I didn't get on it!!.."

And suddenly the realisation hit her. She was safe! She started sobbing hysterically. "Helen, its a miracle! Henry called me just before I was to get on."

"Henry? When?"

"When? Helen, as I said, just a short while ago." Then the heavy silence on the line struck Daphne. "Helen, what's the matter? Have you seen the TV already? It was frightening. All those people!..."

Helen's voice sounded strangled. "Daphne, something awful has happened. We tried to find you. Henry was in an accident. Car accident. In the hospital, he kept asking for you; he was worried about the children. His last words were...." Helen couldn't talk through her tears.

Bewildered, Daphne repeated. "His last words? " Then she screamed, "No! No! He can't..He can't be dead!!"

Helen's voice sank to a whisper, "Yes, Daphne, yes, it was awful. He and Kathy. He was taking her to school. Huge lorry. He regained consciousness for a short while in the hospital..."

"Kathy? My Kathy?"

"Yes."

"When? When did they die?"

"Three days ago!"

VICE VERSA

It was right! Just right! Even the girl in the magazine picture had long, black hair curling smoothly under, just like hers did.

" 'Rah! I can stop waiting for the postman now!" Helen laughed gleefully and hugged the magazine. Almost magic to see her name there printed neatly under the title of the story.

She stared again at the picture. The gaudy lights of the Penny Arcade splashed purple and red kaleidoscope patterns on the sidewalk and the big, yellow bears of nylon fur hung lopsidedly on the open doors. The noise and laughter and blaring carnival music were all there, captured in the bright splashes of the artist's colours.

Slowly her smile ebbed away. Of course her story had a happy ending. She leaned against the corridor wall blinking hard. Peter had always told her that the first stories - they had to be about oneself, they just had to be.

Helen sighed. Peter had been wrong. No happy ending for her yet. The quiet, thin boy she had brought home seven long years ago for peanut butter sandwiches after school had never said much so she had remembered that."Yup, all the first stories just have to be about yourself..." He had repeated doggedly and he had taken her down to the movies on his bicycle.

"I wonder if Peter were five years older? I wonder if that would make a happy ending?" Helen stopped herself short. She was talking out loud again, like she had been doing early in the mornings before going out to work while writing and rewriting her story.

She burst out laughing. "What a funny idea!" Peter five years older and she imagined him five inches taller, but with the same serious face under the same tangle of sunburnt hair, exactly like she had seen him a year ago.

And not since. When he had come home on vacation from the university she had pretended that she was too busy to see him then. Most of her friends had gone on to university or poly but she had had to go to work and she had drifted away from them.

She felt she was much older now, much older than Peter and she didn't want to hurt him. Next time he called she was again busy, always busy so that he stopped calling and somehow no one else had come along to take his place.

"Hey, Helen!" Her brothers' voice resounded in the corridor. "Supper is ready."

Helen's long hair swayed as she shook away her thoughts. She pushed open the door into the dining room. Without saying a word she propped up the open magazine in front of her mother's plate.

Even the Barratts next door heard the shouts and Bob's whooping! The Barratt boys came running over and her mother was wiping her eyes laughing and crying at the same time, it was such a surprise.

It was even noisier in the evening because the grapevine had passed the news around. "Helen has sold her first short story!" The telephone too was ringing constantly, at least it seemed to be. Helen was glowing happily in the centre of the hubbub. That is, until the telephone rang again and Bob answered it.

"Yes, sure, sure Peter, she's here. We're celebrating! What? Oh., sure, come on over." When Helen heard everything suddenly became still inside her, just quiet and still, and somehow afraid. She had to put on extra armour in the way of an extra-sparkling smile and she was puzzled at herself.

He was the same except taller and his hair had even learned how to stay down. He had on his orange and brown striped sweater from the university. He looked around for her as soon as he opened the door; shouted his "hello everyone!" right across the room and all at once he was beside her, pumping her hand up and down, congratulating her.

"So, you've done it! Good girl! I want an autographed copy of the story." He was grinning just as if he was so happy being with her again and he did not notice that she was quiet.

Her mother came up smiling and started asking him about his classes. He laughed, shaking his head. "No, nothing about me tonight. It's Helen's night. I'm not famous."

He put his arm around her shoulders. He wouldn't have dared before. Then gently but firmly she felt him push her towards the door. Before she could protest he had turned waving to everyone.

"I'm kidnapping this celebrity for a little while. Got to get my copy of the magazine autographed!" The door slammed shut behind them.

They were out together in the dimness of the porch. He let her go and turned to look at her again, hardly smiling except for the slight twinkle in his eyes, the way she remembered him. Helen thought desperately for something to say to him, to span the long year. He chortled as if guessing her thoughts.

"Come on, get on the old horse. Lets go get a coffee." She forgot her stiletto heels and sheer tights and climbed up behind him on his old bicycle with the crooked handlebars. She held onto her skirt with one hand and onto his shoulder with the other, feeling his thin back through his shirt.

Everything slipped back into its proper place for a moment and the wind brushed her hair in the old familiar way. He coasted down the hill towards the town centre, just missing the manhole cover at the third turning.

A car swerved out of a corner and Peter skidded to a stop. "Five more blocks to the Corner Bar. Lets walk." His voice was a little gruff.

She nodded and he wheeled his bicycle onto the sidewalk and left it leaning at a crazy angle against a wall. No one would take it. It was too old.

He shortened his footsteps to match hers. "Well, what's the plot of your story?"

Helen shrugged her shoulders. "Oh, you know, the usual boy meets girl type." She stared down at the cracks in the sidewalk and again felt that year in-between. So finally he did all the talking.

"You know, I'm writing a novel for the lit class. I've got the main outline done, first five chapters written." He waved towards the large brick house that stood back from the road, partly hidden by a row of tall, silvery spruces. "That's the place of action, except I'm calling it Edgemonton in the novel."

Helen glanced up at him. He continued enthusiastically. "Old Walters is in it and Mr Hans and Dame Ellen, though, of course, they're all camouflaged. You've got to write about oneself, you know. At least for the first few times. I bet your story is really all about yourself!" Helen shook her head emphatically, but he did not even notice.

In the bossy way of Central High, except that the bossy way had been hers then, he told her that she just had to read his chapters.

"Got it! Tomorrow is Sunday. We'll go down to the river in the morning and I'll read it to you. You can tell me what's wrong." He smiled down at her, but she felt bewildered. She kept trying to find the boy who had followed her around with his eyes full of puppy love only a couple of years ago.

Peter stopped her suddenly. Laughing, he pointed to the rows of fuzzy teddy bears hanging outside the amusement arcade. "Hey, Helen, that one's for you!" He reached for her hand and squeezed it tightly, then pulled her into the loud brassy noise of the arcade with the blinking, coloured lights painting patterns on their faces.

Peter grinned as he paid the barker. "I'm planning to win the biggest bear. Might as well bring him over right now!" He handed one of the orange stripped balls to her and pointed at the clown she had to hit.

She aimed carefully, concentrating hard, but just as she threw the ball, Peter put his hand on her shoulder. Her ball careened wildly, spun around and hit the side. She frowned at him, but he just guffawed.

"So sorry! Just couldn't let you win the bear yourself, you know." He winked at her. He threw the ball and the bell on the clown's head clanked loudly as the clown toppled over. He threw again and the bell clanked.

He missed only one ball and that was when Rose, the girl who worked in the lingerie department of the store where Helen was secretary, came up and jostled his elbow.

"I say, Helen, who's your friend?" she crooned, smiling brazenly up at Peter. Helen suddenly remembered what the other girls had told her about Rose. She could sell the most glamorous, expensive negligee to any man. Peter grinned and Helen felt she disliked Rose intensely.

"You owe me ten cents for that throw," Peter laughed at Rose, but his eyes roved appraisingly over her figure. Helen recognised suddenly that purely male stare.

Peter glanced back at her, but she couldn't smile back somehow.

He turned to Rose. "Now, you run along, huh, like a good girl. You disturb me too much!" He shook his head and gave Rose a little familiar pat on the shoulder. Reluctantly, she wandered off and Helen almost sighed with relief, almost as if she hadn't been breathing while Rose was there.

"Well, to win the bear now!" Peter's next throw was smooth and true. Clang!

After ten balls the barker stopped him. "Too good, much too good. You'll put me out of business," he growled, shaking his head. "You've won the bear, the one you said." He pointed to the large, cuddly bear hanging in the showcase, his beady eyes staring straight ahead and his mouth sewn into a funny grin.

"You know," the man grumbled as he shuffled towards the case, "This is for kids, not for men like you!" He shook his head again and opened the case door, stretching towards the bear over the purple vases with glossy painted flowers and dancing girl statuettes bedecked in pink feathers. Peter stopped him.

"Hold on, hold on. You know it's your choice, Helen." He turned around to look at her. "Would you rather have something else?" Helen squeezed between the barker and Peter to look at the array of prizes.

The barker was still grumbling. "Take the bear, he's the best bet, you know. And look here, Miss, you just keep that man of yours out of here from now on...." Helen suddenly turned her face up to look at Peter, the barker's phrase ringing inside her. Peter was looking down at her seriously, not even a twinkle in his eyes. She caught her breath and looked away fast, down at the prizes again.

When she saw it, she was so startled that she dropped her handbag. Just like in her story a small silver ring lay in a cheap plastic case on a piece of imitation velvet.

Peter bent down to pick up her bag. "Well, have you decided?" he asked handing her the bag, but she realized that he didn't mean the prizes. She glanced again at the bear and the vases, but she didn't see them. The barker had said "that man of yours...that man...."

Suddenly she laughed, free, easy, the way she used to be with him. She nodded. The stillness in her had vanished.

"That's better! I won't bite you know," he grinned, feeling the change. Impatiently the barker reached for the bear.

"Oh, yes, the teddy bear of course," and she looked up at Peter, her eyes shining. Perhaps after the day at the river or when he came back for summer vacation, perhaps then they would be there alone for each other as Peter would choose the little ring to put on her trembling finger. She giggled. Her idea was so funny- he wouldn't think of a Penny Arcade ring now.

Peter looked down at her enquiringly, but she shook her head. "I'll tell you my joke someday, later on, that is maybe." She teased him and hugged the soft bear, cuddling her cheek in his long silky fur. "It's something to do with writing stories about oneself, you know, the way you told me, except this one is all backwards!"

EMERALD GREEN

"Why, you don't really think that the French here will turn traitors, too? Go over to the Germans? Become Vichy! Surely Lebanon is too far from France." Ann Harden, impeccably dressed all in dark blue, was the wife of the American consul stationed in Beirut. She passed a cocktail over to one of the guests. As the perfect hostess, she could carry on more than one conversation at a time.

"Aileen, dear," she turned to the vivid, dark-haired, young woman standing beside her, "If you want tales of the Arabs, of the Bedouins, you should ask Paul there. He's our Lawrence of Arabia, you know. Oh, but you haven't met him yet. French sculptor, quite fascinating! Come, my dear." Ann politely stalked through the party crowd.

As she followed Aileen gazed around. Being here was a rare occasion for her. The room was huge, decorated with fine geometric designs in a typical Arab style. The arched windows opened onto the colonnaded veranda that looked out to the sea. It had been built several centuries ago as the summer home of some rich Egyptian family. Lebanon was used as an escape from the greater heat of Egypt.

In the late nineteen twenties it was bought by the US government to be the residence of their consul. The Harder's home was in complete contrast to the modernistic, three-story concrete block that served for the USA legation.

Ann talked over her shoulder as they made their way across the hall. "He's a great traveller, been collecting sketches of Bedouin women. His sculpture of an "Arab Woman at a fountain" won a prize at the French Colonial Exhibition."

Aileen interrupted, "Why did he return to Beirut?"

"He said he's returned to make a statue of a Venus instead of a Cleopatra!" Ann smiled. "You watch out, though, he's quite a womanizer!"

As they passed him, Harry, one of the personnel at the legation smiled. "Did you warn Mrs Taylor that no one knows how much of the Arab philosophy Paul Alain himself really believes? He's lived so long in the East that he's, perhaps, well, you know, sort of different."

There was a group of interested listeners around Paul "our Lawrence".

"You don't really believe that man has no freedom, as this tribe of Bedouins believes! After all we're not born into slavery!" The protester was young and vehement.

Paul smiled and shook his head. He talked with a slight accent, and his long hands were never still. "I never said whether I believed it or not. It's their philosophy. I am repeating it. By the way, you have forgotten one of the crucial points. You do have liberty, freedom, whatever you want to call it, but only for one moment of decision, and on your choice depends your whole life!"

Ann pushed Aileen through the group. "You see, Aileen, he's already talking about the Bedouins! Paul, I'd like you to meet Aileen Taylor, and remember, no idea of building up your harem, she belongs already!" Ann chortled and moved on.

Paul Alain was stocky, shorter than he seemed and his face, bronzed by the desert sun, seemed startlingly alive with intense black eyes. Somehow one could imagine him trudging along in the desert, dressed in the flowing garbs of a Bedouin.

Aileen was fascinated. "Mr Alain, you mean we have one crucial decision to make in our lives and that otherwise all is destined? But what kind of decision?"

"That, Mme Taylor, nobody knows." He smiled at her. "The desert people themselves do not. But, that decision can change the whole course of a person's life, bring him out of the harmony that has been decided for him." Paul became engrossed in lighting his pipe, although he kept glancing at this fresh-looking, young woman in her silky green dress.

Harry laughed. "You see before you the enigma of the desert! No one knows- and you, Paul- won't tell us more! " He turned gaily to his pretty companion as she lifted her glass to drink. "Oh, no, Mrs Taylor," he arrested her action by the shocked tone in his voice, "You must think your decision over. Have you really decided to finish your cocktail and eat the olive on the bottom?"

Everyone laughed and Harry continued," After all, your decision to drink, perhaps, Allah knows, it is crucial. From this point on you will drink more and more and finally become an alcoholic!!"

Paul joined in the general laughter. "To Mme Taylor, her health!" he raised his glass and the company joined him.

She half-laughed embarrassed, flushing slightly, and pushed back her heavy black hair. It was flattering that such a man had noticed her. She knew, of course, that she was pretty, that her figure was almost that of a fashion model and that her face had clear-cut regular features. But still, she felt it wasn't for that that Paul Alain had toasted her. She was really interested in what he said and he must have sensed it.

The room was getting too crowded. People shifted around, someone called Paul and he moved towards a window. Aileen wished she could have continued talking with him. But he was now surrounded by a flutter of elegantly dressed women.

James Moore, the greying historian from the cultural attaché's office, interrupted her thoughts. "Mrs Taylor, you've been in this part of the world for almost a year now. Have you managed to get to Greece?" Aileen shook her head.

"You must go! The Parthenon is the greatest ancient temple ever built!"

"But what about Baalbek?" Aileen had read a great deal about the ancient temples, but Walter, her husband, was always too busy to take her there.

The historian would not even hear her argument and launched into a lecture on the beauty of the Acropolis of Athens. Aileen smiled and held up her empty glass as an excuse to move towards the table laden with pungent Arab and typical American party foods.

Miss Elliot, the long-serving secretary inherited along with the legation by each succeeding minister, smiled at the historian and moved closer to hear him better.

She interrupted him in mid-stream to extol the beautiful piece of brocade she had bargained for in the Souk Tawile. Exotic, unique! It had taken almost an hour to get the price down, and carried away by her own ardour, she started gesticulating, mimicking the Arab seller and almost knocked the host's glass out of his hand.

The host, Archibald Harder, was a large, red-faced weighty man, uncomfortable in the heat and the very correct formal suit. He kept wiping his face with his huge handkerchief. Going from group to group, he finally came up to a tall man who seemed hardly to be listening to the group he was with.

"Well, Walter Taylor!" He gave Walter a hearty bang on the back. "How's everything? Here, another drink." Archibald took a glass off the tray that the dark servant was carrying and thrust it into Walter's hands.

"You know, you mustn't let the heat get you down! Spring is awfully hot this year." and Archibald, wiping his perspiring face again, moved over to the next person, not waiting for an answer.

Walter had almost dropped his empty glass when Archibald had slapped him on the back. He had had only time to nod and disentangle his thoughts, but the consul had moved on. Walter balanced himself on the other foot for a while and wished he had a chair. He tried to catch his wife's eye, he wanted to go home, then she moved so that someone was standing in the way.

Aileen had gone towards the buffet to get away from the historian. Perhaps unconsciously, she had followed Paul Alain. He had fled from the questioning flurry of women towards one of the windows.

As she came up he moved over for her to stand next to it where there was a slight breath of air coming in.

"You've come back to Beirut recently, Ann Harder told me." Aileen smiled. "Do you know most of these people?" Paul shook his head.

Aileen continued, " Over there, that's Archy Harder, the head of the legation."

"Yes, I've met him."

"Next to him is Harry; I don't know his name, but he's also from the legation. Next to him is Walter, Walter Taylor, my husband, then...."

Paul listened politely to her, looking in turn at the people she pointed out. Then, quite brusquely, he turned his back on the rest of the party and stared straight at Aileen.

"But you, Madam, you are by far the most interesting. I do not wish to listen about others." The compliment was said earnestly. "I believe in knowing the individual, not hearing of him. Knowing and seeing and the seeing is the medium to the knowledge as well. Now, please tell me of you."

Aileen shrugged her shoulders. "But there is nothing exciting about me. Nothing at all."

"No, no, there must be. You come from America, from where?"

"Hartford, Connecticut."

"Oh, I have heard of the place. It must be beautiful since you live there."

"No, just an industrial city. The usual factories and dust and smoke." He detected the slight aversion with which she spoke.

"You did not like it there? No. I feel. I am sorry" and he seemed almost to be giving his condolences for someone's death. During the conversation he had been watching Aileen very attentively, every expression on her face.

Now, suddenly he exclaimed, "I think I have it now! It is your face that I need! For the beautiful statue that I have here in my mind. You will model for me, will you not? Yes! Yes! Please turn so, for the light" He motioned with his hands.

Laughingly Aileen obliged. Her profile was regular, almost classical.

Excited, he grasped her hands and raised them to his lips. "Exactly, exactly the profile! Mrs Taylor, Aileen, I may call you that a l'Americaine? Please?" Aileen nodded. "It is more than the pure Bedouin. It is exquisite!" and he kissed the tips of his fingers in the air.

He suddenly stopped and added apologetically, "It is wrong, Madame, that you should do this to me. You see, I am training to be cool, but the artist, he returns even though the Bedouins are good teachers of the calm." At first he started telling her of his life in the desert, but then he became quite enthusiastic.

"Aileen, there is nothing so great as a lovely picture or an exquisite statue. It is the soul of an artist shown in... in all its beauty! You see a block of marble! Misshaped, perhaps distorted, having lain in the ground for centuries and then- Yes, I can see it! An artist strokes it, he feels it." His hands stretched out, gesturing, curving in the air, as if really feeling a piece of marble. "He discovers in it the lovely shape of a woman or perhaps the torso of a gladiator! Can you see it, Aileen! Can you?" He was begging her to follow his thoughts.

And Aileen was caught, entranced by this man. It seemed to her that it was possible he had the power to awaken stone. He could convert a block of marble into life. This was so far from Hartford and her friends, far from the party guests.

"You must love beauty too, for you are like me!" Impulsively, he took her hands again. "These others, they do not understand! They are Anglo-Saxon. Their feelings are below in the cold of their soul. Like the Bedouins. They too cannot understand when I lose my mind for the beauty of their women. Ah, pardon me! You, of course, are Anglo-Saxon too, but you are different!"

"Who is different, pray tell?" Harry had come up to them and had caught the last words. "I don't believe that basically anyone is different. It only depends on the clothes one is wearing," and he comically jerked his tie.

"No, Harry, it is not the clothes. We say it is the soul that counts."

"Fine sentiment, Monsieur le Frenchman, but have you got a soul? That question has been bothering me lately." Harry laughed.

Aileen smiled, "Paul, I think that's sooner a question for your desert friends. Do we have a soul if we have no freedom?"

"But of course we have a soul. Harry, he questions because the English word for it is lacking in feeling. L'ame, that is much better. That has depth. And it is l'ame that one condemns or saves in the one choice."

"Do you really believe that we have but one crucial moment of freedom? It seems so unfair that one moment should decide so much."

Paul shrugged his shoulders. "Who knows?"

For a while the three were silent. Aileen sat down on a couch and the two gentlemen followed her example. Paul carefully lit his pipe and Harry offered Aileen a cigarette.

She shook her head. The Frenchman thoughtfully picked up a silver ashtray and examined it closely, his fingers running over the fine filigree work. He was the first to break the silence.

"I believe, perhaps, these Arabs they say the truth. All our actions, they are from circumstances and then perhaps we can choose."

Harry interrupted him. "But tell me is this philosophy widely believed in?"

"I really don't know. I heard it of one tribe near the Euphrates. Their sheik is a great man, very wise."

Aileen was intrigued by this new idea. "Is there some way to tell when that moment comes and what decision is the crucial one?" She watched Paul's hands turning and playing with the ashtray.

"No, there is no way except, they say, that the sages can tell."

"The sages?"

"You know, Hollywood would film them in huge golden cloaks, with long, flowing beards, white of course!" Harry's interpretation made them smile.

"Yes, the wise men of the tribes. For instance, the leader of the tribe I mentioned before, he has found the right way to approach death. Something intangible, but I felt it when I was fortunate enough to talk with him."

Aileen's imagination flared up- a huge expanse of desert stretching away into the distance. In the foreground, the low black tents of a camp of Bedouins, their sheep and camels grazing near by, above them a few palm trees of the oasis...

In one of the tents an old Arab, sitting cross-legged on his mat, the sage, the wise man to whom the peoples of the desert come to get answers to their problems and to get comfort from their hardships.

Paul had to repeat his question to Aileen twice before she heard him. He was asking her how long she had been in the country.

"Almost a year now and there's so much to see and learn! But Paul, returning to our former conversation- you said the sages knew when the crucial point in a life is reached, right?"

"Yes, this is more of the mystical- why people call the desert an enigma, a puzzle. The sages they interpret the heavens and they believe a green star falls when a man has made the wrong choice. It is an exquisite idea! Most poetic."

Harry echoed him, "Most romantic! I always thought the Bedouins were level-headed."

Ann Harder swooped down on the conversation and promptly reduced it to the 'comme il faut' of a cocktail party.

Soon the banter disintegrated into "goodbye","had a wonderful time" "thank you so much."

Harry in saying goodbye to Aileen wished her luck in finding an interesting Bedouin to talk with, while Paul, not saying a word, bent down, kissed her hand and left, forgetting his hat.

Archibald Harder and Walter came up to Aileen arm in arm and Archy was still talking.

Walter felt talkative as they walked home. "Party was okay, after all. Harder is a good guy."

"Wonderful party!" Aileen replied with fervour and looked up at the star-filled sky, perhaps hoping to see a green star falling. "You know, Walter, Paul Alain is a sculptor, a real sculptor, and he wants to use me as his model!"

Walter yawned, "that's great! "

"Yes, and he told us all about the Bedouins. It's intriguing that those nomads, moving from oasis to oasis, seem freer than all other people. Yet they believe there is little freedom." Aileen was wide awake.

"Strange, isn't it?" Walter unlocked the door to their apartment and yawned again.

"I'm going to ask him to take me to the museum to see the section on the desert". She turned to look at Walter. "Dear, you'd like to come, too, wouldn't you? He knows so much, it'll be fascinating!"

"Well, you know I'm so busy." He yawned again. " And anyway, it'll be sort of boring for me. Can't see what you like about museums, sort of graveyards for old things."

Aileen tried to wake him. "But, Walter, don't you want to know about their life, their art?"

"Frankly, darling, not in the least." Walter kissed her on the forehead, put a finger under her chin to kiss her on the lips, but she moved away, annoyed. She remained sitting in the living room after her husband went to bed.

It seemed strange that she should be so different from Walter. What had Paul said? She was different from all those other people and Walter was one of them. They had their feelings below in the cold of their soul, he had said. She understood what he meant. If she tried to tell them about her enthusiasms, they would laugh. Only Paul would comprehend.

The heat persisted several days after the party. When Walter woke up he felt as if he'd awakened from a heavy stupor. He rolled over to try and find a cooler length of sheet. It was all hot and sticky, even the pillow was wet.

He could hear that Aileen was up already in the next room, quietly singing to herself.

He caught a few of the foreign words, "Libiamo, libiamo"...from some opera or other. He felt like shouting to her, to kiss her good-morning. It was pleasant to hear her so cheerful again. There hadn't been any quarrel, but she had wanted to move over to the next room.

"Its too hot sleeping together and we've the guest bed." And she had collected her night-clothes and moved before he could protest. After all, she was right. It was hot.

"Aileen! Hello-a! How goes my darling?" He appeared in the doorway to her room- big, hearty, his hair crumpled and his shorts hanging at his hips. It was too hot to wear anything more than shorts.

Aileen looked up from the book she was reading. She smiled wearily as he put his arms around her and half-lifted her from the chair, grinning and hugging her to himself.

"Walter, please!" And he felt the rigidity that was in her. The cool silk of her gown crushed against the heat of his skin.

"Say, haven't I the right to kiss my wife good-morning, any more? Relax, baby," and he wanted to pick her up again, but she moved out of reach over to the dresser and started filing her nails, meticulously, carefully.

"Its about time you grew up, Walter. You're always acting like such a child."

"Well, I like that! You mean because I want to kiss you, I'm a child!"

"Oh, no, that's not it. It's just you're always behaving like a....I don't know, completely without manners, no culture, nothing. I don't know. I've got a headache," and Aileen annoyed, threw down the nail file and started furiously brushing her hair.

Automatically, he bent down and picked up the file and then stood staring at her back, at the way her hair curled up every time she lifted the brush to start a new stroke. He wasn't thinking of anything. There was just a blur of bewilderment in him and he felt as though slowly a wall was going up around Aileen, keeping him from her, something intangible.

She had banished him from her. No more playing or kidding around. It got on her nerves or she had a headache. But then, it was probably the heat. He moved his bare feet and left wet footprints on the floor.

He tried to sound cheerful. "Well, darling, why don't you take an aspirin? Take it easy today. I'm off to the office shortly. Will have breakfast in the cafeteria there."

He waited for a reply, but she only nodded and didn't even look up at him.

He ached so badly to take that slim figure in his arms. He took a step forward and then was ashamed that he should think so impulsively. He turned as if he wanted to see what book she was reading.

It lay open at an illustration of an ancient Greek temple. He shook his head and then leaved through a few other pages. There were photos of other temples and altars with broken statues displayed in museum cases. On one page there were illustrations of fine jewellery with intricate designs. He carefully turned back the pages to the one that Aileen had left open.

"Interesting? Huh?" There was no reply. He left quietly, dressed and went out. The man at the legation gate noticed that his usual friendly smile was missing.

"Mr Taylor," he always pronounced the name in a strange way, making it sound almost Arabic. "Mrs Taylor, she is okay? Not ill?"

"She's got a headache!" Walter mumbled, "It's the heat, Abdullah."

"You make headache go away. Get the beautiful madam a beautiful present. She forget headache then!"

Walter raised his eyebrows. "You know women? Abdullah, I think you've hit it! Very good idea. It's her birthday soon."

"If you go to the Souk, the bazaar, of Gold, you find many beautiful jewellery there." Abdullah grinned conspiratorially. "All women the same. My wife, she is the same. Headache goes away fast! Take car to Place de la Concorde. Just before the Rialto, the cinema, small street with gate. You go there...."

Walter took the afternoon off. The legation car dropped him just in front of the small covered street that Abdullah had described. Few people came here- only those rare ones who wished to sell their golden heirlooms or those, more numerous, who wished to buy.

Separated from the market by the gates that shut out at sundown all the rest of the world, this cobbled street had the quiet of established prestige. Those who wanted the best knew it would be here.

Walter stopped in front of one of the jewellery shops vying with each other in the brilliance of their wares. Long golden earrings, ancient, heavy with design hung from a wooden peg. They looked almost Mexican copper except that the design was finer and the pattern more exotic and they were made of gold.

A small man, in a leather apron, came out of the shop. "Good? Pretty, you buy?"

Walter thought he looked almost like the Lebanese jeweller back home. Perhaps it was his brother who had got a visa in Walter's office and immigrated to the States.

The man was waiting for an answer, patiently watching an unseen insect crawling along the vault of the street ceiling.

"No, no, I'm just looking," and Walter moved on. Aileen would look strange in those long pendants. Her college friends wouldn't recognize her in them; they were too exotic, almost cheap-looking. She'd probably prefer a bottle of Chanel.

It was cooler in the covered street and Walter meandered from shop to shop. Was it cool enough for a game of tennis later in the afternoon?

Again the same array of golden earrings, bracelets, necklaces. Why had he come to this street anyway? He could have bought her a present in one of the modern stores on Bab Edris.

No. He wanted to find something really special and Abdullah had said that this is where he could find it- a beautiful present for the beautiful Mrs Taylor.

In the next shop window he noticed a bracelet on the very left, it would suit Aileen. Then he remembered that he had given her one almost like it when they had first arrived in Beirut, almost a year ago.

A delicate jewel box attracted his eye. On the polished wood a fragile design of a crescent moon gave it an exquisite charm. He wondered if that would be a good choice, but she had a beautiful silver case they had bought in Damascus only three months ago. Perhaps the shop had other treasures and Walter went in.

Fatma, a young girl of about ten, was alone. Sitting with her arms crossed, playing the little shopkeeper. She arose and asked the tall American, politely, in Arabic, what she could do for him, gesturing so that he'd understand.

Walter pointed to the jewel box in the window. He had never joined the courses of Arabic that were given at the Legation. He had meant to but somehow hadn't got around to it. So many people knew English that it didn't really matter and if they didn't, well, there was always sign language.

The little girl carefully took out the box and wiped it against her dress, then she set it primly on the table. With obvious pride, she rubbed her finger over the inlaid gold and looked up at Walter for approval.

Walter smiled and nodded . "Adesh?" How much? He knew a few phrases. The little girl looked blankly at him. Shop keeping had its complications. Suddenly she explained something to him and disappeared into the back door.

Walter examined the jewellery in the window, then turned to the little box-table with its glass top, standing in the corner. Here were the precious and semi-precious stones, great turquoise necklaces, brilliant sapphire rings. Some of the jewellery was covered with cotton wool and there were a few Egyptian scarabs on a small silver plate, but they weren't as brightly green as the ones one can buy on Fifth Avenue in New York.

He heard footsteps and a veiled woman came into the room, followed by the little girl. The woman had no shape, no human form, as from head to ground she was bundled in loose black garments. She raised her top veil and two shrewd eyes looked appraisingly at Walter. He felt that she was noticing all. He wished he had worn his old black shoes instead of the creaky new saddle ones.

"Saide, good-day. What is it you wish to buy?" She went briskly up to the table and picked up the jewel box. Efficiently, she turned it this way and that making the gold glitter as it caught the light. She thrust the box into Walter's hands. He looked at it closely and she turned away as if wanting to rearrange the chairs, but still she watched him sharply. Did he like it? Did he smile? Or did his grasp lack eagerness?

No, he was not very happy with it. Perhaps a ring would please him better and she brought out of a drawer several gold rings. The buyer shook his head. Perhaps he'd like a silver belt? She told Fatma to fetch the turquoise one from another box. The belt was beautiful but Aileen needed another colour to match her evening dress.

He wanted something else and then she guessed what would please him and for what he would pay three times the price.

Out of a smother of cotton wool at the bottom of a little cardboard box she took out a silver chain with a precious emerald pendant. She held it out to him, she dangled it in front of him and a star glimmered in its cool green depths.

When he came home that evening Aileen was very enthusiastic about something for her blue eyes sparkled.

"Walter, its so exciting! There's going to be a trip to Petra this spring. We must go!" He nodded, but wasn't quite sure what Petra was. Somebody had mentioned the name before. It was a city or a lake or something…

"And just think, the Nabotheans built it long before the Roman Empire. Thousands of years ago!" Puckering her eyebrows she tried to calculate exactly when.

Walter poured himself a glass of lemonade. "Where on earth did you pick up the Nabotheans?"

She ran her fingers through her hair, impatiently, piling it up on her head to cool the nape of her neck. "I told you that Alain was going to talk on Petra today and you weren't even interested!" Walter bent down to kiss her on the back of the neck, but she pushed him away.

"But Aileen, why would I want to hear about your Petra, anyway? I hear about all these dirty little villages every day, from the villagers themselves when they come for visas."

"But this isn't one of those dirty little villages, as you call them! This is PETRA, don't you see? Its ancient and really exciting, all cut out of rock."

114

"Well, what of it? Haven't you seen the pueblos in New Mexico? Anyway we'll talk about it nearer the time. Right now, you better get ready to go to the Harder's, meeting about tomorrow. Plan is to stay in Baalbek overnight."

"Isn't it exciting! Finally, finally I'm going to Baalbek!" Aileen waltzed out of the living room to dress. Walter smiled, thinking how fortunate he was with such a beautiful woman!

Next day they walked over to the legation and joined the group getting ready for the drive. It took almost three hours to reach their destination.

Baalbek was a green oasis of gardens. Rising above the trees were silhouettes of tall slender columns- all that remained of the great Temple of Jupiter. The ruins were a little to the side of the village, and the party decided to stop for dinner at the hotel where they had reserved rooms.

Aileen was impatient. "Doesn't anyone want to see the temple right now? Its not too late!"

Paul immediately offered. "Please, may I accompany you? I know it well!"

Walter was weary after the trip, but it was Miss Elliot who convinced him that he didn't really want to go. "Poor Aileen, she'll be bored with him," she predicted. "Being a sculptor he'll want to stop at every pedestal and every carving!" Walter heard her and shook his head, glad that he hadn't volunteered.

The ticket seller at the bottom of the huge platform on which stood the ruins warned Aileen and Paul in his poor English. "Only half hour light, then night comes. But beautiful moon soon!" He winked at Paul.

Smiling, Paul assured the man that "Yes, of course, we'll use the moon to the full!"

Aileen blushed.

Before them stretched the temple ruins. They didn't need a guide. Paul gave a brief history of Baalbek before they had reached the top of the stairs. Heliopolis, of the Greeks and Romans was built on top of the sacred temple to Baal. Then came the Christians who built a church in the centre.

He stopped Aileen when they reached the great courtyard. It was littered with broken columns and cornices and sections of the enclosing walls. At the far end, on a still higher platform, towering over all were six great columns, grandiose, solitary-all that remained standing of the Temple of Jupiter.

"You must imagine, Aileen, that we two, we are pilgrims of long ago, come to worship at the Temple of Baal, or Zeus, or Jupiter, the greatest of the Gods! You and I, we have come together from our home far away." He took her hand and pulled her into the sacred grounds.

"You must imagine this great courtyard as it was then-full of colour and marble, beautiful colonnades, and peoples from far away, clothed in white Greek togas, multicoloured Indian gowns!" As Paul talked his voice became richer, as if he was indeed seeing what he described.

Aileen interrupted him pointing to a beautiful sculptured cornice lying in front of them. "Please, Paul, what is this stone. Where does it fit in?"

He quickly raised his hand and covered her eyes, gently, for a moment. "No, Aileen, you must not see the little details now. They make the whole perfection, but now it is the feeling, the spirit that you must feel." He remained silent, looking up at the six columns.

The last rays of the sun lit them up and they seemed to flame scarlet.

Gradually the sun sank below the horizon and the columns lost their colour. A coolness arose from the orchards of the village, and Aileen involuntarily shivered. Paul gently put his arm around her and drew her to him. He held her close for a moment.

Then quietly, without a word, they turned and slowly went down the steps into the lower yard. Aileen strayed away from Paul, looking at the huge rocks strewn around. She jumped up on one of them and stared at the moon, just rising between the columns. A small breeze caught her hair, and she lifted her arms to hold it back from her face. She stood motionless there in the moonlight.

Paul turned to see where she had gone, and stopped suddenly. Standing on her marble pedestal was a perfect statue of a woman, of a Grecian goddess, with her beautiful bare arms raised, holding back her hair. He had found his Venus!

Next day the whole group explored the ruins. Not only those of the central court, but also of a smaller temple, that of

Bacchus. It was almost whole having been protected by the massive walls of the courtyards towering next to it.

"Of course, you've all noticed that it's Bacchus that has withstood all hardships!"

Harry said, laughing. "The God of revelry, gaiety, drink, he can take it all, while the greatest of the Gods." and he pointed at the six columns of the temple of Jupiter. "He succumbs. Ladies and gentlemen, kindly notice the moral that nature points out!"

Everyone laughed and soon the party started towards the exit and hence the return trip to Beirut. Walter put his arm around Aileen and led her to Ann's car. Miss Elliot sat down next to a morose Paul in the other car.

Having made good time back to the legation, Walter suggested that as an end to a great day, they should all come back to the Taylors for drinks.

That evening, for all their walking and driving, no one seemed too tired. Only Aileen looked a little distraught

They gathered around Walter and the bar.

"Small gin and it, please."

"Scotch and soda for me."

"I'll have mine on the rocks, please."

"Straight, thank you." Paul gulped down his drink and poured himself another one, then sat down in a corner, staring at a small crack in the floor tile at his feet. He looked up as Aileen came in from the kitchen carrying hors d'oeuvres. For a second their eyes met, and she turned away, agitated. Putting down the plate on the coffee table, she fled back into the kitchen.

Falling into a chair, she pressed her hands against her throbbing temples. She tried to think. She must make herself think straight. But all she could see were Paul's beseeching eyes. What did he want of her? She could give him nothing. She was married and in love with her husband. Of course, of course she was! But then again she saw Paul's eyes. She felt his arm around her.

Walter noticed that Aileen was gone for a long time. He came gaily into the kitchen, a glass in one hand. "Hello, darling! I've been looking for you." He smelled of whiskey when he kissed her. She stood up and put her arms around him, and suddenly held him tightly to herself.

Carefully putting his drink onto the table, he hugged her, too, laughing, tried to lift her up in the air, but then her eyes, so serious, arrested him.

"Darling, what's the matter, my sugar plum?"

"Walter, Walter, I love you, I love you. You know I do, don't you? Don't you?" Aileen's look was almost pleading and she held him still tighter. He was so tall and strong. He could straighten everything out.

"Why Aileen, are you sick or something? Listen, why don't you go to bed, darling? You've had a long day." Walter was anxious.

"Walter, please" Aileen stepped back from him and looked up, "Walter please ask them to leave, to go away. All of them."

"I can't, dear. You must be reasonable. Here have a drink. It might help and then go to bed. You aren't well."

Aileen pushed away his glass and straightened her shoulders. "No, it's quite all right. I am well. I'll be reasonable now. One has to be reasonable" and she turned to go back into the living room.

Walter stopped her. "Wait a minute. Stay right here. I'll be back in a moment." He hurried to his room and took out the little box with the precious emerald that he had bought for her birthday. He thought that perhaps if he gave it to her now, instead of tomorrow, she would smile and forget to be melancholy.

"Close your eyes, dear." Aileen dutifully closed her eyes, but her smile was strained. When she opened them, around her neck hung the delicate silver chain with the green stone.

"Walter! It's beautiful! I've never seen such a stone before!"

"Darling it's an emerald, but hold it up. See! Look at it in the light!"

Aileen exclaimed, "Its got a star! Oh, Walter, how absolutely lovely! I must show it to everyone!" She ran out of the kitchen so that he couldn't see that her eyes were still unhappy. "Look what Walter has given me!"

They crowded around her. "Aileen, how lovely!" "Gorgeous green!" "The shape is wonderful!"

Walter watched the scene, leaning against the doorway, beaming. He looked around and saw Paul still sitting in his corner.

"Come on Paul, you should look at it. It's really a fantastic stone, even if I say so myself." He took Paul's arm and pushed him through the crowd.

"Aileen, Paul hasn't seen it yet. Show it to him, dear. Being a sculptor, you know." Aileen kept her eyes carefully lowered on the emerald. Only her hand trembled a little as she raised the stone on it's chain.

Paul hardly glanced at the necklace. He stared at the hand that was holding it up. It was a perfect little hand. Impulsively he bent over and kissed it. She jerked it back as if burnt and for one startled second looked into his eyes.

"Hey, Paul, you don't go around kissing married women! That's not done!" Walter laughed as he put his arm around Aileen.

Miss Elliot shook her head and murmured "These Frenchmen! Can't resist kissing a lady's hand!" and everyone laughed.

Someone turned on the radio and Aileen moved away to get some more ice for the drinks. Unnoticed Paul followed her into the kitchen. She heard steps and started taking out an ice tray.

"May I help you Aileen?" He came up to her and took the ice tray.

Without looking at him, she asked him why he did not leave her alone. The smile vanished from his face.

"I cannot" He shrugged his shoulders as if trying to cast something off. "It is stronger . You are more, much more than a person to me. You are needed for all, for all the world!" Paul grasped the back of the chair and stared down at his hands.

Aileen shook her head. She couldn't understand. "Please let us be friends. Stop persecuting me. Please, can't we?" Aileen was desperate.

He remained silent. She turned and went to the window. Outside, there was the calm and beauty of a Mediterranean night. There was a slight breeze as the palm trees in the garden rustled. She wished he would say something, anything, instead of staring at his hands.

He moved up to her quietly and putting his hands on her shoulders turned her towards him. She looked straight at him and slowly he pulled her closer.

"Do you really think it is possible that we two be only friends? No, I must know you, know every gesture, every line. And I want you, Aileen." He added very gently "I want you so much that nothing can stop me."

Then his tone of voice changed, became triumphant. "And for the world I will make you a Venus, a Venus such as none have ever seen! You will remain forever, my Venus, my Venus!" He buried his face in her hair and then raising her chin he kissed her passionately and held her so close that she could hardly breathe. She did not kiss him back, nor did she resist, but remained bewildered and miserable.

He tried to kiss her again, but she gently disengaged herself and he let her go, watched her leave him without a word.

She went to her room and threw herself on the bed and lay there motionless. Then slowly, through her numb misery, she heard the radio being turned on louder and after a little while, the raising of voices, of some commotion.

Walter burst into the room. "Aileen, we've got to get out of the country immediately! The Vichy have given us twelve hours to get out!" Aileen turned wearily and looked up at him, not understanding.

"Darling, I'm so sorry. You aren't feeling well. I'll do the packing myself. You just stay there and I'll tell everyone that you wish them all goodbye. Poor darling!" He kissed her on the forehead and hurried out of the room.

They would be leaving in eight or nine hours. Only the Americans would be leaving. Slowly Aileen realized that Paul would remain. She would probably never see him again.

She got up and, patting down her hair, walked into the living room. Archibald, Harry and Walter were huddled together discussing what should be cleared out of the legation. All the ladies had gone home to start packing.

Paul was still standing next to the radio. He looked intently at Aileen, noticing every detail about her, as if to keep it in his memory. As she moved slightly the beautiful stone on her neck caught the light and the green star in its depths came to life and seemed reflected in her eyes.

He decided in that one brief moment that he wanted her too much, that he could not let her go without saying a word.

He came up to her and shook hands, anxiously trying to look into her eyes, but she would not meet his gaze. "Please Aileen, stay," he whispered, his voice intense.

Without looking at him she shook her head, "My place is beside my husband."

The door closed gently behind him. She stepped towards it, then turned back.

Walter went with the others. For Aileen there was so much to do, to pack only what was essential before the few hours were up. A concentration camp would not be pleasant, and they had to reach the Palestine frontier by nine. They would be safe there in the British-run country.

She worked nervously through the night, directing the maid, packing the china and the small pieces of furniture, the extra clothing. And it kept her from thinking of anything else.

It was past five when Walter drove up to the house and the sun had already risen. He looked pale and there was a streak of soot on his cheek. His hands, too, were grimy going through the ashes of the burnt papers to be certain that nothing readable was left.

Both tired, they hardly talked as they piled the suitcases into the car. Mustafa helped tie the bigger ones onto the car roof. Tearfully, their maid put a bag of sandwiches into the front glove compartment.

Aileen went up to take a last look at the house to make sure that nothing vital was forgotten. She glanced out of the living room window at the beautiful scene she loved- the azure sea and in the distance the mountains…

She put her hand on the windowsill and noticed a little piece of carving lying on it, a little marble leaf that had been chipped off some column. She recognized it as a piece from Baalbek. Someone, probably Walter, had brought it as a souvenir.

She held it in her hand and Paul's words came back to her- "Two pilgrims going to worship, we two, together" and now it seemed so natural that that should have been so. He had taken her hand and led her to where art and beauty were worshiped.

Walter called to her and in a minute anxiously appeared in the room. "We are ready to go. Have to hurry!"

"Walter," Aileen was calm now. "I'm not going with you."

Walter stopped astonished, then chortled, "Well, what a time to joke!"

"I'm not joking. I'm staying in Beirut."

"Don't be silly. We can't stay here. You know that as well as I do."

"No, Walter, you are going alone. I am staying here."

"You can't! I can't leave you here alone. You'd be in a concentration camp immediately." He took her arm and wanted to lead her out, but she stepped back towards the window, clasping still tighter the little marble leaf.

"Listen, Walter, I mean it. It's silly going on this way. I can't stand it any more."

"What nonsense! Come along now and we'll discuss it on the way." He started pleading with her, knowing that it was getting later all the time.

She shook her head.

"Well," he hesitated slightly, "If you insist on staying I'll stay too. I can't leave you alone. I'll tell Mustafa to unload." But she stopped him.

"No, you're going. I'm staying and I'm tired, tired of you and Mr Harder and with his stories and his wife who pretends she loves art. With a capital A."

"Listen, I wish you'd stop talking like that. You know perfectly well you're my wife and I love you, cherish you and all that. Now, please, Aileen, be reasonable. I know you're tired. Both of us are so, please, don't make it worse."

Abruptly, Aileen pulled off her wedding ring and taking his hand she thrust it into his palm. He stared at the small golden ring shining on his hand and then looked at her bewildered.

"You don't really mean it, Aileen, do you? You're just joking, aren't you?"

"No, I'm not." and her voice was hard.

"Aileen," there was so much hurt, uncomprehending hurt on his face. "Aileen, what have I done? I'm terribly sorry, if I've done anything wrong. Please, Aileen, give me another chance."

He took a step towards her pleading, but she turned away from him. The knuckles of the hand holding the stone leaf were white from the pressure, but she didn't feel the marble's sharp edges cutting her.

"Oh, Walter, you've done nothing. It's me! I can't stand just eating, drinking, laughing at somebody's stupid jokes, thinking I'm living when there is nothing else!"

"I don't understand. What do you mean- nothing else?"

"My God, Walter, you can't understand me even now! It was silly of me to think I could love you." She laughed, harshly, unnaturally.

"You don't love me anymore?" Walter stepped towards her and clasping her shoulders turned her around to face him. "Did you love me before? Tell me, did you? Or did you marry me to come out to this land of romance?" He shook her furiously and involuntarily she gave a cry of pain.

Letting her go he stared down at her, his face pale and intense. "Well, aren't you going to answer or are you going to say you've a headache now and please don't touch me! Except this time it won't work."

"Yes, I did love you then. I don't know why but I did."

"Now, I suppose you're in love with that Frenchman, with that soft-talker! Knows everything about everything... Is that true? Is that who you're leaving me for?"

Aileen nodded. "At least he has some interest beyond just existing!" Walter took a step towards her and raised his arms as if to shake her again, then laughing mirthlessly, he turned away from her.

"Have him! You're welcome!, I'm sure. Have fun , darling, looking at statues with him! But I better not see him before I leave," he added furiously, "the underhanded little rat!"

"Walter!"

"What's the matter, Aileen?" he said sweetly, too sweetly, "You want more than just living, you want art, museums, but poor Walter doesn't care for dead mummies so you throw him over for the first soft-talker. Well, I'll break his damn neck if I see him!" He turned away and left her.

She could hear him walk heavily down the stairs and slam the car door. For a moment there was silence, then the engine started and the car lurched into motion. She saw it go down the street at a crazy speed and for a second she was frightened.

Then she noticed a man standing still against the wall, on the other side of the street opposite the house. The man turned and slowly walked away. Aileen was grateful to Paul that he didn't come to her at once.

The wonderful days, and months, and years that lay ahead- there would be time then to be with him. She wanted a few more moments to think of Walter, pitying him going away alone.

It rained and rained and rained, heartbreaking sort of rain. The tin roof of the shed next door kept beating a monotonous tattoo. The gutters were full of dirty water, mud in the streets, bedraggled beggars too miserable to beg and wet dogs pawing at the overturned garbage cans.

Aileen wearily pushed back a straggling wisp of hair and remained seated as motionless as before. The walls of the room seemed to come closer, to shut her in. It was grey everywhere. The terra cotta models arranged on a lino-covered table were grey. The patch of sky in the window was grey. Aileen too was grey, the colour of a person sick and weary.

The ticking of the clock hanging on the wall became louder as the patter of the rain quietened. She glanced up at it and painfully got up and heavily moved towards the door.

"Its too dark, here, much too dark!" She sounded almost hysterical as she turned on the central light and then walked around the room turning on all the other lights. The brightest light shone on a beautiful marble statue of a woman with a perfect figure.

"What did Paul, my darling, call it?. Yes! Of course I know! Venus before her night with Neptune." Abruptly Aileen began to laugh, mirthlessly, almost crying.

"Yes, yes, waiting for him to come to her!" She picked up a photo frame standing close to the statue. A smiling Aileen looking at an adoring Paul...a picture taken a year ago and it dispelled for a moment her grey thoughts.

They had had wonderful days. He had loved her and cared for her. He had almost worshiped her when he saw her posing there before him. Day after day as the marble took her form, the exotic happiness in him had lasted. He would throw down his tools and clasp her to him. Immortal days when only they two mattered and the war, the world, remained unseen, outside.

In the nights, when the bombers came droning over the city heading for Beirut's harbour, he would hold her close and caress her, his hands feeling her shape. Then, gently, with the tips of his fingers he would follow the contours of her face, whispering how much he loved her. When the sharp sound of bombs exploding in the harbour reverberated and the house trembled, they laughed and held each other closer.

 Then one morning she came back to their bed, nestling close to him. She remembered it all so clearly.

"Paul, my darling, guess what's happened! The most wonderful thing possible!"

He had looked up at her smiling and suddenly rose and turned away to the window.

He had seen in her eyes the first gentleness of motherhood.

"Aren't you happy, Paul? We're going to have a child! Oh, its so wonderful!" She wanted to hug him, but he pushed her away.

"What's the matter, Paul? Remember, you said little Jacques was so cute, that we should have a child! And now?"

He took her hands then and held her off at arm's length. "Yes, of course I want a child. Of course! But not at this price!" Then he had added viciously, "How could I do this to you?"

"But, darling, a child is the goal of every woman! What ever happens, I'll never regret it! I'm no different from other women!"

His muttered reply was that they could have adopted a baby.

"But I want our own child, yours and mine. We could find a second-hand crib in the bazaar. I'll paint it bright yellow, to add more sunshine to the house. Darling, it'll be lovely!"

Paul didn't listen to her. He sat down and held his head in his arms. She came up to him and rumpled his hair, kissing him.

"Tell me, what is it? Why aren't you happy?" She was close to tears.

He stood up, facing her. "Happy? How can I be happy? You are going to become bloated, ugly, and I should rejoice!"

"That's only for eight months, Paul." She had answered gently, "And then you could make a statue of me with the child! Paul, think of it- a Madonna and Child!" She had added joyfully, sure that she had found the right argument.

He had looked at her with infinite pity in his eyes. "No, that is impossible. You must forget all that." Then he added furiously, "Oh, God, that I should have been so selfish!" He stormed out of the house without another word.

But his unfinished work drew him relentlessly. Aileen groaned, remembering the long sessions of standing on the upturned box that served for a plinth. He insisted that she pose for longer stretches.

"But, Paul, I can't! I must sit down."

"Just a moment more. See, I've almost finished this hand." And half an hour later, she sank down onto the box.

Paul tore at his hair..."How can I work with you sitting down!. Get up, get up!" She burst into tears. He pulled her up. Held her close.

"Please, Aileen, please!" He pleaded with her. "There is so little time left! Forgive me Aileen, but you can not understand. I love you so much, you are my reason to live! But I need some more time. See, the body is almost finished..." He kissed her passionately, held her close. And wearily she stood up on the box for another half hour.

Then, at least, he was at home with her and for all his sharpness there was so much of the old Paul left. Now all that had changed.

When the last bit of polishing of the statue was finished he wrapped up the chisels and other tools and put them away.

And he himself left in the morning and came back so late that she could hardly stay awake to greet him."Hello, Paul," rising she went to him and he kissed her absently.

He never looked at her now. And he slept with his back turned to her.

Aileen stared at the statue, then almost like a sleepwalker she slowly turned the statue around so that it faced the wall.

It kept raining outside. She wished that it would stop so that she could go to the neighbour's and talk with her, hear what was happening outside her narrow world.

"A little rain! I won't get too wet." She was talking to herself as she put on her coat and went to the door. Suddenly she stopped startled. The room spun madly around. She leaned against the door so as not to fall. A spasm of pain shot through her and she clutched the doorknob.

Slowly the spinning stopped and the pain ebbed away. She sat down, resting, wondering what had happened to her. The doctor had said there were four weeks before the birth.

Yasmin lived almost opposite her. "If I walk slowly I could get to her house. I'll be all right." Her neighbour always talked to her in the grocery store at the corner. "She won't mind my coming over." Aileen didn't want to be alone; her imagination flared too easily and her thoughts were not happy ones.

She unlocked the door and shut it quietly behind her. The rain was pelting down and there was a flash of lightning. It seemed that her neighbour's house was further away somehow and she was tired when she finally arrived.

The lights were burning brightly in the house. She could hear talking, laughter. Through the grey mist of the rain covering the window she could see that there was a party going on. Someone got up and went to the piano. Aileen recognised her friend. She was dressed in her best clothes, a dark red velvet dress and her hair was arranged differently, professionally.

Aileen pressed her face against the windowpane to see better. The rain was starting to soak through her coat, but she didn't notice. It was so long since she had seen a party. Or been to one. It was wonderful!

It looked so warm and jolly… She hesitated one moment. Perhaps she wouldn't be welcome. Then she noticed Yasmin, smiling happily and talking with her usual wide gestures. Aileen knew she wouldn't mind if her American neighbour came in to watch.

"I've got to put on something pretty!" and as she turned to go home the pain shot through her again. She bent down clutching her body.

"No! I'm going to a party now!" She was going to have a good time, fun. She started walking slowly, bent over, and the pain eased.

It took a long time to get back home and then somehow the keyhole was hard to find.

At last she was in. She moved slowly to the wardrobe and feverishly started pushing aside the hanging clothes, looking for the pretty green dress that she had brought from the States.

She found it at last and held it up to the light to see if it was too wrinkled.

"No, the wrinkles won't show! And my emerald will look just right!" She opened the drawer of the toilette table and easily slipped on the silver chain.

All the clothes on her were wet; she hurriedly took them off and started dressing. She tried to pull on the silk dress, but it didn't fit. One of the seams ripped with her impatient tugging. Throwing the dress down she went back to the wardrobe.

"There must be something, something I can wear". She threw several dresses onto the bed. Nothing would fit. And her slacks were too wet to put on again. Slowly she sank down onto the bed and pulled on a maternity skirt. Her smile faded. She couldn't go to the party. She shouldn't be seen in this state…

But perhaps if she combed her hair, put on some lipstick? "Won't I be all right?" She turned to brush her hair. The reflection of the beautiful statue of Venus gazed calmly in the mirror behind her. Aileen shivered and hid her face in her hands.

The rain had stopped and a wind came up, rattling the shutters. The waves beat on the rocks below the road. Somewhere a cat meowed pitifully, forgotten outside and then she heard quite distinctly the town clock beat out the hours. Eleven.

"Why isn't Paul back yet? He should be here with me." Her imagination jumped- "He's with another woman!" Perhaps he was at this very moment taking her in his arms, kissing her. She could see him. Aileen staggered to her feet. "Yes, that was it! He left me for her!"

She clutched the edge of the table, brutally, as if it were that other woman whom she grasped. That other woman, he would leave her too. He would give her moments of ecstasy and then he would leave her alone in the rain and the dark!

Aileen grabbed her coat. She would warn her. "Yes, I'll warn her!" The sharp pain again zigzagged through her. "Have to hurry, tell her that this man is a beast!" Warn her before she falls under the hypnotism of his passionate eyes and sensitive hands. Long hands, fine hands, delicate for coaxing marble to take the soft shape of a woman.

Flinging open the door Aileen felt the cold wind catch her in its wet embrace. Almost staggering, she turned to the left for that was the direction that Paul went every morning. She had watched him leave so often.

"Have to hurry, must hurry," she repeated hysterically. She almost cried it out loud and the wind laughed derisively as it tugged, pulled at her in the deserted streets.

Paul came in quietly, hoping not to wake Aileen. The kitchen light was on, but she hadn't left him anything for supper. There were usually some cold cuts and bread. Tonight there was nothing.

He groped into the dark of the bedroom and undressed silently. Aileen was surprisingly still. She would usually turn in her sleep at the slightest movement. The bed wasn't turned down either. He suddenly felt that everything was too quiet.

Gently he put out a hand to feel the blanket. Aileen wasn't there. Switching on the light, he saw that the bed had not been slept in and Aileen's coat was not hanging on its hook. Several dresses were strewn on the bed and crumpled at his feet lay her silk party dress.

He turned to look at the clock. It was two-thirty, too late for her to be at the neighbours. But perhaps she had fallen on the way home from her friend.

It had started raining again and a cold wind was blowing. He crossed the road to the neighbour's house, but there were no lights showing there. Anxiously he hurried down the street looking in the dark corners near the houses.

It was useless wandering around like this and he turned back to their empty house, debating whether to ask for help from the police. He sat down at the kitchen table trying to think where she could be. All her friends had left Beirut. He started pacing the floor. Something must have happened to her.

Of course, why hadn't he thought of it before? The poor girl must have been too lonely and had decided to see if there was somebody left at the American legation. Perhaps on the way back she had sprained her ankle and was sitting shivering on some dark stairway waiting for daylight to ask somebody for help.

The trams had stopped running for the night and he was alone, walking rapidly up the street. On either side, forming an impenetrable wall, the wet black-windowed houses stared dumbly at him. The streetlights cast a few weak circles of light onto the wet pavements, but beyond those the street was dark.

Turning into a short passage, he stopped horrified. Someone was whimpering in the darkness under the low balcony of one of the houses. He bent down to look. It was the huddled form of a dog, licking its wounds. Relieved, he went on. Relieved and yet it would have perhaps been better to have found her there, even hurt.

The fear in him started growing. He remembered that Aileen had been strange these last days, but the woman next door had laughed at him. Shrugging her shoulders she had told him that Aileen was probably lonely. He should stay at home more. He had been angry with her and as he remembered a small anger came up in him again, but this time tinged with guilt.

Telling him to stay at home with Aileen! To see her there before him accusing him silently at having destroyed her beauty! He gave a short bitter laugh, remembering Aileen's suggestion that he make a statue of her and the child- a Madonna and Child.

He could not forget when, as a boy, he had admired so much the youthful figure of his sister. He had always thought of her as a youthful Apollo. Gentle, but strong, with beautiful limbs. It had been his one great ambition for years and he had studied sculpturing, working in every spare moment, waiting until he was skilled enough to make a beautiful Apollo that would have rivalled the world's best.

And then his sister, his model, had married and when she had come back for a visit, for the long awaited visit, she had come with a baby in her arms and her figure was plump and matronly. He could not understand the egoism that could have preferred ordinary happiness to immortal glory. She had laughed at him, teasing.

And he had found another goddess.

He crossed a street and the walls of the legation loomed dark in front of him. The gravel crunched under his feet as he walked up the driveway. He went through the garden, around the house. The lawn was uncut and the rose brambles had spread on the once neat path. As he stopped for a moment the night silence again blanketed all. The wind had stopped. Only the water from the drain of the roof kept dripping.

"Aileen!" he shouted hoping that perhaps a miracle would happen and she would answer, but the night remained mute and full of foreboding.

Perhaps she had gone to the sea! Perhaps he had driven her to kill herself!

A night watchman saw him running down the street and shouted for him to stop. Paul went on. He had to reach a police station. Perhaps they would find her before it was too late.

Breathlessly, Paul explained to the sleepy policeman on duty that his wife had disappeared. He gave him a description of Aileen. She was pregnant and feeling unwell.... Someone started phoning. An officer came out and Paul repeated all that he had said before.

He hurried them. She must be found. The officer reassured him that they would, not to worry. Paul was asked to stay in the station just in case they would need him.

Paul sat down on the hard bench. The naked electric bulb glared down into the bare room. He did not know how long he sat there, but the black outside turned to grey and a tram passed noisily by. The policeman awoke and left the room. He came back with two tiny cups of black coffee. Paul gulped the hot liquid, scalding himself.

Another policeman came in and Paul eagerly looked up, but the man passed him and went into the room where the officer in charge was still sleeping. Paul heard them talking and soon the officer came out, buttoning his jacket.

"Monsieur Alain," Paul looked up and seeing the expression on the officer's face, he turned away towards the window, staring out at the grey coldness. He knew that Aileen had been found, but too late.

"Yes?"

"A woman has been found. A woman with a baby. They are now in the hospital. Will you kindly come with me to identify the bodies? Perhaps it's not your wife. I hope not, Monsieur Alain." and he sympathetically grasped Paul's shoulder.

In the car going to the hospital the officer explained, " She must have fallen down in the street. She was brought into the hospital, but they couldn't save her.

The officer had to shake Paul to make him get out of the car. They walked silently up the steps and through the hospital grounds. The long corridor was white, completely white, spotless and the nurse that came up to them was dressed in white. She led them up the white stairs to a small room. A sheet covered Aileen's form. She too was the colour of marble, cold, lifeless.

The officer insisted on taking Paul home. It was still night in the rooms and automatically Paul threw open the shutters. He looked about him dazedly and bent down to pick up the silk dress still lying on the floor. He smoothed it out on the bed, folding it a little so that the torn seam wouldn't show.

It was so silent in the house. The grey terra cotta statues seemed grotesque and hesitantly, he approached the marble statue of Aileen. His fingers gently outlined every curve trying to convince himself that this was real, but the stone was cold and lifeless.

Paul retreated into the bedroom.. Something glistened under the bed. He bent down and saw it- the silver chain and the emerald pendant. As he held it up the green star glimmered in its depth and he remembered what the old Bedouin had said.

AN ORCHID CALLED SANDRA

The woman who opened the door, grunted, incredulous. "Someone who lived here fourteen years ago! And you expect me to remember?" She was ready to slam the door shut closing out the tall, pale man who had rung the bell.

"I think you may remember her. Her husband, a fellow named Masters..." Jim hesitated. "He was murdered."

"Oh, that one!" The door opened wide. "Come in. Yes, I remember her now. The one you mean. A cold fish that one. Never as much as cried about her husband."

"Wait, maybe that isn't the same woman." He shook his head. "I'm her cousin, from Australia. Sandra wasn't a cold fish!" He pulled a yellowing newspaper cutting out of his trouser pocket and held it out, his thin hand shaking.

"Here's a picture of her. This is her." He looked down at the woman as she took the tattered piece of paper from him. Her finger poked at the photo of the dark-haired girl.

"Yes, that's her alright. Never looked you in the eyes, that one, while the trial was on, almost as if she had done him in herself. That's what we all thought." The woman sank heavily into an armchair, leaving Jim standing awkwardly just inside the door.

"She left right after the trial for London. Left a forwarding address for her solicitor, I think, or insurance company." Jim stepped forward eagerly, but she stopped him, holding up her hand.

"You don't think I kept it, do you, for fourteen years? Sure, the trial did create a stir here, talked of nothing else for at least a week. So strange, no body ever found." She looked up at him. "Oh, but then you'll know all the details."

He started and backed towards the open door. "Me? Why me? Why should I know anything about it?" Then he smiled, a forced pale ghost of a smile. "Why, yes of course. We read about it in the papers in Australia and her being my cousin..."

He glanced at his watch as if there was someone, or somewhere for him to go. "Would you remember where in

London, at least the street or... or...? It's very important! I must find her." His voice was so intense that the woman looked up at him suspiciously.

"You know, you haven't got much of an Australian accent. I thought you said you'd been there long." He stepped towards her putting his hand out for his newspaper cutting.

"Where to? Where to? I must know!" He uttered the words slowly, distinctly, completely English.

"No, I don't remember." The woman pouted and got up, moving towards the door, but he moved between her and the corridor. She drew her cardigan closer to herself, as if she suddenly felt cold.

"Try and remember!" He stared down at her.

"I don't know." She moved away from him. "Yes, hold on. Some strange saint's name. Jeremiah? No, a shorter name. In Kensington. That's all I remember. That's all. Go away now. Just go away." She almost pushed him out of the door and he heard the bolt slam to.

He walked slowly down the steps looking at the worn grey stone and feeling, more than seeing, the dark red curtains moving in her parlour as she stared at him moving away. He could almost hear her gossiping with the neighbours.

"Yes, he said he was from Australia. Not a bit of an accent and pale, you know, pale like as if he'd been shut away. And this fellow, about forty, I'd say, and the murdered, he was in his late twenties, you know at the trial. Just right,... kept looking at the open door, too. As if afraid I'd shut it."

He walked slowly towards the end of the street and a man who had been leaning against the fence opposite, slowly turned towards the corner too, still reading his paper. The tall gaunt man glanced back, then started walking faster and turned the corner. The other abruptly rolled up his paper and sprinted after him. At the busy crossroads the second man paused, looking around quickly.

The tall man had disappeared. A red bus was slowly edging away from the stop close to the corner, ignoring the impatient cars behind it. The man with the paper jumped after the bus, caught hold of the platform pole and swung himself onto the platform, at the same time bending down to peer inside at the passengers. The bus gathered speed and was soon engulfed in the stream of traffic flowing swiftly toward the next red light.

Smiling coldly, the man who was called Jim Raymond stepped out of a doorway close by the corner, but then the smile faded. He frowned. He was quite definitely being followed.

But why, by whom? Surely, not just because he looked different, acted differently from other people? That woman in the house who had said Mrs Masters had gone to London... she had looked at him strangely.

The other passengers in the express down to London also looked up curiously at him as he kept opening the door to the corridor every time someone pulled it shut to keep out the draught.

He looked around furtively. The woman opposite looked like Sandra a little bit. Perhaps it was her hair, dark with a golden glint to it. His eyes kept moving towards her then he would look away quickly, whenever she raised her eyes from the magazine she was reading.

Strange what the woman in that house had said about Sandra. She had been so much in love with Masters. It must have been a great shock to her, and yet, the woman had said she was a cold fish.

And now, to finish with his past, he had to find Sandra, to tell her what had happened, to tell her the truth.

London. It frightened him. People hurrying, people running, people talking, shouting, laughing, so many people. And people not staring at him and that startled him because he had steeled himself against being stared at, thinking he must stand out in crowds. And yet, no one looked at him!

A stream of people pushing towards the underground caught him and he let them sweep him along. He bought a ticket to Kensington High Street. At first, when the doors started shutting, he panicked and pushed almost frantically towards the exit to get out before the doors locked. But a man dug an elbow into him and pushed him back, grunting for him to stop pushing. The man had not even glanced at Jim above the paper he was reading and he did not notice the cold sweat come out in beads on Jim's forehead as he hung on a strap.

Kensington High Street. The newspaper shop right at the exit of the underground sold maps. Jim bought one of London and folded it so that Kensington was in the centre. He leaned against a wall and studied the maze of streets and names. From Kensington Park across Holland Road over to Kensington Gardens and then from Notting Hill down to the Old Brompton Road.

All these black lines had rows upon rows of houses on each side. Tall brown Victorian houses, broad, modern buildings with white entrances darkening into grey and others with rococo pillared entrances, discreetly marked as hotels. Each house three, four or more stories high, and each floor four, five rooms and some with four-five flats and that was not counting the new blocks. And how many people in each house? And among them all to find someone who had known a dark-haired woman named Sandra - fourteen years ago!

"Fourteen years ago, one woman fourteen years ago!" Jim muttered to himself and clenching his teeth, he rubbed his chin roughly with the back of his hand.

"Mad!" he exclaimed aloud, "Mad, mad, mad!" and he snorted. An old man, his watering eyes narrowing to focus better, turned to stare at him and a small, freckled urchin, mouth gapping, followed him till he crossed the busy main street.

The flickering name of a cafe caught his eye. "Peter's Cafe". Couldn't be in Peter Master's memory, could it? Jim guffawed mirthlessly. Millions of Peters. He glanced at the blue, plastic covered menu on the window, then pushed the door open. The hot air smelling of cigarette smoke and frying chips enveloped him. He sat down at an empty table in a corner, facing the door.

"Fish an' chips, sausage an' chips, beans on toast, egg, sausage and beans..." The waitress in her green overall stood above him, chewing her pencil.

"Come on, I can't be stood here all day!" she grumbled. He looked up at her and smiled hesitantly. Food had been decided for him for such a long time, he felt lost reading the worn menu.

"What would you suggest?" He appealed to her, and perhaps he did look lost. The hard lines of her mouth relaxed and she suddenly grinned at him.

"Sausage, two eggs and a double portion of chips. That's what. Chips aren't greasy and you could do with the double portion. That is, if you can pay for them." She added with a knowing wink.

He nodded, "Yes, I can pay for them." She moved away and he let his breath out slowly. His hands were clenched again, the knuckles showing white. Pulling out his handkerchief he wiped his forehead.

He watched the waitress deftly dodging the customers coming in and out of the crowded smoky room, then shout his order through the kitchen hatch to the cook. She looked up and caught him staring at her. She smiled and winked, then turned to the next table.

He pulled out his map and smoothed it flat on the grey plastic tabletop. Taking out a pencil he carefully drew squares across the whole Kensington area, using his knife as a ruler. A square per day to visit. He had a little money that his mother had left him, and until it was spent, he would search for Sandra.

He did not notice the waitress. She came up silently and held his plate over the map, waiting for him to move it. In his flustered hurry he knocked over his glass.

"I'm so sorry! It's not broken," he added apologetically and at the same time he thought desperately of something to say to her to get her to talk to him, maybe smile again.

She glanced down at his map.

"You new here?"

"Yes," he nodded. Then he shrugged his shoulders discouraged. "I've got to find a room somewhere." That seemed such an insurmountable problem. He must have shown how lost he felt.

She smiled again. "If you come back at six, I'll take you over to my place. The landlady's ,got a small room up on the fourth. Forty pounds per week. Robbery, I says, but if you're desperate? Its about here." She jabbed her pencil at one of the tiny roads leading off Old Brompton Road. "All right! All right! I'm coming!" she exclaimed impatiently over her shoulder to another customer.

"An' for you- tea with a large piece of black currant pie and custard." She did not ask him this time.

He nodded, "thank you" and his smile had lost a bit of its hesitancy.

He was outside the cafe at five-thirty, he was so anxious not to be late that he had wandered the whole afternoon close by not to lose his way back. It was past six when she came out. He did not recognise her without her green overall. She came up to him, smiling and he turned to look behind him.

She burst out laughing. "Its me and I'm just saying 'hello' to you. Yes, you!" She pointed at him. "That's the way we says hello in Kensington. We smile. And my name is Flora. What's yours?"

"Jim." He looked down at her. She could not have been more than five feet tall but somehow all of her seemed bursting with confidence. Her hair was dyed a flamboyant red and her face was covered with a layer of make-up, strong and raw, but it did not hide the deep wrinkles around her eyes and mouth. He noticed that her eyes were grey, soft and gentle clashing with the harsh make-up, almost as if the make-up was a mask or a shield.

She took his elbow when they came to the road and steered him through the wall of on-coming pedestrians. "You're not used to city life, are you? Huh?" Flora grinned again at him and he nodded, hoping she would not drop his elbow when they had crossed and trying to take smaller strides because of her high heels. She held onto his arm and led him along, chattering about her day at the cafe, the strange ones that came in. He wondered if he too seemed strange to her and thought again desperately of some chitchat.

He started saying that he was from Australia, but somehow the lie did not come easily now and she did not even listen to him anyway. Slowly, he realized that she did not expect him to talk and he sighed inwardly with relief.

It was only later, much later when Jim was sitting on her bed in her small bed-sitter, balancing a cup of tea on his knee, that she listened to him, but even then, she kept moving about, lighting one cigarette after another, never standing still. She hardly glanced at him as she cleared up, washed the blue and white mugs in the hand basin, emptied the teapot. At first he wasn't sure that she had heard about Sandra, but then she interrupted him.

"This woman, you still want her as your girl?" She asked as she brushed the biscuit crumbs off the faded rayon bed cover.

"No, she is, was somebody else's wife. I just have to find her..." He finished lamely. No one would accept half a story. He should not have mentioned Sandra. He would have to explain. He stared down at the carpet, waiting, dreading Flora's questions. He had felt so lost that he had asked for her help. Now he regretted it.

"You haven't seen her for fourteen years?" Flora did not sound surprised. " It'll be difficult." She pouted slightly pushing back her bushy hair. "As long as she's not your girl, I'll help you find her." Flora grinned suddenly at him. He tried to smile back, but it was a mechanical smile that did not reach his eyes.

He ran his fingers through his greying hair, looked up at her, waiting uneasily for more questions.

"First, her picture? Have you got one?"

"Yes," He pulled out the worn newspaper cutting and held it out to her. She wiped her hands on the sides of her skirt and took it, holding it carefully.

"Pretty." Flora nodded. "Probably kind. Your type?" She looked up at Jim suddenly, piercingly, as if reading his thoughts, and then looked back at the photo.

She moved towards the washbasin and glanced at herself in the mirror hanging above it. One hand automatically smoothed down her flamboyant hair, her eyes were pensive.

"Fourteen years ago. It's a long time. She could look almost like me by now, if she had to fight for herself." She shrugged her shoulders then strode over to the curtained-off corner of her room that served as her wardrobe.

Jim watched her anxiously. He suddenly felt he had to get that photo back. It was his. She could tear it- or throw it away. He half-rose from the bed. Flora noticed the movement, maybe the strained look on his face.

"Don't worry!" her voice was gentle, as if talking to a child, "I shan't spoil it." She drew aside the curtain and rummaged in the pockets of her black, shiny coat. She pulled out a hard plastic envelope that still had a pink label on it. Carefully she folded the newspaper cutting so that just the photo showed and then she slipped it into the envelope.

"There you are!" Smiling triumphantly., she held up the photograph in its transparent cover. "You should have done that fourteen years ago if you wanted to keep it in good condition. Also much better if folk don't know it's from a newspaper, start thinking of murder and rape and so on."

Jim's face remained expressionless, only a nerve twitched on his temple. He stared down at his shoes and then at the threadbare flowered carpet, waiting for her to start questioning him, but she turned back to the small gas burner and started lighting it.

"Fresh cup of tea? Let's see your map."

It was springtime when they started. They explored Kensington together when she had time off work. The small alleyways and side streets opening unexpectedly into squares where the tall elm trees were just uncurling their pale green leaves, the long busy roads, cut up into sections of noisy traffic by the rows of red and green lights, the dark brown entrances of the small boarding houses and the streaked, pseudo marble of the large hotels.

At first it was a game that Flora and Jim played when she joined him- at least she pushed him into playing it. She called it 'MI5 in action' and they took turns asking newspaper vendors and housewives, shopkeepers and reception clerks if they had ever seen the woman in the photo.

By summer Flora realized that for Jim it was no game. He was half-a-man and Flora started hating this unknown Sandra, but she knew that he would remain half-a-man until he found her. At least, the hurt, lost look in his eyes was fading.

Summer crept along and Jim went around alone during the day and Flora joined him during her free hours and slowly, painstakingly, they crossed off square after square on the map.

On one particular day it was hot and muggy. Flora kept thinking of the coolness of the Serpentine. Her pink nylon blouse clung to her and her shoes were dusty, her feet aching. She could not even joke anymore.

"Look, enough of all this," she waved at all the people jostling their way somewhere urgently. "Lets go to the park." She took his arm and pulled him along, but he stopped her.

"I can't go. You go." He looked down at her. She dropped his arm and took a few steps forward, then turned to face him.

"Look, there must be someone who has her address. She couldn't just disappear." Flora suddenly looked up at him full face, something she did rarely, as if to let him have his privacy.

" Jim, people won't remember her if you don't tell them why they should remember her. I was wrong about the plastic envelope. We should show her photo in the paper, say why she is there."

Jim drew in his breath waiting for her to ask.

She came up to him and put her hands on his shoulders, forcing him to look straight at her. Her hands tightened on him.

"Jim, she wouldn't be there if it wasn't newsworthy. If it wasn't a case or something..." She felt him cringe, but she kept on. "If you don't want to tell, all right, but then write to the clerk of the court, wherever it was. Write! You can't find a thimble..." She tried to joke but even her smile was taut. "Heck, there are seven, eight, I don't know how many million in London, you can't ask them all! And even if you did, they wouldn't remember."

She stepped out of her high-heeled shoes and bent down to rub an ankle. He looked down at her and saw her for the first time in many months. Saw that her hair was no longer flamboyant red, but her natural burnished chestnut, and the hard make-up was gone. Her face was gentle and open, matching her eyes, instead of being shielded and the wrinkles around her mouth were laughter-lines, not bitter.

He pushed his hand into his pocket feeling for the tiny square box he had been carrying around now for weeks. Passing a jewellery shop, suddenly, impulsively, he had gone in thinking that perhaps he could find a silver thimble for Flora, as a joke. She had joked that they were looking for a thimble. Then, standing there, slightly bewildered, he looked at the glass cases and all he could see was rings, hundreds of rings lying neatly in rows on red velvet. A young couple stood in front of him, their heads bent close together, the girl giggling, trying on rings.

The assistant's stringent voice cut through, "Yes? May I help you? Engagement ring? Wedding? Friendship?"

Jim had bought her a ring with the money he had planned to buy himself a coat- a small ring with a cultured pearl, neat and simple. But he had never had the courage to give it to her.

Now he looked down at Flora, his fingers curling around the box. Her grey eyes stopped and held him. Her face was tilted up to him, eyes hostile, cold. For once, Flora was not smiling at him. She was looking up at him and into him.

Suddenly he knew it was very important that she smile at him again. He felt panicky, lost. He couldn't lose her now!

"Yes, yes, you're right," he mumbled, not really hearing what she was saying. His hand reached down to her and brushed a curl of falling hair gently from her forehead. She caught his hand to keep her balance as she slipped on her shoes.

Hesitantly, his eyes not leaving her face, he pulled the little white box out of his pocket and held it out to her silently. Slowly she opened it, cradling it in her hand.

For once she too was silent, but only for a moment.

"Oh, Jim!" Her smile was radiant. She threw her arms around him and stretched up on her toes to kiss him. "Jim!" And her eyes were full of tears.

Awkwardly, he put his arms around her and held her tightly against himself, and then buried his face in her hair, still holding her body against his. She knew instinctively, that he had awaken, he was now a whole man. And the passers-by smiled, seeing a tall, middle-aged man blushing, but still grinning happily as he hugged his petite woman.

Later, much later that day he drafted a letter to the court clerk to ask for Sandra's address. It was quite easy to write the lie about Australia, he had repeated it often enough. He then went out to the stationer's at the corner and bought thick, luxurious linen paper. It was Flora who had thought it might impress the clerk more.

Then he started waiting for the postman. Each day, impatiently, watching the hours crawl by till the next delivery of mail. Flora laughed at him.

"You'll be lucky to get a reply in two weeks time! It'll sooner be two months! After fourteen years, what do you think?"

But on the third day the reply arrived. Jubilant Jim ran down to Flora's room waving the letter. "See! Here it is!" He tore it open. Before the postman had even time to walk up to the next house Jim had memorized the address: Mrs Peter Masters, c/o Miss Judy East, 30 c, St Jude's Close.

"I'm going right now." He turned to the door, but Flora stopped him.

"No wait. It's too early. It's only eight-thirty." She was frowning. "You know, it's really surprising, you getting an answer almost by return. Almost as if the clerk had recently dug it out for someone else.. Could it be?" She peered into the mirror above the washbasin and started brushing her hair, but she was still frowning. "Strange!"

Jim laughed. "Oh, you're just being a wet blanket! I'm off. By the time I get there...." She heard him run down the stairs, lightly.

He was so sure that Miss East would still be living there that he was not even surprised when the woman who opened the door told him that it was she. She also remembered Sandra well.

"Come in," she opened the door wide and led him into her living room.

"Could you tell me where Sandra is now? What's happened to her?" Jim tried to keep his hands steady, but the vein in his temple stood out pulsing nervously. Perhaps this would be the end of his search.

Miss East shrugged her shoulders, her mouth creased into a long bitter droop. "I don't know what happened to Sandra. We were so close before, and then she just disappeared."

Jim sat up startled. "You say Sandra just disappeared? Vanished?"

The woman sighed and her whole body seemed to sag even more into the over-stuffed chair. "Yes, here one day and then disappeared without saying anything to me, and me who had given her shelter and all."

Jim interrupted, "Did you tell the police?"

"Police?" Her eyes squinted suspiciously at him. "The police? Why? Get me a bad name, huh? Police coming, asking questions. None of my business." Her tone was belligerent at first. Then she added sadly. " She left me her things, left a note saying I could have them, she didn't need them."

"No, as I says, we were close, so close." She held up her hand with two fingers crossed. "And then this man appears and Sandra just seemed to change. As if she was afraid of him, she was. And she was always one for a nice bit of conversation, but with him about, she just stopped talking to me. Come to think of it, she never did tell me about her husband, you know, the one who got killed, and her coming to me, all set to have a baby. Ha!" she snorted, "Was I taken in! I thought she had got herself into trouble, I did, and didn't want to talk about it."

Jim started, then sat stunned, not listening. Sandra was going to have a baby. No one to help her. He frowned and then shook his head as if to clear it. He smiled wryly. Yes, Sandra was going to have a child - fourteen years ago!

Miss East was still talking. "Even knitted her a little coat for the baby, I did, and me with my rheumatism in the fingers, it wasn't easy, it wasn't."

She pulled herself up slowly. "I'll show you the little coat. I've got it right here in a drawer. Hadn't sewn the buttons on yet and haven't felt like giving it away. Used to love Sandra like my younger sister, I did!"

She opened the drawer of the dark dresser and rummaged in it, talking half to herself and half to Jim. "Yes, going away like that, without a goodbye...."

Miss East turned back to him triumphantly, unwrapping a yellowing tissue paper package. She held up the little white coat, smoothing the wrinkles with one hand.

"And you know, I saw her later. She was pushing one of those fancy prams, brand new, expensive. Dressed fit to have tea with the Queen, she was. Skirt like her coat and gloves and all and talking with that man." She scowled. "Same man it was, short, limping, carried a stick, remember it as well as if it was yesterday. When I shouted to her and started running, it was in Green Park it was, she looked up startled like.

"Then she turned to the man and he just grabbed her arm and pushed her quickly to the entrance and right out and across the road. Pedestrian crossing there. He limped but you should have seen him go! I know, she must've recognised me. She sort-of looked at me, almost saying she was sorry, I was that close, I was and then I lost them in the crowd. It was that man," she added bitterly. "If it wasn't for him, I would have given her this little coat, I would have."

She slowly wrapped up the little coat in the paper and then turning to the drawer she thrust it in roughly and slammed the drawer closed with a bang.

Jim rose, frowning. He was puzzled. It was not like Sandra at all. He knew Miss East was right about that.

"Well," he hesitated, not knowing what to do next. "Well, thank you. You can't really help me, I guess, but thank you just the same." He turned towards the door, his shoulders sagging. Then he turned back suddenly.

144

"You wouldn't know of someone else? Another friend who might know?"

"Well," she thought for a moment. "There's Mary, Mary Johnson. She used to work with us in a beauty parlour long ago. You know, before Sandra went up north. Had a Christmas card from Mary last year. Married, she is, living in Barking."

"Please," Jim smiled relieved. It wasn't quite the dead end of the search. "Would you have her address?"

The woman sighed. She was getting tired of him by now. "Yes." She moved over to the dresser and pulled open another drawer. She leafed through her tattered address book. "Can't remember her married name off-hand." She mumbled to herself, "Jones, no, Potters? Yes, I've got it." She held out the open book to Jim. "Thats it." Jim copied down the name. Mrs. Mary Potterson, 7 Grosvenor Drive, Barking.

The woman who opened the door at Number 7 backed away horrified from him when he mentioned Sandra's name. She shouted over her shoulder, her voice high-pitched, hysterical, "John, John! There's a man here wants to know about Sandra.

A man came striding through the hall and pushed her aside. He looked angrily at Jim. "You just get out, will you!"

Jim quite astonished, stared at him, "What's the matter anyway? I'm just looking for an old friend. Miss East told me to come here."

The man glowered at him. "We know all about you, thank you! Just go away and don't come here again. Do you hear? Don't come here again!" The door slammed shut and Jim heard the key turn.

He felt shaken and dismayed. What had he said that had startled them? But the man had shouted that they knew all about him. Who had told them? He walked slowly towards the bus stop, staring down at the cracks in the pavement, pondering. Slowly, the feeling of being stared at started penetrating him. He spun around suddenly. A few paces behind him a man was looking at him, grinning broadly. The smile disappeared and the man crossed the street hurriedly under Jim's stare.

Jim stood looking after the man. There was something familiar about him. Perhaps the newspaper tucked under the arm of his blue raincoat. In a flash Jim saw the man who had followed him in Birmingham when he had gone to Sandra's old boarding house. He too had worn a blue raincoat and carried a newspaper. Could it have been the same man?

Jim snorted. He must be imagining things. There were plenty of men in blue macs and carrying newspapers.

And the Pottersons? Who had talked to them about him? Why? Jim walked past the local pub, just as two men jostled out of it, laughing uproariously. Jim glanced up at the sign. "The Old Bell".

He pushed open the door of the public bar and went in. The familiar stale smell of beer and smoke was reassuring. There was only one other customer there and the publican was drinking with him.

"Pint of bitters, please," Jim leaned his elbow on the bar. "What about joining me?" he asked the publican as he brought Jim his pint. "Am planning to move into the neighbourhood. Any good around here?" He took a gulp of his beer.

"I've heard that a house on Grosvenor Drive may be put up for sale shortly. Want to make an offer before the estate agents come in for their cut. Know anything about it?" Jim felt surprised at himself. He was talking so naturally.

"Don't know of any house for sale, no." The publican turned to the other customer, "Heard of anything, Don?"

The other man shook his head. "No, but it could be the Pottersons moving, after that nasty business with their girl, you know." Jim held his breath and stared down into his drink. He mustn't sound too eager to hear more. "Business about their girl? What, not safe for families around here?" He looked up calmly.

"Queer business that. Just the other day it happened." The man named Don paused and raised his glass. "Their girl disappeared on the way to school. Picked up by someone. No, no maniac apparently. Nothing happened to her, but they had a phone call, just when she should have arrived at school. She's about ten, I guess."

The publican interrupted, "More like twelve-thirteen, I should say, or else she's one of them very forward ones!" He guffawed.

"Phone call, saying this fellow had the girl. Not to call the police and the girl would be returned at ten, let out in the park." Don shook his head. "Queer business! They were warned about something or other. No one knows what. And the girl was let out at ten, unharmed."

The publican shrugged his shoulders. "They never told anyone, the Pottersons, that is. Just sort of leaked out, part of it from their closest neighbour, and then the girl herself. I say, Don, Pottersons wouldn't have been in the MI5 during the Korean war or something?"

Don laughed and Jim tried to smile sociably, but his eyes were cold. Don jabbed the publican over the bar. "You've been watching too much TV!"

"So, its still safe for families? Huh?" Jim finished his drink, paid, waved his thanks and sauntered out. He had heard enough.

Jim went back to Miss East. But first he bought a gun. He knew where to go, he had picked up a great deal of information from his cellmates during those long years. And when he went to see her, he made sure that no one could have followed him. He had learnt enough tricks for that. It cost him at least two pounds for an eighty pence ride as he criss-crossed around in the different buses.

Miss East was puzzled. "Funny that she didn't want to see you. We all used to have good times together." She shrugged her shoulders. "Never can tell with people, can you?"

"Would you know of some other friends, Miss East?" Jim asked hopefully.

"No, I wouldn't. Sorry and all that!" The woman added crossly, "I treated Sandra all right, and see what thanks I got! Gave her my spare room too, and didn't ask for rent and her wearing orchids and too high-up to even say 'good morning'!" She held the door open waiting for him to leave.

"Orchids?" Jim asked surprised. "Sandra wearing orchids, you say?"

"Oh yes, when I saw her in the park with that man, I was close enough to see them, I was. Lovely things, them. Don't see too many about. Two-three pinned on her coat, she had. And she could have said 'good morning'!" Miss East let the door shut slowly behind Jim, as she muttered to herself, "Orchids, orchids! and she wouldn't even say 'good morning'!"

It may have been hours that Jim wandered aimlessly through the streets, stopping automatically when the traffic lights turned against him and the cars rushed past, and then walking on, being elbowed and hustled by the crowds.

Finally he wandered through an open gate into a park where the noise of the city became a background hum instead of a pulsing, all-dominating roar. He sank down onto a bench and leaned forward, staring at his dusty shoes.

Something was wrong, very wrong. Sandra, warm, impulsive, loving Sandra with a man only some three months after Master's death. But then of course! Jim sat up, his face set in grim lines. He must have been Simeon, Peter Master's brother! But still, with orchids pinned on her coat. Orchids which were Peter's and his brother Simeon's obsession.

Jim had heard of the orchids the very first time that he and Sandra had met Masters, several months before all the trouble. Reeling slightly, Masters had pushed his way through the crowded pub from the bar to their table, looking intently at Sandra all the way. He had drawn up a chair for himself, unasked, and dropping into it, he had leaned across the table towards Sandra.

"You're her, no, no, you're the she for me!" He slapped his knee, chortling, "See, I even start talking poetry after seeing you." He pushed his thick blond hair away from his hot forehead and smiled blandly at Sandra. Jim remembered that she had smiled back, even though she didn't usually smile at strangers, half-drunk at that.

"Look, move on, will you?" Jim had growled at him but Masters only glanced over in his direction, his eyes not really focusing.

"Its all right, I'm not really very drunk," he enunciated the words very carefully. "Its only because I haven't got the courage without a little bit in me." He smiled apologetically in Jim's direction. "I've been looking at her now for weeks. I won't fight!"

Jim grimaced, remembering that he had liked Masters then despite himself. A pest, sure, but honest at least.

Later however, Jim had had enough of him. Masters had leaned on their table, his large fingers still grimy from the day's work, curling around his glass of ale. He was a big man, almost oxen-like, with his large, kindly, brown eyes, blood-shot then, but later, when they had met him sober, the kind that look you straight in the eyes, honestly, without a trace of guile or deceit.

In his half-drunken state, he had started talking about orchids then. He turned to Sandra. "You know, you're just the right person to grow orchids with me and my brother Simeon." He took another gulp of ale and grinned.

"You want to grow orchids?" Jim exclaimed. He had seen orchids and that was only once in the downtown shop where the sales girls wore white silk over-alls and flowers in their hair.

Masters ignored him. "They're beautiful flowers, beautiful! And we're going to grow them someday, Simeon and me. Not the large, gaudy purple ones, not those, but the smaller ones, five, six on a stalk. Delicate, beautiful!" He smiled like a little boy. "Or else the slipper ones, cypripediums. No one has ever yet grown a perfect white one! You know, one without the slightest bit of colour somewhere."

The man seemed transformed somehow talking about the flowers, looking intently at Sandra as if convincing her was so very important.

"Look, its all very interesting, I'm sure, but just move along, will you?" Jim had had enough, but Sandra put her hand on his arm and smiled at him coaxingly.

"Wait a minute Jim, its interesting. I've never heard about orchids." She looked back at Masters. "You've really read about them?"

Masters nodded, his face suddenly very serious. "Yes, everything on orchids they have in the Birmingham Library, the main one. Next place, the British Museum Library. My brother Simeon, he'd be the brains of the business, you know, the works. All we need is you. Needs a woman's touch, you know. I can make anything grow. Green thumbs, you know!" He grinned staring down at his huge thumbs. "But I haven't got the instinct, the flower instinct to know what would be perfect, which flowers to cross-pollinate. You would." He nodded, sounding positive.

"What do you do now?" Jim asked suddenly.

"Me? I'm in the car works." Masters glanced vaguely in his direction then turned back to Sandra, his eyes focused intently on her, forgetting Jim completely. "You know, it's a long, long job. Takes five years for an orchid plant to flower, then you cross-pollinate, grow seeds in a kind of jelly, then transplant the seedlings into tiny pots with osmunda fibre. Best comes from Japan, you know. Then you put sphagnum moss on top... must be the right kind. Delicate job, long job but then you have it! Simeon and me, we've thought about it for years now."

He smiled shyly. "Its like a dream! Can you imagine it? Row upon row of flowering orchids, beautiful, delicate, exotic!" His arms extended, he rose towering above them, swaying unsteadily, but his eyes were glowing and looking far away into the distance. "And among them you might have a champion, one of a kind never grown before!" He bent down over Sandra, suddenly. "What's your name?"

"Sandra. Why?" She was fascinated.

"Sandra." Masters scratched the back of his head, reflecting. "Hum, Sandra." He cocked his head to one side as if listening to the sound of the name. "Yes, that would be all right for an orchid, but not white. Red. Red to go with you. Definitely red. We'll have to work on the reds first then." He nodded. "Of course it's for Simeon to decide. He's the brains. But can you imagine it?" Master's face was shining not only from the drink.

"Snow outside, but inside the hot, steamy glass houses - a dream, a magnificent dream come true!" He stood still for a moment beaming, then he sat down heavily. His face clouded, its excitement extinguished. "Haven't got the money. That's all. Haven't got the money." He raised his glass and did not lower it until it was empty. Then without another word, his head sank onto his arms and he was asleep.

That was the first time Jim and Sandra met Peter Masters.

They met Peter again next evening at the same pub, but this time he was sober. He stammered apologetically, "I'm sorry about last night. I'd had a little too much. I'm sorry." and he backed away from them to the bar. Sandra had smiled at him encouragingly, as if he were an old friend and he had smiled back at her, almost gratefully, like a hungry St Bernard being thrown a bone.

"What are you beaming at him for?" Jim asked annoyed.

Sandra turned back to him. "I can smile at him, if I want to, can't I? I'm not yours, you know!" Her chin tilted up and her eyes were sparkling dangerously.

"Yes, you are! We're going to get married, aren't we? And I shan't have you picking up every drunk who talks to you in a pub!" Jim moved his chair closer to hers and put his arm around her, looking down at her.

The fighting sparks faded in her brown eyes and she looked up at him, her perky face, soft, her eyes glowing. "When, Jim? Please when? Lets make it soon, next month. That's April. Lovely for weddings. I've waited so long." Her voice too, was soft, entreating.

"Well. soon, sure, soon, but not that soon." He felt rather than saw her shrink away from him. "We'll wait a few months more. You know, till I've saved a little more and then I should get a rise, what with Jones retiring." He looked at her, but she was staring down at her hands, twisting her engagement ring around and around. He could only see her profile, her cheek flushed.

"You've said that before. You've said that ten times, a hundred times!" Her voice was low, but there was a hysterical note in it. "I'm sick of waiting. I'm sick of it. If you don't love me enough..." Abruptly she pushed back her chair and grabbed her bag. He did not even have time to get up before she had run halfway across the room towards the door and she let the door bang shut behind her.

Jim sank back into his chair. He might as well finish his drink and let her simmer down.

It was late when he knocked at the door of the house where she lived. The landlady opened the door scowling. "Its late, much too late..." she grumbled. "Oh, its you, Mr Raymond." She smiled, then shook her head. "Sorry, Sandra's gone. And she asked me not to give you her address. Sorry, but she'll get over it, I'm sure." She closed the door and the light in the corridor went out.

Slowly Jim walked down the steps into the deserted street. She'll get over it. She'll get in touch with him.

But she didn't. Two weeks later he saw her. She was with Masters, sitting at the bar at the Cock and Crow. She had smiled guardedly at Jim and then turned back to listen to Masters. Jim noticed that Masters was completely sober and yet talking animatedly to her, his hands gesticulating, explaining something. Morosely Jim had wondered if he was still talking about orchids.

Jim followed Sandra that evening and they did not even have a quarrel. It was a very polite, cool conversation, almost as if they were talking about the weather instead of their lives. No, Sandra had had enough. She did not think she loved him anymore.

"Well, if you prefer that Masters fellow, that's it, I guess." He had felt numb, as if he was talking about someone else. Half-heartedly, he asked if she wouldn't change her mind about coming back. He did not add that he was lonely without her, so lonely that he wandered about in the streets in the evening rather than face his empty room.

They even shook hands politely and wished each other good luck- and it was only later, outside in the street, that he kicked viciously at the hedge, furious with himself. He could have talked her around, he would have married her immediately, only to have her with him.

After a while the hurt faded. His own radio churned out the music hers used to blare out in the evenings. Then there was always the Cock and Crow.

That evening, two months after he had talked to Sandra, the pub was crowded and the smoke and smell of beer hung low. John, the publican was in rare spirits, his hand over-generous on the tap and his jokes saltier.

"Hey there, Jim, come on over," he shouted over to him and Jim, still squinting to see in the smoke, pushed his way through to the bar.

"Here, son, to give you courage." John pushed over a mug, the foam spilling over. "Heard that dame of yours, gone and got married yesterday. You heard of it? Hey?" He jabbed Jim in the ribs as if it were a joke. "Pour it down, pour it down. Give you another on the house."

John turned back to serve another customer. "No good for business if a good customer gets married. No good at all." He grunted to Jim over his shoulder. "But that Masters fellow, he'd nurse a pint the whole evening, not like you, Jim old boy."

The smoke seemed to be choking Jim, but he was glad it cut him off from the noisy, laughing crowd. He suddenly wanted to be alone. He could see her laughing, teasing him that

152

day long ago by the river at his favourite fishing spot, right under the Captain's Rock.

He had struggled with her on the grass and had stifled her teasing by kissing her violently, passionately. And she responded. Her whole body responded to his so that for a timeless moment they were one. Then they had lain still, completely at peace. Remembering in that hot, stifling bar with the ceiling of dark oak beams pressing down on him, Jim felt sick, sick because he still wanted her.

That was the last time he had heard of Sandra, except for a couple of times, mentioned by a strange fellow with a squint who seemed to have followed him about.

The man had worn loud clothes, the kind that shouted for attention. The bright yellow check of his trousers looked almost like a tartan. And he carried a cane with a silver knob that hit the floor loudly, decisively, as if the man knew exactly what he was doing.

Jim was in the queue in the local post office when this fellow had sidled up, his chin sticking out aggressively, one hand doubled up into a fist and the other brandishing his walking stick and he kept his head tilted as if expecting Jim to hit out at him.

"Hey, you!" Jim had turned around to look behind him to see if the stranger was addressing someone standing there, but the stranger came towards Jim, pointing with his stick.

"You're Jim Raymond, aren't you?" The voice was loud, pitched high, dramatically, so that all could hear him. He didn't wait for a reply. "You leave my brother alone, see? He ain't a bully, and just because he's married your girl, it's the best man who's won, see?" Jim, astonished, stared at the stranger. The crowd in the post office had fallen silent, gazing at the two of them.

Jim frowned. "What do you mean? I haven't seen Masters or Sandra..." he managed to stammer, completely surprised, but the man had turned and limped rapidly out, his stick tapping quickly down the steps. Jim turned back to the window. "Never seen the man before," he muttered to the post mistress and she shook her head disapprovingly.

The second time it was again the same fellow, and Jim now knew that he was Peter Master's brother, the one Peter had said would be the business side of orchid growing. The Cock and Crow was full, convivial, the drab greys and blues of the usual customers pointed up here and there by the bright hues of dresses.

Jim was just raising his mug when a high-pitched voice, so high-pitched that he recognised it at once, shouted across the room, killing all the talk.

"Hey, there he is, that's the fellow I was tellin' you about!" and through the smoke the fellow with the squint pointed towards Jim, brandishing his walking stick.

"That's the fellow. Jim Raymond's his name." He was shouting and the crowd in the pub hushed, expectantly, staring at the two of them, clearing the space between them. "Hey, you, you just leave my brother alone, see?"

He turned to the two men standing beside him and muttered something to them, then turned to face Jim again. "He ain't done nothing to you. It's the girl who's chosen him and if you go menacing him, we'll call the police, see?"

Then expressively, in the dead silence, he drew his finger over his throat, and then shook his stick again at Jim. Furious, Jim strode across towards him, but the two companions stepped forward and barred his way.

"What do you mean anyway?" Jim glowered down at the squinting man over the shoulder of one of his bodyguards. "I haven't seen your brother or Sandra for ages now. What are you trying to stir up?"

But Simeon bared his teeth in a semblance of a smile and backed towards the door, his guards moving between him and Jim.

"You know what I mean," he turned around to face the room, his hand behind him on the door latch. " We don't want no violence, my brother and me, so you stop following him about, Jim Raymond!". The thick door swung open and then slammed shut behind him. The other two men leaned against it, their hands nonchalantly in their pockets, but their eyes alert, watching Jim's every move.

"Get out of my way!" Jim grabbed the shoulder of one of the men to swing him away from the door, but the other moved in immediately and expertly pinned Jim's elbows behind his back in one fast professional move. Jim kicked out at him, but the fellow gave him a violent push and sent him sprawling across the room into the group of men watching silently, leaning against the bar. Jim was up immediately and rushed to the door, but the two had slipped out. A motor revved up and tyres squealed as their car took the corner out of the pub's car park.

Jim turned back to the bar, shaking his head, frowning. He downed his drink and asked for two more in quick succession.

"What on earth does he want with me?" Completely puzzled, shocked, Jim told the publican about the incident in the post office.

But it was the third time he met the limping man that he became really troubled.

Jim was returning home from the factory. Friday evening, his pay cheque in his pocket, a sunny weekend forecast for his fishing... He'd try the river, right under the Captain's Rock this time. It was a good name for it- the hard granite crag jutted straight up out of the river, controlling it. The water swirled around it, leaving a deep quiet pool behind the rock so that it was just right for fish.

Except it was also the favourite spot for courting couples. His own memories of that still hurt in a vague, yearning way... And sometimes there were boats there. They could moor in the straggling brown rushes and no one would see the vessel until they were right on it. If he got there early enough... Then suddenly his thoughts were dispelled.

A stringent voice, by now familiar, cut through.

"Hey, you Raymond! I told you to leave off." Jim spun around. The little man was leering up at him, his cane half raised and beside him towered Peter Masters, embarrassed, not looking at Jim, his hand on his brother's shoulder, restraining him. But the stringent voice went on.

"I told you to leave off, didn't I?" His chin stuck out and the little eyes, squinting, were evil, goading Jim on. He laughed mirthlessly. "What you fighting my brother for all the time?"

Jim grabbed at his shoulders and lifting him up, shook him furiously. The stringent voice suddenly became terror-stricken, and whining, almost crying like a frightened child.

"Peter, Peter, He's hurting me! He's hurting me. Let go, let me go!" and the misshaped legs thrashed out helplessly in the air.

Jim felt the clench of Peter's fists around his hands, making him drop the little man. He ducked under Jim's arms and stood back.

"He hurt me, Peter! He hurt me! Hit him Peter, hit him..." The voice was no longer terror-stricken or whining. It was ordering and Peter listened. He drew back his right arm and slammed his fist into Jim's chest. Jim staggered back and Peter followed, his fists hitting out, and in the background the stringent voice, half-hysterical now, was shouting.

"Hit him harder, Peter. He hit you first. He's been fighting you all the time... He hit you first....

Furious, Jim hit back at Peter, trying to get at the little man protected behind Peter's broad back. Trying to get at that goading, hysterical voice.

A policeman stopped the fight and before Jim could straighten his torn jacket he heard the whining voice.

"Yes, officer, that man there. Jim Raymond, his name, he started it all. Grabbed Peter, he did. Peter married his girl, that's why." Slowly the policeman pulled out his notebook.

"No, no," the little man shook his head. "Peter won't want to bring charges. No, just a fight. Not to worry, officer, but just in case, officer, what's your name, you know, just in case?"

The policeman took the pad the little man held out to him.

"Constable Jones, Andrew Jones from the Twelfth."

Thank you, thank you very much." Peter's brother pushed the pad into his pocket and backed away as Jim approached.

"That man is lying" Jim growled and started explaining that he had just been going home, but the policeman shook his head when he heard the story, and Jim knew it sounded ridiculous.

Next day- the Saturday- Jim would remember for the rest of his life. Each detail stood out clearly, like an indelible photograph etched in his memory.

It was a lovely morning, crisp, sunny, perfect for sitting quietly at the edge of a pool listening to the thrushes singing above the gurgling of the cool water. Jim was up and out early. He waved jovially from the street to his landlady as she shook a dust cloth out of a top window.

"Will bring back some trout for dinner. You just wait and see!" he shouted to her and threw his bag onto his shoulder.

"It'll be more like catfish, I reckon, Mr Raymond," she laughed and pulled the window shut.

At eleven o'clock, when she had finished making the beds and tidying the lounge, the door bell rang.

She was really shocked when she opened the door. Jim stood there on the step, bruised, his clothes torn, and his rod, the one he was so proud of, broken, dangling from his shoulder. A nasty purple blotch stretched down under his left eye and the blood was still ousting from the cut on his forehead.

"Some bastard attacked me!" Jim was fuming. "Crept up on me and attacked me!" He swore violently, but the landlady shook her head incredulously as she wiped the blood gently from his face. She had a son of her own, she could guess what could have happened. Mr Raymond had had a fight yesterday too.

"Really, Mr Raymond, you should behave better! It must be the company you're keeping!" And she just shook her head again when he repeated that someone had crept up behind him, someone he had never seen before.

The same day, as he was watching the TV, he still remembered the programme about a murder in a grimy Welsh mining village, the police came.

There were two men, one close to retirement age, the other young. They cautioned him and then asked him to pack an overnight bag. They took him to the police station. That was when he heard that he was accused of the murder of Peter Masters.

He did not have long to wait for the trial. The constable who had stopped his fight with Masters was called to the witness stand. After all, the little man, Peter Master's brother, had written down his name. And the postmistress, and John from the pub, and Sandra, they were all there.

The last time Jim saw Sandra was at the trial. She never glanced in his direction. She had stared straight ahead and answered the questions in a monotone, almost as if in a daze, or under strong sedation. Her face seemed thinner, drawn, pale.

"Yes, Jim and I were planning to get married," Her voice was lifeless.

"By Jim you mean the accused, I presume?" The emotionless voice of the prosecutor could have belonged to an automat.

"Yes," Sandra seemed to be hardly breathing, her words were so low.

"Then please say so." There was a cold, calculating glint in the prosecutor's eyes as he glanced at Jim. "When did you meet Masters?"

"Jim and I...I mean, the accused and I," she stumbled over the word and Jim wished she would at least glance at him, but she kept her eyes fixed into space. "We were in the Cock and Crow, having a drink when Peter, that is Peter Masters, my husband..."

The prosecutor interrupted her, "Your late husband, Mrs Masters," and for once there seemed to be a human being talking as the words were spoken gently.

"The man who became my husband, later on...my late husband," Sandra corrected herself, "he joined us and kept talking to me. Jim, that is the accused," her whisper was hardly audible, "wanted me to go home then. Peter kept making jokes and Jim got angry."

"What kind of jokes, Mrs Masters?"

"Well, not quite jokes. He kept talking about me." Her voice faded away and she stared silently at the floor, her shoulders drooping and her face hidden in the shadow of her dark hair, so different from the usual bubbling, gay Sandra, that Jim felt a surge of pity for her, and love, and he wanted desperately to put his arm around her, to protect her from all of this. He glanced at the faces of the jury and he saw there printed on the faces of the men, exactly the same emotions as his own.

The prosecutor interrupted his thoughts. "What kind of jokes, or rather, what did he say about you?"

"He said he wanted me to come and work with him and his brother. He said he needed me."

"Were you engaged to be married at that point to the accused?"

"Yes."

"Had you been engaged long?"

"Two years."

"Why didn't you get married? I believe that is the custom nowadays. Short engagement period.

"Jim, that is, the accused, didn't want to. He kept saying that he didn't have enough money yet." Sandra's voice seemed firmer suddenly. She repeated louder, almost bitterly, "The accused did not want to."

This court scene with the judge sitting on his dais in all his medieval regalia, the drably dressed jury, behind the dark-red mahogany barrier, the crowd of spectators, rustling newspapers, coughing.... This whole scene had seemed so unreal to Jim, as if someone else, not him, was on trial and he was watching it.

Suddenly, in a shuddering flash it became grimly real. It was really him, Jim Raymond, sitting there on the hard straight chair with a policeman standing behind him.

"The accused did not want to." Sandra seemed to be condemning him with those words. He shuddered again.

"The accused was going to marry you, someday, and then the late Peter Masters won your affections and you were married, I believe, quite soon after you met him. You left the accused. Correct!" The prosecutor's tone was final and seemed to be addressed more to the jury than to her. For him the case was clear cut.

At the court, only John the publican had tried to defend him.

"Yes, he came back to the bar after those fellows left. Never seen them before, I hadn't."

He described the incident in the pub when Simeon Masters had shouted at Jim and then disappeared. "Simeon Masters, him. yes, he'd come into the pub a couple or so times. Couldn't help remembering him, him always dressed like a peacock. But never seen those other fellows before, I hadn't, and in my business it pays to remember faces. Jim sure looked shocked. Real puzzled too."

The prosecutor interrupted him then. "The accused could have been feigning surprise, couldn't he?" Several of the jury nodded.

John shook his head emphatically. "No, not Jim. He was really worried then. He told me about something that had happened in the Post Office, with the same fellow. Its a put-on job, that's what."

The prosecutor had sent John out then and the next witness swore that on the morning that Masters had disappeared a man had rented a boat from him.

"Was it the accused?" The cross-examination was brief.

"Well, it could've been, and then again, it could've been someone else."

"Please look at the accused carefully. Was it someone similar? Same height? about six feet?"

"Height? Well, yes, about the same. Wore a dark jacket."

What about the face? Same face?"

"Well, could've been." The boatman shrugged his shoulders.

"Please look carefully at the accused."

"Well, yes, could've been him. Same height, could've been him all right. Have some ten-twenty people coming in and out in a day. But, yes, it could've been him."

Mrs Parsons, Post Mistress at the local Post Office was much more emphatic.

"Yes, it was the accused at the Post Office and you should have seen his face! Real angry he was. His horrid plan seen through, that's what he must have been thinking!" She glared at Jim, ready to continue, but she wasn't questioned further. Reluctantly she left the witness stand and several of the jury exchanged knowing glances.

The judge summed up the case at length. The day Masters disappeared a man who could have been Jim Raymond had rented a boat. The boat was still missing as was Peter Masters. That Saturday Raymond was seen returning from the river, his clothes torn, his face and arms bruised, as if after a fight. He had complained to his landlady that he had been attacked at the river's edge by some fellow who had crept up behind him. He'd been peacefully fishing at a place locally known as the Captain's Rock.

The accused could not identify his assailant, claiming he had never seen him before, and no one else had seen anyone locally who fitted his description, the judge added, almost sarcastically.

When Peter Masters failed to return from his fishing, Mrs Masters had searched for him as he was usually punctual. His brother, Simeon, had called the police.

At the river's edge they had found signs of a scuffle, bushes broken, the wet ground churned about. In the reeds close to the water's edge, they found a shoe with dark stains on it that were later identified as blood.

The shoe was one which Masters had put on that morning, the blood on it was found to be of the missing man's group. The footprints in the muddy ground were those of Masters and the accused. Also in the quiet pool behind the rock the reeds were bent and broken as if a boat had been pulled up there not too long ago.

The judge paused in his summing up. For a moment a heavy silence, like a smothering blanket lay on the court. But suddenly, the silence was broken by a stifled sob. Simeon Masters, brother of the missing man, presumed murdered, had his head down on his arms, and his shoulders were moving convulsively. The three women in the jury stared down at him, and then exchanged glances, shaking their heads, their eyes moist.

Simeon Masters, the judge continued, had testified that his brother was in the habit of going fishing, had started going regularly about a month ago, and that Saturday he had gone as always down to the river.

Everything was repeated, briefly, and to the point. There could have been only one verdict after that. The jury were out for about twenty minutes.

Jim shuddered, remembering those ominous minutes. There seemed only one minute of silence between the tap-tapping of the stick that the third juror had carried. It had faded away for what seemed like a very short time... then he heard it again, growing louder as the man had walked back along the long, bleak stone corridor.

That tapping had haunted Jim during his years in prison. He would wake up in the middle of the night in a sweat, hearing it again, and it was only his cellmate snoring.

And now, fourteen years later, free, he shuddered remembering. That tapping stick, just like Simeon's, almost as if it was Simeon who had found him guilty and had sent him to prison.

The park was slowly emptying of people as the lunch hour passed. Jim rose and stretched himself. He had gone through all the details so many times. He couldn't continue like this and Sandra was his salvation.

And Sandra? Something was wrong. Very wrong. She could not have been wearing orchids and talking happily to Simeon only three months after Master's death!

Orchids were for celebrations, not mourning... Surely she could not have liked misshapen Simeon? And yet the three women jurors had all looked sympathetically at him, dressed in his sober greys.

Brusquely, Jim pulled out his map of London and sat down again. Frowning with concentration, his finger followed the main road from the park up towards the British Museum, his lips forming the names of the streets as he memorized them. He still did not like taking the underground.

The stillness of the British Museum Library and the shuffling feet and quiet whispers made him uneasy. He stared about him - at the several personal computers with their screens blinking with instructions how to use them. Hesitantly, he walked up to the enquiries desk; his shoes seemed to be creaking so loudly.

"Pardon me, I..." The young lady continued reading her notes and didn't even glance up at him. He cleared his throat. "I wonder, please, could you help me?" His voice faded away.

The young lady marked her place decisively with a pencil mark and looked up at him. Her smile was quite friendly.

"You've never been here before? I'll help you." She rose effortlessly and came around the desk. Her voice was efficient, well-practised.

"These numbers here show you the screen; the subjects are all according to these other numbers. So, you choose which you want." She pointed to the screen, pressed the shift key, "And here you have the classification according to authors."

Jim interrupted her. "I would like some newspapers, please. Old ones. Fourteen years old. Would you have them?" He almost stammered.

"British or foreign?"

"The Times, please, and the Birmingham Chronicle from September 5th to September 12, 1982." Jim's clenched hands were perspiring and he told himself to relax. No reason why this young girl should know what happened during that period in Birmingham.

He carried the heavy awkward volumes into the Reading Room. He held them gingerly, as if they were fragile.

The Reading Room also made him uneasy at first. There was a constant, muffled noise of pages being turned, of stifled coughs, of whispering... He settled himself down at an empty table and hesitantly started leafing through the first volume, reluctant to reach that decisive day of September 5th.

Finally he reached it. He glanced over his shoulder to make sure that no one else could see the photograph of himself staring blankly and bewildered from the front page of the Birmingham Chronicle. It was big news then for them and the photograph covered a third of the page. The murder trial had lasted for four days and the newspaper had covered it fully, to the last broken twig, it seemed, under the Captain's Rock.

Jim found nothing new. He had remembered everything, after all. No new leads. No names of relatives given. Then suddenly he stopped at one paragraph. His defence had stressed that the man presumed murdered had been insured, heavily insured , but Jim was startled to see the figure. Impossible, not Masters, not Peter Masters.

Jim slumped down, thinking, his elbows resting on the closed volumes. He could not imagine Masters insuring himself, even if he had loved Sandra so very much. After all, to Peter Masters, all the world was kind, why should he ever worry about such a thing as life insurance? No, not Peter Masters.

Simeon? Jim shuddered. Simeon with his cane tapping... no, it wasn't Simeon on the jury that had found Jim guilty, no, but it could have been and Jim shuddered again.

Suddenly he gasped. Orchids cost a great deal of money. Surely orchids were not worth the life of a brother?

His hands went cold and he sat stunned at the thought. Simeon.

Slowly the whispering and rustling of papers, the small noises of the library penetrated through to him. He rose slowly and gathering the newspaper volumes together, put them on the return shelf.

He went back to the enquiries desk. The same young lady looked up.

"Yes? May I help you?"

"I'm...I'm interested in orchids. Would you help me please?" He followed her as she marched in front of him to one of the computers. Quickly she ran her fingers over the keys and a continuous list of names appeared, shifting slowly enough to read.

"These are all on orchids and related subjects. Any particular author?" She looked up at Jim.

"Yes, well, no not really," Jim frowned, not quite sure of what he wanted. "Is there perhaps a magazine for orchid growers, you know, the kind that would give all the news, who has started in the business or won a prize for a new type or something of that sort? " He finished hesitantly.

Efficiently, her fingers again tapped the keys and she stopped the screen at a range of magazines. She handed him a pencil and a blank card from the top of the cabinet. "Here, from this number onwards. If you want to see the rest you just press this key. These are all the periodicals on orchids from the time they first started. You need this number here to order the magazine. Alright?" She smiled automatically at Jim but her eyes were appraising the queue gathering in front of her desk.

Slowly, thoroughly Jim read the entries, reading all the details. He finally picked out the magazine which had the highest circulation and carefully noted down the number and the title. "The Orchid News". He took another blank card and wrote down the exact number of the screen for next time.

He collected three bound volumes of the magazine and went back to the same table in the Reading Room. The volumes covered the three years after the trial.

He opened the first volume and stared fascinated at the deep red orchid glowing on the cover page of the first magazine. Vibrant, exotic, its petals embroidered like the wings of some tropical butterfly.

Then he settled down and steadily, methodically, went through the magazine. It was the last few pages of each issue which carried the personal items, and the prizes page was the one right in the centre. Pulling out a pad he started scanning through the journals.

"Mr Perry Kinder selling his orchid business in Hampshire...the Brown Nursery offering beginner's collections. Be an Orchid Specialist and Grow Prize Orchids Only Five Years After Starting With Us!" Jim grimaced. Masters had said it took at least five years before an orchid flowered. "Peterson Nurseries selling their stock of rare cypripediums collected in Brazil..." Would they have kept a record of who had bought them?

It took Jim three afternoons and evenings to go through five years of "Orchid News" and "The Orchid Specialist". His pad had been replaced by a notebook and that too contained pages of addresses and notes. In the mornings he read his notes out loud to Flora and she commented on them as she washed up their breakfast things before she went to work. He had never told her the whole story, but she knew some of the details.

"No, they couldn't have a prize orchid by then- only four years, even though the fellow's name is Simeon." She turned the hot water tap off.

Jim continued reading, " A new orchid business that promises much has just been started by Mr and Mrs S. Allinson on the outskirts of Reading..."

"Possible." Flora came up to Jim and bent over him, reading his notes over his shoulder. "Mr and Mrs...No, I doubt it. Mr and Mrs, though, sounds good doesn't it? " she added wistfully. She kissed the top of his head and he muttered something as he wrote a large question mark against that entry.

He closed the notebook and turned around to her as she sat down beside him on the bed. She had taught him to smile again, not just automatically with the lips, but with his eyes as well. It was peaceful, but he glanced at his watch.

"Off to the library." He rose and stretched, then pulled on his coat. "You know, there is one volume I just can't get. Every time I ask for it, someone else has it. Its the "Orchid News" volume of two years ago. I think I'll ask them to reserve it for me as soon as its turned in, then I'll be able to see it tomorrow." He smiled at Flora.

"You're on late shift tonight, aren't you, Flora? I'll have some tea ready for you up in my room, alright?" The door slammed closed behind him.

At the library the young lady at the desk shook her head. "I'm sorry, Sir, but that volume has been reserved already for today."

"But I can see it there on that shelf. Could I just glance through it and as soon as the person who'd reserved it comes in, I'd give it to him."

"I'm sorry," she shook her head, "That's against regulations. It's reserved. But if you wish, I could reserve it for you for tomorrow? Would that help?"

Jim nodded and wrote down his name, then strode into the Reading Room with another volume tucked under his arm. He wondered if he could ask the man reading the "Orchid News" if he could borrow the volume for just an hour during lunch break. But no one came into that Reading Room with the volume.

Next morning Jim was at the desk as soon as the library opened. The volume was there. Eagerly he carried it in to the room and started from the first page. This was the last volume that he had to examine and then he would start eliminating all the question marks in his notebook. He and Flora would go visiting the places.

Then he stopped abruptly. In the March issue the page on which the Royal Horticultural Society awards were announced was torn out. He shook his head. No, of course, that did not mean anything, but somehow, he could not help wondering.

Jim carried the volume to the desk. The young lady was very sorry. Yes, he could have another copy of the same volume tomorrow morning. A man standing at the desk looked up at Jim suddenly, with narrowed hostile eyes.

Jim looked back surprised and the man immediately looked away and walking over to the computers started keying in as if engrossed.

Jim ran down the library steps and turned as he always did towards the street where he lived. Then suddenly he changed his mind. He still had time. He would go shopping. He hesitated a moment then plunged down into the underground with the crowd of pushing people. He kept hold of himself as he watched the doors close, then smiled. He had almost conquered that horrible feeling of being helplessly shut-in. He would soon be normal again.

Still smiling to himself, he pushed his way out of the train and strode briskly through the tunnels to the other platform to wait for the connecting train. People kept pushing and jostling him. His smile faded.

It was unpleasant after all. He tried to let those hurrying pass him, but one man seemed most impatient. Jim moved sideways, however, somehow in the crowd, it was too difficult to let everyone pass. Jim found himself at the very edge of the platform. A small blond with a turned-up nose looked up sideways at him, her full, bright red lips half-smiling.

"Too many people, huh?" She wriggled her shoulders as if to free herself from the crowd. The rest of her conversation was drowned by the drumming noise of the approaching train.

Jim felt the cold rush of stale air and the noise of the train became louder and louder. Suddenly Jim felt a sharp jab in his back. He staggered, frantically grabbing at the elbow of the man standing next to him. Someone grabbed his shoulder and jerked him back just as the train burst into the station.

A shriek tore the air and the little blond was flung by the first carriage like a laundry bundle, in front of the screeching wheels.

There was a dead silence for a single moment when the train had stopped and then pandemonium broke lose. A woman screamed, someone sobbed hysterically..."Oh God! Oh God!" The crowd surged towards the front of the train.

Jim stumbled further back, gasping, deathly pale, his shoulder still firmly held. He turned to the man holding him. "That...that would have been me....thank you, thank you." He could hardly gasp. Someone retched and the smell of sickness made the air even hotter.

The man let go his shoulder. "You all right now?"

"I guess so. But that poor girl!" Jim felt sick in the pit of his stomach. "I...I feel somehow it was my fault. I could have grabbed her perhaps."

The man shook his head. "No, it wasn't your fault, really. It was an accident. Horrible. It's the crowd. You're obviously not used to the rush, but it wasn't your fault. An accident." The man, too, looked shaken. "Lets get out of here." They walked up the stairs and onto the escalator.

Guards were stopping people from coming down. As Jim glanced back, he saw a policeman standing next to the front of the motionless train and a group of people on the track looking down.

"I say," Jim stammered, "I..I haven't really thanked you properly. And, do you think I should make a statement, give my address or something? After all she was standing next to me."

"Yes, perhaps," The man was gripping the escalator bannister tightly. "But I'd watch out, if I were you." He looked back at Jim over his shoulder. "That man behind you, standing next to me, a fellow in a blue raincoat, I'd almost say that he wanted you under that train, not the girl. He seemed in such a hurry, pushing."

The man raised his hand in a gesture of goodbye and disappeared at the exit into the crowd. Jim walked over to the policeman standing at the ticket window and told him the details, gave his name and address.

Jim still seemed to feel the cold rush of dead air as the train had burst past him so very close and he could still see that little blond being dragged under the wheels. And her shriek was still vibrating in the air, mingled with the screeching of the brakes.

Jim shivered. What had the man said? Someone in a blue raincoat right behind him, "I'd say he wanted you under the train.. he was so pushy."

He would walk from now on, or take a bus. He stared around at the people passing him. No, there was no one wearing a blue mac close by. Jim started walking briskly in the direction of his home.

He passed a small, limping man whose walking stick kept hitting the pavement hard and decisively. Jim shivered again, remembering. He had thought that he had only to find Sandra and he would be free of his past! Perhaps tomorrow, Saturday, when he had that volume.

And Flora, tidying up Jim's room before getting dressed to go to work was also somehow caught in his past. She sighed. Sandra and her dead husband Peter, and his brother Simeon...they had all become part of her life too, those ghosts from Jim's past and she did not know how they all fitted together to make the correct pattern.

That Saturday, after Jim had gone off early to the library another person from that past, but very much alive, intruded on her life.

The young boy looked up at the front of the house and then at the slip of paper he was holding. It was still only ten past nine so it had been worth getting that early train from Didcot. He was trembling inside, but he did not know whether it was from hunger or fear. He did not know whom he'd find at this address- and he hadn't had his breakfast.

The landlady was kind, very kind. Gave him a broad, motherly smile. "Sure, sonny, mister Raymond, he lives up on the fourth floor, at the very back. You go on up, but remember to knock on the door, you know." She patted him on the back as he passed and the boy winced.

Flora opened the door. "Yes?" she pulled her dressing gown closer. She had not expected a young boy.

"Is, is mister Raymond here?" The boy blushed violently and tried to hide it by staring down at the floor boards.

"No, I'm sorry. He's gone out." The boy looked up at her in dismay.

"Gone out? Already?" His face fell. Then it brightened again. "Will he be back soon? Could I wait maybe? It's Saturday- does he work today?" He looked at her anxiously. He was taller than she was and there was something appealing about him, almost familiar to Flora. Perhaps it was the colour of his eyes that reminded her of someone she knew, but she couldn't think who.

"No, he doesn't work on Saturday, but I don't think he'll be back before noon." She glanced at the boy and was sorry for him, he looked so disappointed. "Come downstairs to my room. I'll be making a cup of tea. You'd like some, wouldn't you?" She led the way down and opened the door wide.

He came in hesitantly and sat down on the very edge of the chair she pushed towards him. He stared down at his brightly shining shoes. He had plastered his light brown curls smoothly down, and put on his best suit. Flora looked at him and again felt as if she had met him before or someone very much like him.

He gulped down his tea and quickly wolfed down the buttered toast she offered him. With his mouth still full he started talking.

"Sorry for coming this way, but its very important. Life and death really. Well, almost." he added as he saw the look of amused disbelief on Flora's face. She turned back to the teapot so that he would not see her smiling. His face was so serious.

"Are you Mrs. Raymond?" he asked and she smiled openly at him.

"Well, almost," she passed him another piece of toast. He hesitated. "Go on, have another piece."

"Thank you." He held it ready to bite. "Almost Mrs. Raymond?" He was puzzled. "Are you a close friend then? Could I talk to you?" The blue eyes looked troubled.

"Yes, anything you'd have told mister Raymond. And whatever you want to tell him, I'll pass it on. Alright?" She looked back at him as he examined her and she could almost read his thoughts. Finally he nodded and she knew she had passed.

"I'm John Rogers. My mother's name is Sandra." Flora jumped and her tea cup clattered violently on the saucer. The boy grinned. He'd got the reaction he had been hoping for. She would listen now.

"Sandra Masters?" Flora barely whispered, but the boy shook his head.

I don't know what her name used to be. It's Rogers now. My Uncle Simeon also changed his name to Rogers after all that affair. So I don't know."

Flora shuddered. The boy had said "all that affair" so matter-of-factly when it had affected all Jim's life. But then again, Flora did not know the whole story. Someday, she thought, Jim would be ready to tell her and here was this young boy shrugging it off- and presumably Peter Masters had been his father. He could not have cared less! Flora shuddered again.

"Please, please, could you help me?" The boy's voice had suddenly changed. Now he was very unsure of himself. "I got mister Raymond's address from Uncle Simeon. That is, I got it from his desk. He doesn't know I got it. None of them know I'm here. They'd probably thrash me if they did." He glanced at the half-open door and Flora got up and shut it. The boy swallowed hard.

"I heard Dad and Uncle Simeon quarrelling yesterday. They've been quarrelling for years, but it was worse yesterday. Almost fighting. Dad kept saying he'd had enough. He said he'd find Raymond and Uncle Simeon didn't tell Dad that he had mister Raymond's address. Uncle Simeon just told him that mister Raymond would kill my mum and him too." The boy's eyes filled with tears and he brushed at them furiously.

Flora got up and moved to the window, staring out unseeing. "Why should mister Raymond want to kill your mother and father?" The boy shook his head.

"I don't know. I just don't know. And Uncle Simeon said that if he went to prison, he'd just die. He couldn't stand living in prison. And after all he had done for Dad...." The boy gulped again, and even in his retelling, Flora could imagine the frightened boy overhearing his father and uncle talking of life and death, the way the boy had said when he had first come in. She wasn't smiling now.

"I think Uncle Simeon knew I was listening because he even opened the door to the next room and he didn't look in, or he'd have seen me. He's the kind who always looks behind doors, just in case, Uncle Simeon is that type." He added harshly.

He paused and shook his head. "And if he wanted me to hear, I don't know why, I just don't know." The boy sounded desperate. "Maybe mister Raymond could help. It's horrible at home now. Uncle Simeon is always ranting at Dad that Dad no longer listens to him. And mother hardly laughs any more."

Flora did not turn from the window. She could hear the tears in the boy's voice. "And what do you want Mr. Raymond to do?" She thought of Jim and she could not imagine him as a killer, then she clasped her hands together suddenly.

She had remembered the gun that Jim kept in his brief case. He had laughed about it when she had questioned him. "Just in case," he had replied, "just in case." Then he had asked her to go for a walk with him, and the next time she was cleaning his room, the gun was no longer there.

"I don't know. I thought perhaps I could ask Mr. Raymond, convince him, that is, not to kill Dad. Dad's the kind who wouldn't hurt a fly. It almost hurts him when he has to cut an orchid... he couldn't have done any harm. Not to anyone." The boy was pleading with Flora. She turned around and moved up to him.

"Please, please," he caught her hand, "Please," his eyes looked up at her begging. "Talk to him, he mustn't kill my Dad. I don't know why he should want to, but he mustn't!"

Quite suddenly, the boy smiled at Flora and his voice changed completely, almost conspiratorial. "You know, I'm not even his real son, he adopted me after the affair. We just call it the affair, I don't know what it was, mother asked me never to ask – and I've tried not to be curious. Well, Dad married mother and adopted me when I was a tiny baby and mum told me, oh, ages ago, but Dad doesn't know I know."

Flora stared down at the boy then looked away, half-smiling, she suddenly felt relieved. So Sandra was married again.

The boy continued half-laughing, "He's the kind who'd be afraid I wouldn't love him anymore! Best Dad in the world, he is!" the boy's chin stuck out, proudly, but the smile faded quickly. He remembered why he was there.

"Perhaps Mr. Raymond would see me first, before – I mean, if he…" The boy stammered, "Oh, he can't want to kill Dad!"

Flora put her arm around the boy's shaking shoulders and he hid his face in her skirt. "Look, he won't kill your Dad," she tried to sound reassuring, but in the back of her mind she kept seeing that smooth, well-oiled gun. Slowly she raised his tear-stained face up, her hand under his chin so that he was looking straight up at her. "I promise you, he'll talk to you first, all right? Where can he find you?"

"At the Stafford Orchid Nursery, Upton, near Didcot." He stopped suddenly, dismay darkening his eyes and his hand clapped his mouth shut. "He didn't know our address before! He didn't know it before, did he? And I've told you!" he stared up at Flora with horrified eyes, as if she had suddenly changed into a viper. "And I've told you!" he shrunk away from her, but she calmly walked away to the window and turned her back on him, trying hard to keep her tears back.

When he had looked up at her just now, she had suddenly realised whom he resembled. She shook her head to push the thought away.

"You say that you got Mr. Raymond's address from your uncle's desk? Was it just lying there in the open for you to take?" she was trying to think of something constructive.

"Yes," the boy sounded completely miserable, subdued. "Yes, I had wondered why he had left it like that, he's always so secretive."

"Perhaps so that you would come here?" Flora asked brusquely. "Perhaps your uncle Simeon wanted you to give Jim your Dad's address," she added coldly. "Perhaps your uncle Simeon wants Jim to do his dirty work for him?"

"His name is Jim?" the boy's eyes opened wide. "Jim Raymond? You know, my father's, that is, my real father's name was Jim, I remembered that. And it was something like Raymond, Mum told me long ago. I can't remember more."

The boy's face went pale and he stared at Flora's back. "Could he be my real father? I've wondered about him so very often!"

"Yes, yes," Flora hated the sight of the boy now. She wanted him to leave. "Yes," she almost shouted the words at him, "He's your father, yes! now go away, go away!"

The boy jumped up and backed away from her towards the door, his eyes frightened now. But he stopped just inside the door she was holding open for him. He looked at her steadily for a moment.

"Please, I don't know what my father means to you, but my Dad, he's the only one I've had, don't let father kill him." He turned and ran down the stairs.

Flora slammed the door shut after him and then slowly, all the hate and anger left her face and she sank down onto the bed sobbing. That was why Jim had wanted to find Sandra. He had a son and he had never told her.

She sat for a long time on the bed and stared down at the carpet at her feet. The pattern had smudged and the pinks and purples had faded together – she could just make out the outline of a flower, right next to her left slipper. It could almost be an orchid, a purple orchid. She kicked at it viciously, and then snorted at herself for being so silly.

She got up and slowly, like an automat, started getting dressed. She went up to the basin and stared at herself in the mirror. She patted some cold water on her eyes, she grimaced at herself, her eyes red, her nose red, and the wrinkles around her mouth drooped, making her look so much older.

Not thinking, she rubbed her usual cream gently into the skin, patting under her chin, pinching her cheeks to make the circulation better, all the many little jobs that she always performed in the morning so that she would feel cheerful and well groomed and ready for a hard days' work.

But today nothing helped. As she looked in the mirror she seemed to see the young boy looking up at her with Jim's eyes –

pleading eyes. "Please, don't let him kill my Dad. Don't let my father kill my Dad..." it was funny really, the mix-up, if it weren't so dreadfully real. Flora sank back onto the bed, hiding her face in her hands.

What was she to do? Tell Jim the address? Tell him that his son had come? She shuddered, and then burst out crying again. Why had he not told her about the boy? He had sworn that Sandra wasn't his girl...

When Jim came in late that afternoon he found her sitting on the bed in the darkening room, the ashtray on the bedside table was spilling over with butt ends, he came in boisterously, turning on all the lights.

"I've found her! I've found her! Just listen to this!" he pulled out his notebook and started reading, "The orchid committee of the Royal Horticultural Society,' that's the tops in the orchid world, anyway, they've awarded a First Class Certificate to a beauty. There was a photograph of it, dark red, glowing, and called -you guess!".

He was laughing lightheartedly. Flora looked up at him surprised. She had never heard him so gay before.

"Sandra!" She kicked at the faded flower on the rug.

"Right!" He seemed years younger, he was almost grinning. "Cypripedium Sandra, grown by Mr Rogers, the Stafford Orchid Nursery, Upton."

Flora nodded, "That's correct."

He had not heard her. "So, will you come with me for the ride? You know, just to check first?"

Flora's voice rose hysterically. "There is nothing to check! Its correct! You go, just go!. Upton, near Didcot, Berkshire."

Startled, Jim stopped striding about the room and stared down at her. Her tear-stained face looked up at him, the eyes miserable, but the chin jutting out , unbeaten.

"How did you know? What's wrong?" He looked down , his eyes anxious.

"Sandra's boy came here looking for you." She paused, waiting for some reaction, but he just continued staring down at her, obviously troubled.

"Sandra's boy! Why?" He was astonished.

"He came to ask you not to kill his mum and dad." Flora's voice was flat. "He had your address from his uncle Simeon." She looked up at him again. "Don't you want to

174

know what he looks like?" Flora asked furiously. Perhaps Jim would tell her now, about the boy, ask her to forgive him for not telling her before.

But he ignored her question or perhaps didn't even hear it. He strode over to the window and stared out, frowning. "But why? Why did he come?"

"He told me that he was adopted soon after Sandra married his present dad. And I told you, he came to ask you not to kill his dad. I promised to ask you to see him." Her voice rose hysterically again. "Now go, go and see the boy and Sandra! Go and leave me alone!" She couldn't stand seeing him there staring down at her. All this time she had spent with him just for this.

He took a step towards her, his hands reaching for her shoulders, but she swung away from him. She tore his ring off her finger and flung it at him. "Here, take this!" He stared at the ring lying at his feet. "Give it to someone else!"

"I don't want to give it to someone else." His voice was flat.

"Get out"" He froze as if hit. He looked down at her back for a moment then turned and walked out, closing the door very gently behind him. She heard him walk slowly up the stairs to his room.

She listened, completely still. There was the scrape of his key, then the sound of his pulling his suitcase from under his bed.

There was a moment's silence.

She heard him walk out and lock his door, then his running steps down the stairs without even a pause in front of the landing or in front of her closed door.

Then he was gone, she jumped up and rushed to the window impulsively, to call him, but he was already at the corner. In the dusk she could just make out his silhouette, and he had no suitcase with him. Slowly she turned around and slowly sank down onto the bed again.

And then she realised what he had done. He must have hidden the gun in his suitcase and now he had it with him... Her face went white, her eyes staring frightened at the dark square of the window.

The boy had pleaded with her not to let Jim kill his Dad. She hadn't really believed him. "Oh, my God!" she groaned and her hands clenched convulsively. She had sent Jim out to kill. What did she know of him? Nothing, nothing at all, not even that he had a son, she thought bitterly. But at least she could perhaps stop him from becoming a murderer, he couldn't have been one, no. She shivered haunted by that gun. The last thing she could do for him was to stop him from becoming a murderer.

She grabbed her coat and handbag and rushed down the stairs. At the ticket office in Paddington the unhurried clerk yawned and leafed leisurely through the timetable, "Next train for Didcot, in two hours time, Miss, at 9.05. You've just missed one."

"When does the train arrive in Didcot? I mean the one that I've just missed?" she tried to stop shivering and the clerk looked up at her inquisitively.

"The one you've just missed, Miss?" he shrugged his shoulders and glanced at the next person in the queue. She could almost read his thoughts. That train will be in Didcot at 8.13."

Flora turned away from the window and stood motionless staring up at the huge clock in the iron girders of the station. Relentlessly one of the huge hands jerked through the minutes....She could do nothing.

She wandered aimlessly around in the crowds hurrying through to the various trains, and then she stopped transfixed and stared at the row of red telephone booths. What if she telephoned and warned the boy? But then perhaps the police would be there, perhaps Jim would be picked up and she would be the informer! But better that than Jim a murderer.

The enquiries operator seemed to take hours, but Flora could see through the glass door that the clock hand had not even moved two minutes when the polite voice told her the telephone number: Upton 45983. Her hand was trembling when she scribbled down the number.

Far away in the distance she heard the bell ringing. A woman's voice answered and she wondered suddenly if that was the Sandra that she had helped find.

"Could I please speak to John Rogers? It's important." She was pleased that her voice sounded almost normal.

"Why certainly, but I'm his mother. Is it something that I should know?" Flora almost screamed, "Yes! Yes!, The father of

176

your son is coming to kill you and your husband..." but she bit her lip and wondered what the woman at the other end of the line would have thought.

"No, I'd like to speak to Johnny, please. Hurry, please." In three quarters of an hour Jim's train would be arriving at Didcot.

Johnny sounded strange on the phone, grown up and calm.

"Yes, thank you very much. I'll meet the train, go down on my bike. Brown raincoat? He'll want to get a taxi so if I hear of someone asking to go to Upton...I'll ask the taxi drivers ahead of time to let me know."

There was silence for a moment and Flora heard him gulp, "Gee, thanks, I've got to try!" he added suddenly in a tone that sounded very much like that of a desperate little boy, and suddenly Flora's eyes filled with tears for him.

She hung the receiver up very gently and slowly walked out of the station and back to her room. There she sat in the darkness and shivered, wondering what would happen.

Jim sat unmoving in the corner of the compartment staring straight ahead, feeling himself shaken by the rhythmic beat of the train. Unconsciously, he held his right elbow close against his jacket pocket, pushing the hard shape of the gun against himself. He sat not thinking at first, almost as if someone else had given him a push and there he was, Goring, Pangbourne, unknown names, then Didcot... He read two signs flitting past the train window before standing up. The train stopped with screeching brakes.

The cold air grasped him and shook him awake. He stared about at the scramble of passengers pushing toward the barrier and the ticket collector. He couldn't face the bright lights now. He turned and walked slowly into the darkness along the line. He felt the ground trembling underfoot and jumped off the high embankment as an express came thundering through – its brightly lit windows blurred into a long line of light.

Most of the store windows along the main street of Didcot were lit up. He wandered from window to window, staring at the hot water bottles in the chemist's and the tinselled chocolate boxes in the next without seeing anything.

He did not know what he was going to do. A murder of a brother unpunished? He felt the gun in his pocket.

He passed a constable trying the doors of the stores. Jim stopped and turned back to him. "Could you please tell me the way to Upton? Is it far?"

The policeman was thorough. He explained the exact way and then added that it was too far to walk. "About three miles it is, easy to find, but its three miles. Taxis at the station, down that way, if you wish." He pointed down Station Road. Jim shook his head.

"Thank you, I'll walk, I think. Thank you, officer. Goodnight."

The constable moved on down the road and Jim stopped to stare at another shop window. The photographs of pork chops and shish kebabs looked quite appetising, he thought Perhaps he should try to find a pub. He still did not know what he would do.

It was past midnight when he walked quietly down the main street of Upton, past the little Post Office and around the corner, staring at the sleeping houses on both sides of the road, hoping that the light of the moon was bright enough to show him the sign that he was looking for. The Stafford Orchid Nursery. No, the nursery would be at the edge of the village with its greenhouses probably stretching into the fields around.

He walked down to the end of one road – a field of gently swaying corn stretched out toward the distant lights of Didcot. No greenhouses.

He turned and walked back into the village and turned right past the church under its dark cypresses, past the concrete yard of the school, the cottages; three roads came together at that spot. He chose the one to the left. No, only houses. He came back and turned into the middle fork; the right one probably circled back to the Post Office.

The high shiny silo of a farmhouse labelled the next group of buildings...A dog barked and a cat scampered across the road in front of him, then turned and came silently towards him, rubbing itself against his ankles. He bent down to stroke the soft dark fur, then the cat melted into a hedge.

He came out onto the main road. It was not the Upton road any longer. A lorry thundered past much faster than its fifty-mile limit. But there were houses on both sides here too.

Further off to the left he saw the sign of a pub swinging on its high post. Then behind it, in some trees he could see a light burning. What if he knocked there?

It was a bungalow, lying sideways to the road. The massive five-bar gate was shut. He looked over the gate towards the house. A tree in front of the house was almost iridescent with white blooms and the smell of flowers was heavy in the air. Under the tall trees on the furthest side of the bungalow he could see the black shadows of other buildings.

As a gentle breeze moved the branches the moonlight reached through the leaves and played shimmering on the glass of a greenhouse.

He could see no signs around. Quietly he pushed himself between the thick gate post and the hedge. The hedge gave way and he was standing on the gravel drive in the moonlight. The light in the house went out. Suddenly he heard the sound like a door opening and he quickly stepped into the shadows of some trees.

He waited listening. A dog barked somewhere far away. There was a rustle of leaves close to him and a mouse scurried across the moonlit drive.

He shivered involuntarily, he felt as if he was being watched, but he could see no one in the shadows of the house. All he could hear now was his own heavy breathing.

Quietly he edged his way through the garden around the drive towards the greenhouse, keeping in the shadow of the trees. A twig broke under his foot; he stopped motionless, all on edge. He waited for a long time, at least it seemed to him to be a very long time before he dared move again.

The back door of the greenhouse was unlocked. He pushed it open and looked in. There was a slight glow from a small heater in the corner and he could just make out the long shelves with the rows of pots standing neatly in straight lines. The air felt hot and humid and smelt of wet moss and compost.

"Mr. Raymond?" Jim spun around, his hand automatically pulling out his gun. Standing in the corner behind him he could make out the shadow of a boy. He stepped forward towards Jim.

"I'm Sandra's boy, Johnny Rogers." His voice was trembling, "Would you mind if I turn up the light a bit?" he paused in front of the heater and adjusted the wick, then slowly he turned to face Jim, looking up at him very intently.

"What are you doing here?" Jim asked gruffly, "How did you know I was coming?"

The boy remained silent and continued to stare up at Jim, Jim felt uneasy and looked down at the gun which he was still pointing at the boy, and he stuffed it back into his jacket pocket.

"Please, I….I just want to ask you, please, I don't know why you should want to, but please don't kill my Dad and mum! Uncle Simeon said you would…" his voice faded before Jim's silence.

Jim stared at the boy, he was being so very brave, because Jim could see that he was trembling spasmodically and it was hot in the greenhouse.

"Why should I listen to you?" Jim finally asked gruffly. "They put me in prison for fourteen years for a murder I didn't commit." His voice was bitter, "Shouldn't I get even?" the boy's face went deathly pale and his eyes stared at Jim horrified.

"No, no!" His voice rose hysterically, "they couldn't have! They couldn't have! Not them!"

"And why not?" A cold, sardonic voice asked from the further side of the greenhouse. Unnoticed, the short man had come in the main entrance and stood there smiling thinly at the two of them. In his hand he held a gun pointed straight at Jim. And Jim recognised Simeon at once. He had hardly changed during all those years.

"Get out, John," Simeon's voice was cold, "I'm going to shoot this thief. Accident, of course." The voice became mocking, goading. "Was it the orchid 'Sandra' that you wanted to steal?" Then he gestured impatiently with the gun to the boy. "Move out, boy!"

"No, Uncle Simeon," the boy moved forward instead. His voice was firm. "You're not going to kill my Father. Not if I can help it!"

Jim gasped and stared down at the youngster standing in front of him.

"So, you knew about him?" Simeon's laugh was short. He looked at Jim over the boy's head. "It's her fault. She insisted on naming the orchid "Sandra" and I knew I couldn't have the "Orchid News" kept from you forever! Fools!" He spat out the words. "Pity Harry bungled that job on the underground. Would have saved us a deal of trouble."

Jim started. "What! You sent that man in the blue Mac?"

Just then a light went on behind Simeon's back in the bungalow, then a door banged.

"Johnny?" a man's voice called in the dark and a man appeared beside Simeon in the entrance, he towered above Simeon, a large, gaunt man, his hair completely grey, his face drawn.

Jim shook his head as if trying to get rid of a nightmare, "it can't be!" he gasped, "You! Alive!" it was Peter Masters.

He stared at Jim for a moment in complete silence, "yes, Raymond, you've found us at last, we've been expecting you." There was a note of relief in his voice. "Well, all right." His shoulders straightened, "you've got an account to settle with me, let's go. You've served your sentence." He took a step forward and then suddenly noticed the gun that Simeon was still aiming at Jim over the boy's head.

"No, Simeon, I've had enough." Peter's voice was weary, he put out his hand to take the gun, but the little man jerked away from him.

"Don't be silly, Peter," Simeon's voice was quiet, as if talking to a child, "you go inside the house and I'll get rid of him, and then we'll live peacefully again, you know, no more trouble."

"No, Simeon, I've had enough." Peter repeated firmly, quite calmly. "I've been dead for long enough now; I might as well really be dead." Jim felt the shudder through the boy's body, for he had stepped back against Jim when Simeon had ordered him out, and instinctively, Jim put his hand on the boy's shoulder, Johnny looked up pleading, trying to read the expression on Jim's face.

For a moment everything else faded from Jim's mind – only the fact that this tall lad was his son and he looked down at him, somehow pleased, he even forgot during that moment that black gun held quite steadily by Simeon.

Suddenly he heard the crash of a body against a shelf and looked up in time to see Peter lunge at his brother and grab the gun from him. The shot rang out startlingly loud and glass shattered close behind Jim. Peter held the gun, Simeon started pleading, stretching his hand out for it.

"Please, Peter, it'll be like we used to dream about it, remember? You growing orchids, and me managing, and you'll be free of him forever. Let me have the gun," his voice was wheedling.

"No," Peter's face was completely expressionless.

Then Simeon became hysterical. "I can't go to prison. I can't! I'll die there if they put me away – and that's what you're going to do – put me away after everything I've done for you!"

Peter stared down at his brother. "After everything you've done for me?" his voice was bitter. "Is that what you said? You told me that he wouldn't go to prison! You said that he'd only be a scapegoat for a short time 'cause my body wouldn't be found! You said that we'd get the insurance money, grow orchids and he'd be free and you'd give him some of it! You talk too much!" his huge hand grabbed his brother's shoulder and as he talked he shook him furiously. Simeon was whimpering now.

"Peter....Peter...." then Jim and the boy saw Simeon glance up at the gun in Peter's hand. Before they could cry out to Peter, Simeon lunged for the gun. Peter rose to his full height, shaking Simeon, trying to free the gun from Simeon's desperate clutching hands. Unbalanced, Peter toppled over Simeon and they both fell heavily onto the board floor between the shelves. The gun fired again.

Jim and the boy stood motionless for a moment, and then with a sob the boy rushed forward.

Shaken and pale, Peter Masters slowly rose to his feet, staring down at his brother lying motionless on the floor, then he knelt down beside him and turned the inert body over, the eyes were still staring, but there was blood trickling down over his cheek.

Peter stared down at the blood, and then carefully he pulled out his handkerchief and gently, very gently, tried to clean the blood off Simeon's cheek.

He was whispering to himself, or maybe to the dead man. "What you have cost us, Simeon, Simeon! What you have cost us!" it was like a dirge and his voice was full of tears.

Then suddenly Jim and Johnny became aware of the banging of doors, the running steps, a woman's frantic voice shouting "Peter! Peter! Johnny!"

Jim turned to the boy, "your mother?" his voice was urgent.

"Yes," the boy glanced up at Jim, "you can use the backdoor." Jim turned and slipped through the door into the darkness just before Sandra ran in.

She stopped horrified, staring down at the sprawling figure on the floor, then she knelt down beside her husband and put her arm around him, holding him tightly to herself, and he turned to her, sobbing dryly.

Johnny stepped forward; he spoke loudly, so that the man standing in the shadows could hear too. "Mum, it's all a horrible accident. Dad thought uncle Simeon was a thief, come to steal the orchid. And in the dark, he grabbed uncle, he hadn't recognised him, but Uncle Simeon had his gun."

He stopped talking and looked at his mother. She was still holding her husband tightly to herself, not looking at her son. She repeated after him, almost as if memorising, "your Dad thought uncle Simeon was a thief, come to steal the orchid..."

She suddenly looked up at Johnny. "Was Jim Raymond here too?" she asked him without taking her eyes off his face.

"Yes, my father was here too," and he said the words loudly, almost proudly, his words penetrated Peter's grief and he looked up astonished at the boy.

"You knew? You knew that I wasn't your father?"

"Yes, Dad, yes, I've known for an awfully long time, but it doesn't matter, you know. Doesn't make any difference."

Peter, crouching beside his dead brother turned back to stare at the white face lying on the floor, he started talking almost as if he were in a daze, but choosing each word carefully, slowly.

"Listen, John, your uncle Simeon had told me long ago that he would tell you I wasn't your father if I didn't do what he told me..."

Sandra gasped, "So that was it! My poor, poor Peter." Her voice broke. Peter did not hear her.

He bent over Simeon and gently closed his eyes. "Simeon, he was born with a crooked body, this way. And then his mind went crooked too....when we were at school, I'd fight all the boys who'd dare laugh at him, and he would do my school work for me, he was the brains, he said, and I was the muscle.

"We used to laugh about it then." Peter stopped for a moment, "but then he started going bitter, hating everyone, he even made me promise never to tell anyone that we were twins."

"Twins!" Sandra's voice sounded horrified.

"Yes, you see why?" Peter glanced at her, "you can't help comparing me with him then, him with his limp, poor Simeon!"

A twig scraping along the roof of the greenhouse in the breeze broke the silence. Peter looked up at the shelves of orchids standing neatly in rows, "This was his dream, always, to grow orchids. It was after we got married, Sandra, he started working on his plan. I didn't know anything about it at first. Gradually he told me bits and pieces. He said Raymond wouldn't be found guilty. My body wouldn't be found and they wouldn't punish him if they weren't sure."

Peter hid his face in his hands, and then he looked up straight at Johnny. "Simeon said your mother wouldn't protest much because of you, you were going to be born soon, and if we told her when it was too late... I refused. Then he showed me the insurance policy, for you, for your mother. He told me he'd tell you when you were old enough that you weren't really mine...." His voice faded and he rose wearily to his feet, his arm around Sandra.

For a minute all three of them stood silent, looking down at Simeon, the wind whistled through the cracked glass and then, distinctly, they heard the crunch of someone walking on the gravelled drive.

The boy immediately turned and pressed his face close to the window pane. He saw the dark shadow of a man walk down the middle of the moonlit drive, swing open the gate and step out into the open road without even glancing back.

Sandra shrank towards Peter and he pulled her closer to him, she stared at the glass, but she could see nothing.

"Will he be back?" she whispered, her voice suddenly filled with fear.

"No," Johnny shook his head, "no, father won't be coming back." He was sure because the man in the shadows had heard the story too. "Come on, Dad," he turned to Peter, "We'd better call the police and a doctor."

The inquest did not take long, but it was a whole week before Johnny could leave Upton to go to London. He carried a present for Mr. Raymond and the landlady opened the door.

"No, I'm sorry, Mr. Raymond isn't here right now, he's getting his papers and so on, leaving for Australia, he is, next Monday so he has plenty to do."

"To Australia?" Johnny wasn't surprised, "would the lady be upstairs? Mr. Raymond's friend?"

"Miss Flora? Yes, she's up there, but I don't think that she's so much of a friend now. Haven't seen them together for at least a week or so, anyway, you run up and see her."

It was only then that Flora heard all that had happened.

The swirling water between the ship and the dock slowly became broader and Jim noticed that it was dirty water, bits of wood and orange peel floating on it, and an oily scum covering it all, slowly he looked up at the receding warehouses.

"Well, good riddance, I guess," he muttered, but his hands were clenching the rail tightly, it wasn't quite so easy leaving after all, the crowds around him pressing to the rails were laughing excitedly, waving, one or two crying openly.

Some woman pushed up beside him on the rail, she was holding a bulky parcel wrapped in brown paper, annoyed, he glanced down at her and then stopped frozen.

"Flora!" she was beaming up at him and holding the parcel up for him to take.

"What on earth are you doing here? How?" he asked gruffly.

"Someone ill, got a spare ticket! On the last boat to Australia."

Slowly his face creased into a delighted grin and his arms went around her, pulling her to him, the rough parcel squeezed between them.

"A present from your son. I'm to wish you good luck from him! It's a book that he's been working on for years." She stopped suddenly and her eyes filled with tears, remembering what the boy had told her.

Then she blinked hard and smiled again, teasingly. "How to grow orchids, he said, and the bulky part, that's album of pressed orchids. He'd worked out a method how to do it." She took a deep breath and added quietly, almost whispering, "And maybe, I thought you and me, we could grow orchids in Australia together?"

Just then the ship's whistle shrieked out right above them, Flora jumped and Jim held her tighter, he shouted to her above the noise of the whistle, but it drowned his words.

And then in the silence, before it blew again, he smiled tenderly at her, "So, you want a dark red cypripedium named Flora? We might have a go…"

BACKGROUND / MEMORIES
REKINDLED

SHORT STORY COMMENTS

WHERE, WHEN, WHY AND
REFLECTIONS OF AUTHOR'S LIFE

With apologies to those who have remembered differently some of the places and events I describe. I keep reminding myself of an excerpt from a 17th Century Nun's Prayer. "I dare not ask for improved memory, but for a growing humility and lessing cocksureness when my memory seems to clash with the memories of others. Teach me the glorious lesson that occasionally I may be mistaken."
I'm still trying to learn !

BYBLOS -THE SITE OF A MATTER OF HANDS

As the Thomas Cook representative told Eleanor and Eric Brook, Byblos is a short drive from Beirut along the coast heading north. It's a fascinating place, steeped in history. Starting from the Stone Age burials in clay vessels or pots it has mementoes of almost all the following ages. According to some archaeologists it is the oldest city in the world as it has had continuous human inhabitants from the very beginning of civilization.

I stress "human" inhabitants as the site is considered closely related to prehistoric gods and goddesses. Much more recently the Greek God Adonis, known by various earlier names, lived hereabouts and drowned in the river just a few miles away. Being young and handsome his legendary death started a whole tradition manifested in processions and public grieving for centuries!

And a son grieving the death of his father contributed to the history of Byblos in another way. In the Beirut museum there is a huge granite sarcophagus and written on its side is an inscription which is one of the earliest examples of alphabetic writing.

It is the tomb of Ahiram, King of Jebail, the Arabic name for Byblos, who died in the 13th century BC and it is his son's inscription, perhaps a lament. The sarcophagus seen in the castle is a copy so that tourists could see it in situ (and to keep the very precious original safely from vandals!).

One day, this was in the middle 40s, when I was still at school, the American University of Beirut (AUB) had a sale of old and ancient pottery and other interesting objects. They had too many of them. Eli, my brother, came home with several small clay lights, the kind which were filled with oil and had a wick protruding from a side hole. Fourth century AD, he was told. He gave me one of them.

Some twenty years later Nigel was sent to Connecticut for three years by ICI Plastics Division. The family went too. The older boys settled at school. So did Mary –after being promoted into an older class. She knew how to read by then while the younger children of her age, hadn't learnt yet.

It wasn't a coincidence that both my older boys were picked out by their teachers for outstanding roles in the school's plays. Nick enjoyed being a Santa Claus with his Ho! Ho! Ho! shouted with an English accent.

And of course it was his accent that had Rurik as the teacher of a small one-room backwoods school! A black, high collared jacket and a wig tied back with a velvet black ribbon made him a splendid newly-arrived New England "puritan".

One day Rurik told me that they were studying the Romans. I dug out the little lamp that my brother had given me, filled it with oil, made a wick from twisted cotton wool and showed him how to light it. He returned from school radiant. The teacher had been really impressed and asked him to show the lit lamp to all the classes! No one had seen such a thing before, not even the teachers!

What a difference growing up in Europe where "old" and "ancient" are quite common! And so back to Byblos, its Crusader castle and Grecian temple ruins.

HOLY WAR – STARTING WITH BEIRUT

Poor unhappy Beirut- the town where I was born! I left the town after finishing the American Community School – third from the bottom and top of the class! (class of only three pupils). The rest had gone to the USA to prepare for college by going to their final school classes there. I followed a year later to go to Wellesley College in Massachusetts. World War II had just ended.

I never returned to live in Beirut, only on visits to my parents as Father was a Professor at the American University of Beirut (AUB). In those days it wouldn't have been the "done thing" for a daughter of a professor to seek employment in the town. The only occupation for me would have been as librarian or secretarial work at the AUB. Hence, I decided to stay in the States and was lucky to find a job at the UN Secretariat in New York.

Thus, I wasn't in Beirut when they had the massacres of refugees, the shootings. Even the president of the university was murdered as he sat at his desk. I heard much later that he had refused a guard. The president, Malcolm Kerr, had been in the class below mine at the school and his sister had gone to Wellesley the same year as I had.

For all the disturbances I believe the town must still be a lovely place! Only a few of the houses will have remained empty steel skeletons and some of the roads still impassable because of the bomb holes and the rubbish.

But picture a town with the blue sea on three sides. A backdrop of orchards and olive trees that terrace by terrace climb up into the mountains; golden beaches on one side and steep hills plunging down to the sea on the other.

I remember the tram used to go from the black and white striped lighthouse at Ras Beirut, head of the promontory, to the far end of the city ending in banana and orange groves.

Often on Thursday afternoons during school term a group of youngsters, me among them, took the tram to the end of the line. From there, under the supervision of a Russian school teacher, we would march off into a side road among the groves for an "excursion".

190

There was quite a large group of Russian refugees in Lebanon. Classes, meeting once a week, were organised for their children. French schools had a free Thursday afternoon so that was when the Russian school took over. My American school allowed me to take that afternoon off as well. And it was on these excursions that I learnt popular marching songs that I still remember.

The photo of Beirut shows the section called Ras Beirut, or the Head of Beirut. One year when I was quite young we were living in the house right next to the lighthouse. Early one morning Father woke us up and sleepily we gathered outside in our garden to watch a full solar eclipse. He distributed a kind of mask to each of us with a pin hole through which we gazed at the darkening disk of the sun.

It was such a mysterious happening as slowly a shadow crept over it.   And then pandemonium broke forth!   The animals, dogs, cats, donkeys became hysterical- barking, meowing, braying, and all our neighbours were also noisy- hitting pots and pans, raising quite a din!. It was quite astonishing! Animals and human beings trying to frighten away the evil that was devouring our sun.

Then the day became night!   And quite suddenly everything, everyone was quiet. Absolute silence. Waiting breathlessly for the sun to reappear.

You could almost hear the sigh of relief as a shining sliver reappeared and slowly, slowly the sun returned. And everyone resumed their own lives!!!!! And I went back to sleep!

In the photo below Beirut was photographed with the French bathing beach in the foreground. The harbour is around the corner to the left and further inland. We lived in a house about three building up from the front. When I was leaving to go to college, after the family had seen me board my ship, my two brothers hurried home and onto the balcony with a big mirror. The sun was setting behind the ship and they signalled to me "bon voyage"!!!!

191

FROM A FILM- FOR BETTER FOR WORSE

An old film – most of it forgotten, but parts still lingering in my memory- somehow turned into this story. It could be that a passing motorbike triggered it. I can't even recall its correct name. It was something like "Clapham Junction" and it had a tragic ending or perhaps it had no ending and left us wondering "what next?" Mine has a definite ending, though I could continue it to the next generation, but then it would stop being a short story! So, mine ends happily right now.

I can't remember if the film mentioned neighbours, though the neighbour in my story plays an important part. Neighbours are, after all, a very important part or influence as to how we settle in our own homes. This includes, of course, our gardens.

Our house in Harpenden had a large garden. We had a road on one side leading to a new close. On the other side lived a family of pleasant neighbours. Then the father planted a row of lilandia right against the dividing fence. "Don't worry, I'll keep them at three feet," he assured me. But they grew faster than he could find time to cut them back. I didn't want to fuss.

My boys thought of several ways of dealing with the trees which were, of course, bleeding my flower beds of water and nutrients. "Mum, we could dig a trench along the fence and fill it with salty water. That'll kill the trees off!" Yes, and my flowers!

I complained to my boss at the National Pharmaceutical Association (NPA) in St Albans. Tim Astill, the Director, was a lawyer by profession.

"No, the regulations are useless in this case. What you need to do" and he smiled mischievously, "Just wait till your neighbours are out and just go chop-chop over the fence!" However, I didn't take his advice as my attention was diverted to a more serious case.

A builder had constructed the estate of two rows of semi-detached houses behind our garden. He was permitted to do so on condition that he left a wooded area between our row of single houses and the new ones in the close. Now he wanted to build a house there.

A two-story building right at the bottom of our gardens, overlooking us, would have been distressing! We formed a protest group. He changed the look of the house; an architect drew a half-under-ground building. He hoped we'd agree.

We were invited to a meeting to examine the new plans. All the members of the group were astonished that council members were willing to consider the new idea, even though it went counter the original condition for building the houses in the close. There was some heated discussion: increase in car traffic, still over-looking our gardens and so on.

However, permission was denied. There was a preservation order on the trees growing there. He couldn't lay a road to the building.

One day my children were playing close by. Seeing a man come with some tools, they hid to watch. The man drilled a hole in the large tree blocking access to the area. He pottered about then left. Intrigued, they investigated. A powder had been poured into the drilled hole. Quite suspicious!

The children washed the powder out. We didn't discover what poison the builder had used, but he never built the house. And, I believe, that tree is still standing!

And the description of the elderly couple, Eileen's father and mother, looking solid and strong together as if they were two old oaks with roots deep down is a rather over-used simile, but it is so appropriate. Probably because for all of us an oak or other heavy tree is a symbol of strength. Two together are a bastion against ill winds. That is the way I remember my parents supporting each other!

A watercolour - houses under an autumn tree, a "simile" for parents sheltering their family.

LIFE STORY- THE BEGINNING

In the autumn of 1994 when my youngest son was 28, I went on a lively, inspiring week to Fen Farm in Norfolk.. It was a week of hobnobbing with other aspiring writers.

Philip Martin, leading the discussions and the critiques, was someone who worked for BBC Radio Drama in Birmingham (BBC - the British Broadcasting Corporation)

We read our various writings to the group and received applause or otherwise, but our leader always ended on a positive note. Nothing was so awful that it couldn't be helped with some sympathetic editing!

One afternoon we were given a subject to write about "Something lost". Due to be read that evening, we were a very varied group and scattered looking for inspiration

I remember going alone along the lane close to the farm. It was peaceful and I had a feeling of being quite safe on my own in a strange place. Having an imagination that often creates frightening scenarios the peaceful country around me seemed to have permeated me with calmness. But for how long?

That's when the idea for my story emerged. Being a disparate group of individuals our resulting subjects were also very different. Most had chosen "lost objects", be it a jewel or a souvenir. I remember someone wrote about a precious casket.

My story was about a woman who lost her feeling of security. Hence my idea was different to the others in that the lost object was an intangible one.

Someone suggested that I should amplify the story, make it suitable for reading on the radio, probably Woman's Hour. As written it was too short for the BBC's usual slot. "Life Story" is the enlarged and amended version of what I read that evening at Fen Farm!

However, it has an unhappy ending, unlike the uplifting ones read on the BBC.

As I mentioned above, my imagination does sometimes create frightening scenarios. In a piece of plywood I saw this fantastic scene that belongs to the Lord of the Rings.

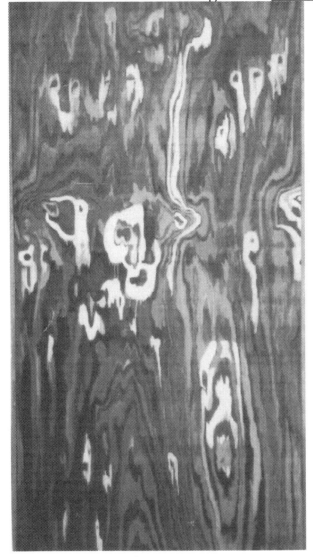

"The Nazgul came caught in the fiery ruins of hill and sky..." Tolkien.

So Eloise alone in her house is afraid, as I would have been.

WHY OMELETTE?

One of my sons came home from school complaining. The teacher told them to write about a snow flake. "Mum! A snow flake! " I don't remember his exact words which expressed his utter disgust, but "How sissy!" was his general feeling about such a subject.

"Sissy? What about a snow flake falling onto the engine of a steam train? You could describe the old steam trains we saw in Didcot at that special exhibition. And the poor snowflake melting, sizzling away to nothing!"

Didcot was several miles from Upton where we had bought our first home. After my husband, Nigel, had been accepted to work for the Atomic Energy Research Establishment (AERE) we decided it was time to put down roots. Our first son was born in a rented house in Wantage- King Arthur's and Rurik's birthplace!

Rurik is an unusual name, rarely used as it is not Christian and most Russian names belong to saints'. I had heard this name for the first time when working at the UN headquarters in New York. Rurik, historically, was the first king of Moscow. He was a Viking and the Slavs rebelled against him and finally kicked him out.

Nigel and I had agreed that our children should have names that are Russian and English. So our first born had William as his middle name.

A telegram arrived from my parents in Lebanon. "Why don't you call him Michael? He was born on Saint Michael's Day...." What, my Father and Mother telling me what to name our son! I was always a bit bolshie...

They neglected to tell me that Rurik wasn't a Christian. He was a pagan- and my ancestors on my Father's side were mainly Russian Orthodox priests! I may have changed my mind, but then again Nigel was delighted with a Viking name!

We had no trouble with the next two children's names Nicholas and Mary, both names international, born in our own house. We found one that suited us in Upton, overlooked by the Berkshire Downs.

It was a bungalow on a large v-shaped piece of land. At the bottom of the V was a pub, the George and Dragon, and at the broad top was a railroad cutting.

It had a vegetable garden down towards the pub, house in the middle and the rest an overgrown old orchard. Finding some rare old types of apple was exciting.

Another discovery was a deep well. "You could use that there well for your septic tank," said the man from the village. I protested vehemently! That would be worse than spitting into one's drinking water. Of course the house was on the mains, but what if ? The well was sealed off with a concrete slab, just in case we would need it in some unforeseen disaster!

We settled in happily. Named the bungalow "Maslina" in honour of the first musical that Nigel took me to in New York when we started dating. Maslina means olive, or olive tree in Russian. We saw "Kismet" in which Howard Keel sang the lovely song about a dream of having an olive, then an olive tree, then an olive grove and finally the world!

Our next discovery was an exciting one and it delighted our children. The trains between Didcot and Newbury puffed by at the bottom of the garden! Great fun watching...but then we found the down-side!

The sparks from the steam locomotive ignited the long grass in our orchard. It meant rushing out with brooms and sticks to beat out the flames. That even happened in the middle of a New Year's Eve party and all the guests gleefully joined in.

Our fire-fighting adventures did not last long as Beeching's railroad cutting hit "our" line. The station in Upton became someone's home. The one store in the village was not affected as most of their customers were locals and the bus did go to the closest town so no one was put off too much.

And what has all this to do with "Omelette" and the "sissy" snow flake subject? I had an inspiration-what about a shy, stuttering boy bringing his "sissy" pet to school? And mention of trains triggered my memories.

Then the lovely development of the "sissy" pet becoming a beautiful butterfly! Perhaps a Monarch Butterfly, like the one pictured here.

GRANDDAUGHTERS AND DEATH

Memories are strange phenomena. I remember a little girl (and I wonder if it could have been me) in church at a funeral. This was long ago, in Beirut. Someone is holding her up to the open coffin, as is the custom in Russian Orthodox ceremonies. He tells her to kiss the dead man goodbye. She screams terrified! Her mother takes her, holds her tightly, soothes her.

Saying farewell. Or is that a euphemism for the need of those who remain to adjust themselves to the fact that that beloved person is really gone, is no more.

In Toronto at the funeral of my nephew Yuri Rubinsky, his wife Holley, had a different way of saying farewell. As the globe-shaped casket holding his ashes was lowered into the ground she struck a silver bell. A very clear and pure sound vibrated in the air. It was a touching leave-taking.

When Nigel, my husband and father of my four children, died the youngest was nine years old, the oldest sixteen. I wanted to shelter them from my grief; I didn't want them to be more upset by seeing my tears. So I hid my sorrow.

That year I was teaching art at a school in Welwyn Garden City. The children, thirteen and fourteen years old, were the rougher elements of the school. I could see that they needed a "cuddle" rather than punishment for disruption.

And coming home, I had my own. So as not to breakdown in front of them I would stop at a friend's house and she would give me a brandy and water for courage.

I didn't realize how wrong I was until many months later. At a parents' evening at school I was told that one of my sons had closed up emotionally, couldn't be reached. I had denied him and the others the relief of sorrowing together.

For many years I felt guilty, but, of course, too late. And one day my almost adult son told me that he had made a friend at school who also suffered a bereavement. They had talked about it. So, "Mum", he said "Forget it! You did what you thought was best then!" These weren't his exact words, but that was the meaning. I was able to put my "guilt" to rest.

A while back a very close friend died. A few days before his funeral I didn't join his family when they went to see him lying in state. Neither did I go with them when his ashes were scattered. Would they have wanted to see me weeping?

Sharing grief as well as sharing happiness ? However, it is my Father who gave me the best answer.

He was dying at home in the flat where he had lived with Mother in Beirut. My two brothers, Andrei and Eli, from Canada, and I, from England, had come to say our adieus.

Eli received a telegram urgently requesting his return to Toronto University where he was teaching. When he came into the bedroom to tell Father that he had to leave, my Father told him not to worry, he understood and he wished his son well.

I burst out weeping.....Father gently reprimanded me- why am I crying? "After all, I shall be living on- I'm in you and your brothers, and am in your children...." And later I thought also of the hundreds of students who had studied under him, how something of him, of his enthusiasm in his teaching would be with them for as long as they lived.

And I thought of friends who had died- how they are still alive in my thoughts.

Russian churches
painted in acrylics
on plywood

INSPIRING IBIZA AND TURTLE OIL

Nigel and I had our first holiday abroad before we had children. We flew to Majorca, then by boat to Ibiza. No airports there at that time.

Our hotel on the edge of San Antonio Abad was the only one on the bay. It was a lovely extensive bay, its exit to the Mediterranean guarded by a long isle named Hannibal's Island. I didn't find out whether it was named because Hannibal really did land there with his elephants on his way to Rome.

The hotel was a long, one-story building . Its white terrace ran its whole length, shadowed by tall pine trees. In front of the terrace and sloping down to the water was a perfect beach punctuated by colourfully striped umbrellas and deck chairs. We couldn't ask for more!

Perhaps we could have asked for our vegetables to be served with the meat course, but then we assumed the correct behaviour- do as your hosts do and don't complain. Not even when tinned peaches were our dessert for just about every dinner!

Close to the hotel there was a large sign – a piece of land for sale. We thought about it! The price was very low. How lovely to have a villa built there right on the bay.

However, we found out soon after that the Balearics are under military jurisdiction. No foreigners are allowed to have land on the sea coast. Someone in the hotel mentioned that he could arrange a deal- have the land sold to a Spaniard (with our money) and in reality it would be ours. Nice deal!!!   Gracias, pero no! …

What I describe in my story no longer exists. I've been told that a whole string of hotels encircles the bay now. Perhaps the Los Tres Guitarres, the nightclub, has vanished, but when we were there we watched the natives dancing and even practiced the pase double with them!

A young Spaniard was one of the conspicuous regulars. With a small moustache and the same swagger, he imitated the well-known Hollywood star- Errol Flynn, the sword-welding hero of many pirate films. The Spanish imitator seemed to be the adored idol of many dark-haired maidens of the town.

Then one day a beautiful, sleek yacht moored in the bay. That evening there was great excitement in the club when the real Errol Flynn appeared there! He had a large retinue with him- so I didn't have a chance to dance with him.

Perhaps I should rewrite the story or have another version. The heroine is kidnapped and taken off in a sailing boat!

This sailing boat is not supposed to be realistic! I drew it in pastels. Its bright colours represent nature- the sea, the sun and the wind-the lovely feeling of freedom of a holiday on the Mediterranean.

MEMORIES OF NEW YORK- LOVE IN A TAXI

1951 - End of Wellesley College and the beginning of REAL life in New York! I was offered an almost menial job in the United Nations Secretariat, the one available then. Having a Lebanese passport meant I could only work in the UN.

Working in the registry I collected the incoming mail from my in-basket, punched holes in it, found the appropriate file (as noted by a more senior worker) and deposited the papers in it.

My first assignment was in the Secretary General's separate registry on the top floor of the building. I don't remember ever seeing Trigve Lie there. However, it was exciting to read surreptitiously some of the letters sent to him though, of course, the important ones were never in the "ordinary" mail.

My first experience of a windy storm while working on that high floor was rather daunting. The building swayed quite noticeably. I kept my eyes away from the windows so that I wouldn't notice that the horizon was definitely moving....

Shortly after I was transferred a few floors down to the Documents Department. Knowing four of the languages used in the UN, although my Spanish was weak, added considerably to my enjoyment. The interpreters and translators humoured me by talking in their own language when they came for documents!

The UN building is on 42nd Street and First Avenue. After several moves I was fortunate to find a flat on Seventy–Fifth Street and First Avenue. The Second Avenue bus went straight past the UN.

The flat was on the top floor of a three-story building. I shared it with a young black woman from Washington DC who worked in the Registry Department. Edith was a delightful companion. We had some good parties there with friends from the UN. They were of varied nationalities which also meant different ways of dancing- French, British and other European quite subdued, South American flamboyant and flirtatious. Our string of empty Chianti bottles in straw baskets hanging at the kitchen door were proof of good living!

I imagined that Sara started her journey in my story right there. John, the taxi driver, waited for her at the door.

The trip up to Scarsdale is straight from my experiences. A college friend's parents lived there and I was invited for a weekend. I went on a train and as it was elevated above the street, you could look into the buildings along the way.

Scarsdale was a posh place to live. Ingrid's father had been a mining engineer in Venezuela and had found large deposits of minerals there. Hence he could afford to retire away from the noisy city.

And it was in the noisy city that I went to a noisy, "literary" party! A friend took me to the celebration of a new author in the making! William Styron's book "Lie Down in Darkness" had been accepted for publication. How exciting meeting a new writer!

And just recently I read his obituary. This brought back all my memories of working at the UN and living through the ups and downs of life in New York. Mostly exciting ups!

LIVING IN NY- WASHINGTON SQUARE BLUES

My first "home" was a boarding house in Brooklyn Heights, right across the East River from Manhattan and a short walk from the subway. The boarding house was under the aegis of a church so very respectable. Young men and women, new to New York, lived in two buildings that were joined by communal living and dining rooms. It was a relaxed atmosphere, friendly.

We even put on a play in the church hall one year. Two performances and the hall was packed both evenings! Entrance was a donation to the church.

Fresh from college, in my enthusiasm of "knowing how", I decided to improve the script and used a cut and paste method to move some scenes around. My version was vetoed. To the anguish of our prompter he found he had the cut-up text to use one evening! The actors, including myself, were quite oblivious of his discomfort. Happily, we didn't forget our lines!

One evening a group of us walked over Brooklyn Bridge and curiosity lead us to the Lower Manhattan Court House. It was a late evening session and we saw several vagrants and drunks brought in, one by one by the police. It was sobering to see the seamy side of the city.

In the 1950s a large population from Puerto Rico lived in parts of central Brooklyn. Brooklyn Heights was the fashionable area, being closest to Manhattan. That also meant all the seats were taken by the time the subway train reached my station. I found out that Puerto Rican food is spicy and oniony. Since Puerto Ricans are generally short, my height above the crowd saved me from much odorous discomfort!

My second "home" was in Manhattan- on Fifth Avenue and 42nd Street. Sounds grand! But this was a squalid part of the city. The flat was in a four-story redbrick building that had once seen much better times. I was glad Mother never saw it!

My flat-mate was a curvaceous Southern "belle", unhappily divorced. She played a guitar and sang love songs. The flat we shared had one very big room with an appendage of bathroom and a toilet. The kitchen stove and a cupboard were fitted into the bathroom. We washed our dishes etc in the hand basin. This aroused the utter disgust of a pernickety boyfriend!

Once a group of us went to a nightclub to hear/see Louis Armstrong, Satchimo, play. We had to wait in the foyer until a table could be found for us. My date started talking-up the check girl. I got bored and decided to leave. Caught the subway and arrived home. My room mate announced that someone had kept phoning to find out if I'd arrived. Just then the phone rang.

I laughed. "Oh, let it ring for a while". The poor man was quite distraught. No one just wanders about at night in lower New York. I don't know what he imagined happened to me.

Washington Square, at the bottom end of Manhattan in an area called Greenwich Village, was just a short trip down by bus or subway. It had a leafy, quiet atmosphere with a few bars, people relaxing on the benches, and an Italian restaurant.

One evening Nigel and I had spaghetti or it may have been pizzas, there. Was he given courage by the wine and mellowed by the intimate atmosphere? Whatever. Nigel proposed to me. This was about six months after we first met.

I remember Washington Square with affection!

This is my impression of New York in pastels being an attempt to catch the atmosphere of the lively city!

MY EXCUSE FOR NESSY

Scotland. Glasgow. It seemed a far distance to go to organise an exhibition, but we went. "We" is the NPA- National Pharmaceutical Association- whose membership is the owners of over ten thousand pharmacies throughout the UK. The NPA, based in St Albans, has a wide range of services and goods for its members and this was going to be our showcase.

Mine was a dual role, firstly, to help put out all the stands and attractions. Secondly, as the Public Relations Officer of the NPA and official editor, to take notes and photos for a report in the monthly bulletin.

A revolution happened in pharmacy the same year that I joined. It was 1982.. The NPA launched a nationwide campaign. A London advertising agency was employed. The motto "Ask Your Pharmacist. You'll Be Taking Good Advice!" was splashed in magazines and on posters. Pharmacists were saying "we are the experts on medicines" and coming out from behind their counters to answer questions from their clients.

My idea was to back the campaign with a weekly syndicated column of questions and answers sent to newspapers throughout the UK. We had a newspaper cutting service sending us cuttings of our Q&As so that we knew who was printing them. The excitement in my office, which included by then my assistant Sally Patterson, grew as the number of cuttings increased. In a December 1984 issue of the "Chemist and Druggist" they estimated that 12 million people read the "Ask your chemist" column in their local papers!

A country-wide anti-head lice campaign was my last idea before retiring. The directors approved the two-pronged educational project: one, to eliminate the stigma of having head lice and the other, how to deal with them properly. "No more shameful than catching flu" and "Head lice love clean adults" and ask your pharmacist for the proper treatment. The campaign took off!

Half a million leaflets were initially distributed, then an additional 50,000 more, some printed in three Indian dialects. Members, with our backing, contacted local radios and newspapers. Among many radio and several TV programs, Jimmy Young etc, was the public "louse search" of an MP!

At that time news appeared that Prince William's school had an infection of lice. I wrote to Princess Diana asking her if she would back our campaign. Her secretary answered that no patronage was possible. Pity. It would have emphasized the message that having lice was not shameful- if even royalty suffered from them!

Then we had a press conference on March 31, 1989. Tim Astill, NPA director, explained why pharmacists were running this campaign. Dr John Maunder, director of the Medical Entomology Centre in Cambridge gave the medical aspects of pediculosis (and I wasn't the only one to learn that new term!).

A lighter touch was provided by Barbara Kelly, the radio personality and one of the original cast of "What's my line?" She described how, as a young mother of 18, she found that her baby son had head lice. And on the three-day train trip across Canada going to meet her in-laws for the first time she spent hours picking off his head lice!

Disappointingly, the audience at our conference was very sparse. Only a few newspaper journalists were present- the others were covering the beginning of the Falkland's war! Just my luck!!!

But back to "Nessy". I'd never been to Scotland. So here was an opportunity to find out whether the bleak, grey reputation was justified. It didn't rain. The company was cheerful so I really enjoyed our trip. I had a bit of difficulty with the accents of our Scottish visitors, but then they were quite polite about my American accent!

We were all cheerful coming back on the coach as the exhibit had proved very popular. The pharmacist visitors, both our members and others, seemed to have enjoyed themselves seeing what else was new and connecting with us whom they knew only by voice on the phone.

Spirits soared and we ended up singing- of course a Scottish song that everyone knew well. "You take the high road and I'll take the low road and I'll be in Scotland afor thee…. I didn't know what it was about and heard that it was a song sung by a robber on his way to be hanged, and he is singing to his sweetheart. Sadly beautiful.

On our way back our coach driver made a slight

detour so that we had a glimpse of Loch Lomond, but no monster. Hence no photograph to show of Nessy.

Instead, a photo of my imaginary cliffs of northern Scotland! Perhaps the mouth of one of the lochs....

WHERE FROM? "SING-ME-A-SONG, OH!"

Music and particularly songs seem to invade my consciousness quite uncalled for. They just appear from some hidden source in me. Why? Haven't a clue!

As I was getting up this morning a song came creeping in- "Mother, must I keep on dancing? Yes, my darling daughter!" and that was all. I can't remember the rest…It must have been a popular dance tune, and those, like "Begin the Beguine" have remained among my "repertoire" together with some classics.

My love for opera (not from the dance floor) stems from my Mother's singing. One of her favourites, and that rubbed off on me, was Verdi's "La Traviata". The Italian "Libiamo, libiamo" sung in Russian!

The last time I heard a live performance was at the Coliseum in London. This was many years after my husband had died. My partner, Hamilton, bought the tickets as a surprise for me. I had told him quite a while before that I didn't want to see "La Traviata" ever again because I always start crying at the beginning of the last act!

Of course, I was fibbing! I was really thrilled. He had a big, clean handkerchief ready for me! There I was, a mature adult, enjoying every minute of it, crying copiously!

But when growing up in Beirut there was no live theatre or concert halls. Very occasionally there would be a performance in West Hall, the American University auditorium, put on by the students. I remember clearly the ambitious and delightful performance of "The Mikado". That was during the French Vichy rule, before the Allied soldiers from Palestine and Egypt took over.

When the French marched out and they marched in, our entertainment world exploded. The NAAFI with its troop of actors and singers came often to Beirut.. As West Hall was used by them, anyone involved with the university also profited. Since Father was teaching in the Engineering Department we always had tickets.

Joyce Grenfell's appearance in her one-man show was an outstanding performance which I still remember vividly. Years later she was the inspiration for a comedy I wrote.

At that time she was touring Australia. I got her address from her agent in London and wrote to her, describing my play. She wrote back saying that all her acts were written by herself, so "thank you, but no thank you".

Not quite that long ago Maureen Lipmann acted in "Re-Joyce". So I wrote to her regarding my much rewritten comedy since it had been inspired by J. Grenfell. Her reply was courteous, but at that time her husband wrote all her material. So much for my theatrical attempts!

The theme of the play was/is that my main character has the aptitude or talent to mimic another personality in everyday life. She uses it to her advantage, pretending to be what she really isn't- and getting away, with it. She puts on a very stilted upper class accent "Oh, my dear!" and bamboozles a builder into thinking she really is the owner of a house in a street in London that is being renovated..

In one scene she is sleepwalking, and talking to all her friends. Having won the lottery she has given them what they had always wished for. A luxury cruise, an expensive outfit, even a football team and as she continues waltzing to her imaginary music all these gifts turn sour! Corny- but I think it could be hilarious! (I would think so, wouldn't I?)

Sadly, I now realize that my poor comedy needs much rewriting AGAIN! .

So now back to the beginning- "Mother, must I keep on dancing...?"Has this song been sung somewhere recently and did I hear it then? Probably not. It just welled up from some long-buried memory.

I surprise my children quite often with my complete ignorance of what I call "really modern" or "Pop" music. But "Mum, that group has been around about twenty years at least!"

How long ago were the Beatles and my favourite ABBA? After seeing the musical "Mama Mia based on the ABBA songs these melodies have become the "hums" for me. I don't remember most of the words even though I saw the show quite recently in London.

London plays an important part in some of my stories. In
<u>An Orchid Called Sandra</u> most of the action takes place there.
Several of the others could be there, but I've not specified their
location.

However, in my own life, not the imaginary lives of my
characters, it does have an important role- such as our wedding
took place in Kensington!

A copy of the above picture, well, almost a copy, was the very
first painting I ever sold! I drew it while baby-sitting for friends
in Beirut. I sketched my original in their living room, based on a
picture hanging on the wall. My interpretation was quite
different from that one. Then I finished mine at home in pastels.
When my friends saw it later, they really liked it and bought it
for five Lebanese pounds!

SUMMER SCHOOL FOR VENTRILOQUIST

It wasn't easy deciding on a college. Finished twelfth grade at the American Community School in Beirut. Most of my classmates had already sailed away to the States to their choice of further education. Switzerland for a finishing school? Too expensive and on the whole I felt that that wasn't quite right for me. Finishing to be a lady?

I choose three colleges in the States to apply for entrance and, hopefully, a scholarship. It was just about Enny Meany Mini Mo- and "Mo" fell on Wellesley, Massachusetts. The other two colleges wanted triple copies- much too much trouble (remember this was way before PCs). And Wellesley offered a very generous scholarship. So they accepted me and I, gratefully, accepted their offer!!! But I had a year to wait till next autumn.

The American Junior College for Women in Beirut was just a short walk up our street. I enrolled for several courses. One of these was chemistry and it included some physics. The woman teacher was excellent in what she taught! I still remember very clearly the details of her pregnancy.

And the other was an unforgettable experiment to teach us about electricity. She distributed pieces of chalk to all of us. "Now, just pass your piece to the person sitting next to you. Keep passing!" And pretend the pieces are electrons!

However, I'm not grumbling. The three credits I received from the Junior College served me very well. Freshman year at Wellesley was an eye opener. Coming from a completely different, international world, I found many of my classmates quite naïve. I knew I wouldn't have the patience to stay for four years till I got my BA. Summer school was the answer as it would augment my credits. I would skip Sophomore to Junior Year and that would mean three years till graduation in 1951.

Harvard University, eighteen miles from Wellesley, in Cambridge was the answer. Wellesley is on a par with it scholastically so they accepted me.

I was lucky in that Professor Robert Blake, a professor in Harvard, and his family lived in Cambridge and I had a permanent room up on the third floor of their house. The Blakes were friends from long ago. So when I arrived to go to Wellesley, I had friends in Cambridge!

Not only did they welcome me, but they more or less "adopted" me for the duration of the time I was in college. The summers I spent with them in their summer home in New Hampshire were delightful.

Their son Igor instructed me in driving. I remember quite clearly my panic when I stalled their bright red convertible in the high street of Newport. Cars started piling up behind us. I begged Igor to please help- take over- but he staunchly refused. It was certainly a learning experience! He just smiled at the drivers and gestured that he was sorry, and shrugged that he couldn't do anything!

My experience of riding was much less harrowing. Tetya Nadia (aunt in Russian) was a patient teacher. And I learnt how to ride their passive horse along the lovely tree-lined paths through the countryside close to their farm.

That summer their house was loaned to Professor and Mrs. La Monte. I became their "niece-for-a-summer" as he wrote in my copy of his book "The World of the Middle Ages".

One of the courses I was taking was based on it and John La Monte was our lecturer. It was a fascinating survey of the Middle Ages and the details made them alive for us.   The front photo of Crac-des-Chevaliers, the famous Crusader castle in Syria, at the Lebanese border, brought it close to home!

So that is the explanation for Edmund's world.

And the ventriloquist? Simply a phase I had when quite young. It may have been seeing a puppet handler, but I became enthralled with the idea of learning how to speak without moving my lips and "throwing" my speech. For a while- until I realized how very difficult it was!

Wellesley College- where I wrote some of my stories. It has a beautiful campus including a lovely lake for boating and swimming. The teaching was/is still, I'm sure, first rate. I hadn't realized when applying to them that it was one of the most prestigious women's colleges in the USA.

Its recent alumna included Hilary Clinton the late president's wife, and Madeleine Albright, his Secretary of State. Hilary is now the Senator from New York who campaigned against B.Obama, the current US president.

Besides the inspiring and stimulating courses, there were the extracurricular activities. And the lovely natural surroundings were a side benefit.

My first winter there was an eye-opener (not only from the educational point of view). Coming from Lebanon I had never experienced the beauty of frost on the grass and on the leaves of the trees. I had skied in Lebanon, but this was different. Walking from the dormitory to the class room in the morning with the grass crackling under my footsteps was quite memorable!

INSPIRATION FOR THREE DAYS

When I wrote this story the Catholic/Protestant Irish troubles were not yet settled Almost daily. the news brought reports of atrocities, of people killed, not only in northern Ireland, but elsewhere in the world.

One afternoon Nigel and I took the train to London. It was probably a Saturday. As we strolled along Park Avenue towards Hyde Park Corner, we were admiring the posh hotels.

Suddenly we heard a loud explosion! The ground underfoot seemed to have trembled. And that bang brought all the news accounts of bombing really close to us.

Through the years since that explosion, with our almost daily ration of atrocities happening in the Middle and Far East, as well as in Africa, a bomb in a plane is, thank goodness, not quite commonplace!

The kernel that brought forth this story was a competition in one of the writers' magazines: a composition for Halloween.

End of the 60s and beginning of the 70s we were living in Darien, Connecticut. Stamford was a few miles down the motorway from us where ICI, the petro-chemical British company, had their offices. During our three years stay in the USA my husband represented ICI Plastics Division.

Our next-door neighbours were two teachers. They taught us what Halloween should really be: "Trick or treat"? They had a supply of sweets or other "Treats" ready for the youngsters that came around in their "frightening" costumes.

In addition to the sheet-covered ghosts and black-robbed witches, some of the costumes were quite elaborate, including much more than a mask or facial make-up.

Our neighbours invited the kids in- and asked for a trick from them! Sing a song? Recite a poem? Someone knows of a good joke? The children, urging each other, would finally come out with a trick! And then they would receive the treat. Sometimes it was more than sweets. So Halloween was fun.

And everyone got in on the act. The large store in the town, the equivalent of Sainsbury in England, was decorated with various ghost and witches' masks and even children's costumes. But the most impressive stand was of the pumpkins!

This store was our favourite shopping centre and, not only because of its wide selection of foods, but because with every trip there we bought, at a discount, another volume of an encyclopaedia. We finally ended up with the complete set of twenty-five volumes. Some subjects are now out-of-date, but I still use it.

Our stay in Darien was eventful. Winter was fun for the children. Having a frozen lake at the bottom of our road and friends close by who lent them ice skates meant learning how to ice skate. (These friends also gave them peanut butter sandwiches after school!). The town had its own private beach and in the summer it was wonderful for picnics.

Other friends took Nick and Rurik fishing in Long Island Sound and one day they came back quite triumphant: they had caught a large fish. It was very much alive in the bucket of water. I offered to cook it, once they'd killed and cleaned it. I left them in the kitchen. Loud banging! No, it still wiggled. Then I heard a shot-they'd finally used their air rifle!

At the end of our three years there we packed up and piled into our second-hand Oldsmobile station wagon for the trip across the States. What exciting and wonderful weeks those were!

So much to photograph to remind us of the fascinating places we drove through. And having four cameras clicking away we had hundreds of snaps to be developed when we returned home. Cities, villages and wide open spaces, through the desert and over the mountains to the Pacific. And back by another route. Incredibly, we drove through an ice storm in Texas!!!

My pastel picture is of a spot found in the Canadian Rockies. Perhaps it was a wilderness like this one where Daphne relaxed .No telephones so she couldn't be contacted for three days.

NOT ALWAYS VICE VERSA

A dream of any aspiring writer is to receive an acceptance letter. I've always been writing something or other. I was/am keen. I took a correspondence course at the School of Journalism in London to learn how to write short stories.

My BA degree from Wellesley College, (in Massachusetts) was in history and English composition. Of course, the latter included writing short stories and drama.

When Nigel, my husband, was seconded to the ICI office in Stanford, Connecticut for three years, the family went too. I enrolled on a year's correspondence course of writing at a New York college.

Back in England, I joined a writing group which met in St Albans. It started when Stephen Jeffrey-Poulter, a BBC editor, gave a talk on writing for the BBC. He then asked if anyone would be interested in a writers' group. We were.

The Maltings Writers' Group, for two years under Stephen's leadership, had outstanding lecturers not only from the BBC, but also known writers, among them Alan Plater ("Barchester Chronicles") and Glen Chandler ("Taggart").

After many changes in membership we have now settled down as Aspiring Writers, meeting at my house in Welwyn Garden City, once a month to read our own compositions.

And what have I learnt from all my courses?

Techniques as to what is required by a women's or an up-market specialist magazine; what to do and what not to do when writing an article or a short story; always study the readership, the market, of your chosen publication; and finally whatever one writes to rewrite and rewrite again.

And the final hurdle is to be in step with the fashion! When I wrote a play for my English class in college, the drama students chose one scene to act out. It was a steamy episode when the audience finds out that the lovely girl wasn't really seduced by the sheik of the palace- as she thought- but by the gardener.

I was in the auditorium and sank low down in my seat to be invisible as the Dean of Foreign students marched past in the middle of the performance, her expression quite disapproving of such crude, distasteful subjects. Lesson learnt that rampant sex is out!

Next- the course I took in New York. My mild, pleasing short stories were quite out of fashion there! There must be a rape or a detailed description of mating, something like that, in every story! So, I just got my subjects mixed. Vice versa- it should have been mild women's magazine first and then hot seduction for New York.

The photograph above is that of Beit-el-Din.

The sheik in the play I had written belonged, in my mind, to this palace of Beit-el-Din, an Arabian Nights type of building. Beit means house in Arabic. A really beautiful example of Arabic architecture and decoration, it is up in the mountains overlooking a lovely valley of fruit and olive orchards and terraces with vines. We spent several summer holidays in Becharre the village across this valley.

EMERALD GREEN – LEBANON IN THE 1940S AND BEFORE

Beirut was, and probably still is, an amalgam of diverse peoples, cultures and languages. Many of our friends were connected with the AUB, (the American University of Beirut): Americans, Armenians, Arabs- Lebanese, Syrians, Egyptians, and further afield, including Saudi Arabians. Europeans were also represented, that is, besides my Russian Father, who taught in the Engineering Department. Then we had friends involved with the French St Joseph University.

So our parties were very cosmopolitan. My parents were, like most Russians, sociable and enjoyed getting together with friends. My brothers and I inherited this trait. I remember at one of our parties we counted how many languages we had between us and we had a staggering seven!

This isn't so surprising because of the history of the country and of the whole of the Middle East. It has always been the gateway between Asia and Europe. The seafaring Phoenicians, ancestors of the Lebanese, travelled through-out and beyond the Mediterranean; Julius Caesar went through these lands on his way to India. Then there were other invaders, some of whom settled here.

An amalgam. No wonder when the Second World War brought a flood of Poles coming from the Soviet Union, the Arab shopkeepers assimilated Polish very rapidly. Good for business!!!

One of the outstanding places illustrating so well this mixture of cultures and peoples is Baalbek, the Greco-Roman city of Heliopolis built upon the ruined temples of previous civilizations. When Aileen, Paul and the others from "Emerald Green" visit Baalbek, parts of it had already been restored, particularly the Temple of Bacchus.

As a useful and very instructive project my Father had his engineering students work on this restoration. He had been experimenting on pre-stressing concrete and had evolved a new method of pulling together the large fragments of marble ceiling tiles. These were then hoisted up into place between the columns surrounding the main building.

As a young girl, I remember visiting ancient Baalbek. Especially exciting was hearing Father's enthusiastic explanation how the huge, heavy stones were raised.

I was in Beirut during most of the war. Lebanon was a French mandate, under the auspices of the United Nations. The French authorities followed the lead of France and became pro Germany, in other words, Vichy.

We were living in a quarter close to the American University so that when the Allied forces advanced against Lebanon from Palestine we felt relatively safe from their bombing. They would know, we hoped, that American property was "sacred".

At night the allied planes would fly over us to bomb military targets and the harbour. Quite exciting to watch the search lights catch a plane in their beams.

One night there was a bright light that streaked down close by. We heard a thud as it hit the ground. A flare had lost its parachute. Father and my brothers, quite excited, went hurrying out with a bucket of sand or earth from the garden to find it. Father was worried that someone would throw water onto the phosphorus resulting in an explosion of fire. Besides it would be a valuable bit of mineral for the university labs!

A classmate of mine lived in a house on a hill. One day she invited several of us to come and watch what was happening in the olive groves to the south of the town. The Australian forces were within gun-shot distance. We went out onto the roof. It was quite exciting to see the puffs of smoke from their guns and then, on the other side, the bang or the splash as they hit or missed their harbour target. Thrilling! Until her parents found us- right below the path of the missiles!

There was one rather frightening rumour. The French, it was said, would turn their Senegalese troupes onto the population if the British didn't withdraw. Quite often we would see these rather menacing, tall, tattooed blacks, marching by. However, in the end, the Vichy French declared Beirut to be an "open"city so that the fighting stopped. The French retreated and the Allied soldiers moved in. Other conquerors? But they didn't stay very long. Lebanon became an independent nation shortly after the war. And then tourists came back to admire the ancient temples and their sculptures.

Interest in marble statues goes back to my childhood when, just before WW II , Father had his sabbatical in the USA. He was going to MIT (Massachusetts Institute of Technology) to supervise the building of his special wind tunnel.

On our way we travelled through Europe. In Paris, he took us to the Louvre. At the far end of one of its greatest halls, standing in magnificent isolation, was the winged statue of the Victory of Samothrace. Mother and Father were full of admiration. "Just look at her robe, how the marble folds seem blown by a breeze." This was my first introduction to great sculpture.

When we arrived in Cambridge, Massachusetts Father settled down to work at the MIT, Mother "keeping home" for us and learning about shopping and cooking in the USA. She also met an old friend from Russia, Nadia Blake. Nadia had been to school with Mother's sister and so they resumed their friendship after twenty years!

My brothers and I attended a school called Peabody School. What I remember very clearly about it was that everyone- that is all the pupils- had to learn a poem to recite in front of the whole school assembly. Of all the poetry that I've read since those many years ago, I still remember parts of the poem I recited then, after stumbling, terrified, up onto the stage! It was something about a purple cow. Two sentences remembered: "I never hope to see a purple cow...But I would rather see than be one!".

All this was long ago. Married, then widowed. The four children all living their own lives and I settled down in Welwyn Garden City. But then back to my story-

Some years ago I joined a Clay Sculpture class in Stevenage. Enjoyed it immensely. Produced a Buddha who now sits in my living room. My chess knight with a clay black and white board received first prize in a Welwyn Garden City Art Club exhibition. I confess that there were very few entries competing in that category!......... Hence Paul is a sculptor. And he and Eileen were in Baalbek together.

Six of the 54 columns of the Temple of Jupiter are still standing, each 75 feet high. Built on the site of a temple to Baal a local sun god, the Greeks identified Baal with their own sun-God Helios. They called the town Heliopolis.

BACKGROUND FOR
AN ORCHID NAMED SANDRA

Much of this story takes place in London. Besides being a fascinating place to visit, the city has a sentimental value for me. Nigel and I were married there.

According to ecclesiastic ruling one has to live a certain number of weeks in the particular parish before a wedding ceremony may be performed. We chose St Jude's Church in Kensington.

And so my parents came from Lebanon, and we settled in Kensington, in a small hotel. It was one of the many others lining a rectangle of a green park, once the breathing space for the elegant three-story houses of the wealthier residents of London. During several weeks we meandered along the streets and felt the bustling atmosphere of the town. Of course, we also visited museums and other sightseers' goals.

My father found an appropriate large hotel, the Rembrandt, for the reception. By August 27th family and guests had congregated. Among them were my matron of honour, Ellie Weld an American college colleague, and my maid of honour, Ira Ostapenko, a Russian-American UN friend.

Just before the ceremony Nigel whispered to me that he hoped the church wouldn't fall on him as a non-believer! Then at the reception, to the horrified amazement of the staff, the guests danced to the music of the sole pianist! He was marvellous and took up the challenge with Lehar and Strauss waltzes as well as more modern tunes! Then off to Cornwall for our honeymoon.

And so during the few weeks before the wedding we had explored the streets of Kensington, ready for Jim and Flora looking for Sandra! Then comes the episode of the orchids.

Nigel applied for a position at AERE, the atomic energy establishment in Harwell. His qualifications were excellent, but there was a long delay . After six months his application was "cleared". Having a Russian wife from Beirut, Lebanon was suspect, hence the hold-up. Beirut was in the news as the launching pad for several British spies who had defected to Soviet Russia.

We settled in Chilton, a small village under the Icknield Way downs- one church, one pub, one grocery store, and our small flat behind it. The previous renters had used the bath tub for storing their coal! The plus was that Harwell was within ten minutes drive.

I had a Canadian lady, Sydney Hardwick, as a companion for our lovely walks across the downs. We met the Hardwicks quite by accident. Driving around neighbouring Upton, this was while we were still living in the rented flat in Chilton, we suddenly saw a really modern looking building in complete contrast to the other houses around the village. It was of timber and its design was quite unique. We stopped and while admiring it, the owner came out and invited us to take a look around.

Bill Hardwick's wife had a family in the timber business in Canada, hence the house. They got permission to build on the condition that the old, tall brick wall in front of the house was not demolished. Presumably, that was to protect the old atmosphere of the village from being polluted by such modernism!

When the weather was good, while both our husbands were working at Harwell, Sydney and I roamed over the downs. Once we came to an isolated farm or, rather, garden centre specializing in orchids. It consisted of the main house and several green houses–and a friendly family called the Ratcliffes.

As their home was a short distance from Chilton, I often wandered over to them where the older daughter was my teacher. I learnt a great deal about growing orchids and found them fascinating.

The green houses were resplendent with the rows of potted flowers. I even borrowed books from the library of neighbouring Didcot to read-up about them.

And I thought I was becoming an expert! Always loving to write and being ambitious, or fool hardy, I wrote to the National Geographic Magazine in Washington DC offering an article on orchid growing in England, with, of course, lovely photos. Negative reply- they had their own internationally famous orchid specialist!

And so, back to my story - I could understand the fascination my characters had in orchid growing. However, I'm glad I didn't find any mystery or any murders for inspiration! Two important ingredients of the story - London and orchids-come from these episodes in my life.

Inspired by Orchids! Pastels on plywood.

POEMS AND DOGGERELS

WORD PAINTINGS, VERSES FOR FUN

EMOTIONAL EXPLOSIONS,

A DIRGE, JUST PASSING TIME

BEIRUT

The sky is blue, so blue it hurts my fog-accustomed, northern eyes
and shimmering the blue of sea reflects the blue of sky.

The pulse, the beat, the clang of breathing, growing city
bursting its barriers of sea-bound land spills buildings onto the stretching sands.

The smell of oil fumes, of countless cars, of drying concrete, garlic, frying oil, fish.

Beirut in toto- its excretions are the tin-can hovels grovelling between car-park basements of its multi-storied Corbusiers.

A decaying garden lingers below my fourth floor balcony.

The ten-foot bamboo bent above the green, quatermass explosion of a loufi plant.

A burst of crimson-red poinsettia flowers –a breathing space,

a touch of purity among the refuse where the unloved cats

prowl to pounce on lizards basking on an old Roman wall.

The palm trees thrust between the houses stand aloof, but their Arabian Nights splendour tarnished with the grey spewed up by concrete mixers.

The sky is blue- its depth of calm quarrelling with the shambles of the televison aerials pell-melling above each other on the grey roofs.

The wail of an Arab song hauntingly rises from a Japanese transistor, beats down, around, about the shouts of workers on the concrete skeleton of a ten-story block,

the laughter of neighbours, the cough of an old man through the thin wall.

And the rising roar of a Boeing crashes through all, destroying any semblance of some peace beyond.

SUNDAY IN BROOKLYN

The afternoon is dragging on
the rain is dripping out
and tedious, and grey, the day
and on and on and on.

The puddles breaking up
the brick monotony of walks.
And whining on the corner roofs
the orphaned winds are crouched.

The darkness covering the chimney tops
and greyness becomes dark;
the childless trees their nakedness hide
and blackness on the black are lost.

Somewhere a growl of horn is heard,
far distant through the night,
and splash of passing car forlorn.
And then again the dark.

HALLOWEEN

Something black and grim and headless
clanked a chain against the door.
Something ghoulish, leering, eyeless
screaming fled across the sky.

Was it shadow or a sorcerer
closed the moon's round friendly face?
Was it sighing of a spectre
made the graveyard cypress sway?

Early Druid in his rapture
watched October's blackness fly,
waving potions in the breathless
seeing Stonehenge pure arise.

Ancient Romans in their thousands
held their torches up on high.
Waiting, soundless, for all evil
from their Forum, cloud-like, rise.

Now the olden days have withered.
Evil ghosts and witches gone.
Only shrilly shout my neighbours
"Trick or treat" ,don't you deny-

YET
Something black and grim and headless
clanked a chain against the door.
Something ghoulish, leering, eyeless
screaming fled across the sky.

TRAIN TRIP TO ST. GEORGE'S

The wheels of the train klik klak quite out of rhythm.
The bare elms spread their skeleton fingers accusing at the
sky
Spring? Summer? The sun shines through a cloud of dirty grey
It is the eyes, the ears of me affected.
The loneliness of single love is like a canker growing-
Dutch Elm Disease? Or engine out of true?
My hand that trembles as it writes, my thoughts-
a box of pills, of tranquillizers.

The track curves on- the only shine above the oily
blackness of the stretching road.
A tunnel looms. An endless tunnel that should be shut
and blocked forever more with me inside it...
with just one face, far distant, unattainable to hold before my
eyes
as slowly darkness takes me and I die.

Why not? Relentless on we go. The train speeds towards
the ever-growing arc of light- klik klak.
The rhythm of the tracks pulls on.

Explosion of the light! I want to crawl, claw back my way
into the darkness, to fall asleep, to never dream and never wake-
AMEN

TRAIN TRIP - ENDING

How dare you scorn the beauty of the day and night?
How dare you think of tunnels where to hide forever
while you glide past in the soft velvet of your seat
past tenements of sprawling London?

How dare you look upon the fluffs of cloud as dirty grey?
The sun bursts through a glory of love-giving life.
Your eyes can see the emerald green of flower-stained field
not like that woman with her cane of white.
Your children laugh and shout and quarrel-
their limbs and minds whole, bright, exalting life
and all its raptures. Not like that child whose mouth
hangs open speechless, silent, his eyes an empty stare.

How dare you scorn the love, affection of a life-long friend,
bringing an apple pie for solace- the pie a mute reminder
of the sympathy and care that lingers in the giver?
How dare you scorn and think that all of this is rubbish
to be exchanged for darkness and for death?

The pills slip through reluctant fingers- still unconvinced,
still trembling. The yellow dye in them dissolves against
the blackness of the cinders. Stop. Listen!
The klik klak of the wheels gains a rhythm....
You're almost there. You have arrived.

WHY YOU?

Why did you come and take my hand and lead me back into the
sun? Why you- when now you do not shade me from its
burning glare? Now leave me naked, burning and alone?
Was it because your hand was but a shadow of a fleeting whim?
Why you? I lived, I breathed. The pain of death had numbed
and left me cold. Why did you come and warm my flesh?
Why did you breathe upon me and alight the embers that were
there? The shadow where I lived was gray but slowly, slowly
light was filtering through.
But now the glare of loving all alone is worse by far than
shadows of my softly fading grief. The harshness, piercing
coldness of being on my own -the coldness being greater for the
heat-the harshness doubled having known once more.
Why you ? Did you but sense that I was naught to you before
you stepped so blithely in my path and made me look and see
and feel again- and looked yourself, and saw, and took, then
spurned and left and laughed perhaps. Why did you come to
lift me high? Did you not guess what havoc the music of your
life would shatter upon the numbness of my shadowed self?
Did not your inner self realize your hand on mine undid all
spoken words? Your lips on mine undid all warning signs,
you being one with me undid all vows professed? Or did you
sense but did not heed? Perhaps another would have
understood that burning suns like ours are rarest of the rare-
Perhaps another would have taken the whiplash of disdain, of
hate, the burns, the pain as payment for the joy realizing that the
depths of oneness are the deepest of the true - Another one,
perhaps, but then 'another' is not you. For you, perhaps, the
depths of oneness was of two. The burning sun was but a comet
passing through…The numbness starts to dull about me - A
coldness has eclipsed the sun…….

YOUNG AGAIN

We've had our fling, Peter my love
Sadly, we've had it and thrown it away.
Our middle-age fling with your beard almost gray
and my hair with its silvery tinge.
So now when time passes you'll remember afar
how we acted, the two of us, "laddie and lass",
young in heart, young in love, as if seventeen,
forty-six, forty-nine – one hundred between.
Yet young in deed, young in thought
and breathless with love- too careless to think
of the pain that'll last.
Laughing and loving in the dark of the car,
loving, caressing in the wind of a lane
with the jewels of the airport alit from afar.
Picking straws from a hayrick, milk-maid and her swain,
A walk through the dyke with its light and its shade
glimmering just like Titania's glade.
But its passed, my love, it has passed, it is gone.
Cold and gray and lustreless lies the long day.
No laughter for lunch, no deep glance, not a spark.
Just a nod, just a wave, two strangers you'd say...
when my heart is begging for just one more touch,
one caress, one more kiss , one more love- but its no.
Its no more, its all negative now. Close my heart, close my eyes,
my whole being must sleep. Not wait for the phone that won't
ring, for the touch that's not there, for the love that had stayed
buried and locked-And the trip to the stars has ended in pain.

STORY FRAGMENT

Sweep of the emptiness glimmers through the rooms
on the millions of particles of dust.
And the shadow of stale tunes
rides the banister to the parquet hall.
Sightless, the drapes hang nailed in their sentry's post
closing in the dusk of an endless day.

Yet a slight breath of life is caught in the leather of a crop
thrown to mildew on a foyer chair.
And the sigh of a woman lies entangled enmeshed in the lace of
a fan.
Whisper of petticoats, taffeta rustle, the rudeness of boots on
the floor.
"Randolph!", the surprised cry and the flurry of welcoming
steps.
And then the sudden silence of a shriek.
Randolph has come, the tall and the gaunt, but his eyes are
blank
of the knowledge of man..........

PEOPLES' REVOLT

Was there a man here once?
His sinewy arms grey-streaked from work,
hair tousled from the furnace blast
who from break of day till gloom of night
toiled in the great cauldron of the plant.
And yet survived with laughter in his eyes,
a smile for those less fortunate.
His was a simple life, a life of bread,
a handful of white beans,
a woman whom he called his own,
a hut of corrugated steel.
He was a listener. He could not talk to move the souls of men.
But he could listen, comprehend.
Some promised him in whispers that a change will come,
a change in those black uniforms.
A shadowy, moving whisper of a group of men:
a plan, a knife, a bomb, just one.
Then freedom from the menace of the octopus
whose black tentacles wormed into people's hearts
transforming brothers, sisters, even parents into spies.

He was among that swelling mass of men who listened,
heard the moaning undercurrent of despair
and hoped to change the darkness into light.
"Brothers, the rich grow richer while we search their refuse for a
rind to eat.
Why has a just and loving God forgotten us?"
Another interceded: "No, there is no God. It's us alone
who hold our future between dark and light."
"Why do we wait?" asked one.

"We wait for Judas," someone said.
He came, but not alone.
With him they came, the uniforms.
White faces drawn in chalk, with glassy eyes,
and rifles on the draw.
They say five hundred died that night.
The papers and the TV sneered: "three rebel leaders
were captured on the fifth…"
The rest, the scum, were swept away.
The woman came, with others, many others
to touch the browning stains upon the flagstones of the square
and wash them with their tears.
While coldly, the black uniforms stomped by, not seeing them…
Was there a man here once?

THE BERLIN WALL

Honour belongs to fire.
The eternal flame flickering for souls long dead.
Fire, the symbol of achievement, the Olympic Torch
The burning hearth of home.   FIRE
Water is life.
Mud paddies of rice, the Nile overflowing.
Captured in fountains of great beauty
Taps runith over.WATER. H2O
Now walls.
Prosaic of brick, of stone, of concrete.
The wall of China seen by an astronaut
Buy a piece of broken wall for ten pfennigs
Priceless, like fire, like water
like a breathe of spring.
No longer holding in, holding out. A broken wall- now
signifying FREEDOM.

THE GLIDER

The sun was burning triple images in the
brightness of the dying pink.

The clock was ticking in the car...
a plane roared noise into its stillness and
engined past, its empty glider hook a glint
of gold against the azure of the sky.

And then it came- silently, its long
tapered wings whispering
windlessly in the effortless glide.
It swooped, it turned, the glimmer
of the setting sun glanced off its silky sheen.
Quietness, ticking of the clock; the silence
of companionship with no one there.
The dusking space- the swish of glider
and an expanse of endless blue.

The glider turned, one wing dipped down
Salute to you, earthlings down below
Mine is the space, the blue
the silence for a moment more.

And then it landed, slide, and stopped upon the green.....

DARIEN '72 – TO NIGEL

St Valentines commemorates
the day that birds accept their mates

FOR- Night owls peering in the dark
are quite unsuited for a lark.

Small chirping birdies like a wren
would certainly not choose a hen!

And a fast streaking gliding hawk
is really quite wrong for a strutting cock!

SO- presumably we are birds of a feather
Must stay together through all sorts of weather.

And the birds will remind you of various things
(besides the discomfort of tightening rings!)

One Robin Red-Breast is just like another
That's just to remind you that I'm the mother
of the four little fledglings in our nest.
(My goodness, dear, we could do with some rest!)

And us, sparrow-like searching for worms
while all they can catch is the horrible germs!

Quite unlike the eagle in his eyrie-
you've got a mate that's rather weary!!!!

BUT BASTA!

St Valentines commemorates
The day that birds accept their mates…
So, cooing like a morning dove:
"You, my dear pigeon, are my love!"

HERE AND THERE – TO RURIK, NOV 21, 1995

Here the autumn leaves are carpeting the lawn with yellow.

There the snow has blanketed the trees with white.

The sparrows still are searching here for insects

There the grizzlies are going off to sleep.

A letter from England to Calgary

needs fully five days to arrive;

A passenger flight takes seven hours

A phone call a minute to make.

But thoughts, my son, are much faster

for they do not need to move

IN MY MIND I CAN SEE YOU SMILING-

IN MY HEART FEEL THE WARMTH OF YOUR HUG.

AD: THE UNIVERSITY OF THE THIRD AGE

AS YOU ALL KNOW- THE AIM OF U3A IS TO INTEREST
AND STIMULATE PEOPLE—
Not just any people, but those of 50 +,Like me, like you, like us!
You'll need an autumn programme
That'll give you all the gen
What's best for the ladies; What's best for the men.
What classes you'd like to take; What music you'd like to make.
Could it be history for your family's sake?
Or learning the progress of Hogarth's rake?
Philosophy must make you think.
So then relax with pen and ink.
Traviata may be for an opera buff;
While gardening demands that you be tough!
Sci-Tech or Latin what a mix.
Play reading requires more than six.
And some go to art appreciation
This needs wholehearted participation!
Classical music may make Vivaldi real.
Playing recorders? Don't let them squeal!
Melodious Italian makes you want to sing.
While creative writing might be just your thing.
Wildlife watch might be cold and dreary
If nothing creeps by – you'll be very weary.
Then tango and samba with your dancing troupe
Or join the reading-for-pleasure group.
I've not yet mentioned German conversation;
Nor French which needs a good pronunciation.
Knowing languages makes travelling fun.
Will the travel group take you to the sun?
There you would pastel, paint and draw-
Watercolour nicely whatever you saw.

SO NOW WE'VE COVERED MOST ON THE LIST
IT'S YOUR OWN FAULT IF YOU HAVE MISSED!

A LESSON IN EGYPTOLOGY

The principal pharaohs of Egypt, as our concise table cited

seem to end with Cleopatra whom Anthony delighted.

But from 2000 BC the Old Kingdom- we think-

With succeeding dynasties has a strong link.

Narmer, Raneb, Djoser, Huni and Khufu

Nefere, Unas, Teti, Pepi and Sobkneftu

But the names that will always spring to our mind

Are really outstanding and easy to find:

Hatshepsut was a mighty pharaoh.
She built an obelisk tall and narrow.
Then along came Tuthmosis the Third
and Hatshepsut's name was no longer heard.
Her statues he toppled as he sat on his throne.
Even her obelisk he hid among stone.
In the nineteenth dynasty lived Ramses the Second.

"I'm by far the greatest!" he always reckoned.

So he lived till he was ninety-nine

Siring sons and daughters, ensuring his line.

Tutenkamun owes his fame to a golden mask

When Howard Carter completed his amazing task.

And so we remember these famous names
But cannot decipher their arrogant claims!

WILL POWER

Too late the yoke appears as
Time droops withered from its drying stalk.
And thought, unharnessed, gallops past,
is gone...   Too late the yoke appears.

PRAYER

Oh God, oh Doctor of us all!
wash clean the festering sores of this
our deeply wounded Earth.
And may disease of War
infect us not, once more, and guard us, Lord,
from scratching at the healing scabs of Peace.

CITY LONELINESS

Just the sobbing of the storm in the hills,
the whine of the edges of sleet.
Just a soul in the vortex of the winds
And the stretch of the endless seas.
Just the crying of the crowds in the streets
the drone of a passing car
Just a heart in the care of the town.
And the cold of the concrete walk.

DESOLATION IS......

An elephant skull sun-whitened
Tusk-less it lies on the ground.

Desolation is ......
The churned mud of yesterday's waterhole
Dusting away into space.

Desolation is ......
The shouting silence of a familiar laugh
Missing among the chorusing party.

Desolation is......
An empty sheet stretched cold to the hand
With no warmth of the other gone wandering.

Desolation is ......

BALLAD OF THE DRAGON
(For Nick's birthday-05)

Puff the Magic Dragon
Lived beside the Lea
Underneath the shadow of a mighty tree
Nick took a photo of that mighty tree
Never saw the dragon sleeping by the Lea
When the snap was printed
Nick was very glad
But the magic photo made the dragon sad.
Puff could now no longer
Linger by the Lea
"Look that mass of people all are crowding me!"

Puff the Magic Dragon flew off to the sea.
Never more would Nicky photograph that tree.